Outsiders

Class, Gender and Nation

DOROTHY THOMPSON

VERSO

London · New York

First published by Verso 1993
© Dorothy Thompson 1993
All rights reserved

Verso
UK: 6 Meard Street, London W1V 3HR
USA: 29 West 35th Street, New York, NY 10001-2291

Verso is the imprint of New Left Books

ISBN 0-86091-490-9
ISBN 0-86091-650-2 (pbk)

British Library Cataloguing in Publication Data
A catalogue record for this book is available from the British Library

Library of Congress Cataloging-in-Publication Data
A catalogue record for this book is available from the Library of Congress

Typeset in Sabon by Leaper & Gard Ltd, Bristol
Printed and bound in Great Britain by Biddles Ltd,
Guildford and King's Lynn

Contents

Acknowledgements

'Chartism and the Historians' is an expanded version of a lecture given when I was Andrew Mellon Visiting Professor of British History at Pittsburg University in 1976.

'The Early Chartists' was originally published as the introduction to the volume of that name by Macmillan and the University of South Carolina Press in 1971.

'Women and Nineteenth-Century Radical Politics: A Lost Dimension' was originally published in Juliet Mitchell and Ann Oakley (eds), *The Rights and Wrongs of Women*, Penguin 1976.

'Ireland and the Irish in English Radicalism before 1850' was originally published in James Epstein and Dorothy Thompson (eds), *The Chartist Experience: Studies in Working-Class Radicalism and Culture 1830–1860*, Macmillan 1982.

'Queen Victoria, the Monarchy and Gender' was given as a lecture organized by the Institute for Advanced Research in the Humanities, Birmingham University. A small number of copies will be printed as part of the proceedings of the Institute.

Introduction

These essays were written over a period of twenty-five years. Another twenty years can be added for years in which I was carrying on research and teaching but not publishing. Publishing has not in fact ever been the major part of my work as a historian, not necessarily because research and teaching have seemed more important, but more because in a life which has involved bringing up children, running a household and taking an active part in contemporary politics some things have had to go.

Most people who read this will be more familiar with my husband's work than with mine. This is not only because he has been more prolific, but also because he has been one of the major historians of our generation. Although he and I have by no means always agreed on questions of historical interpretation, in general our approaches have been similar and his work has been of a higher quality than mine. I suppose that if I had not thought this to be so our relationship could have been more conflictual than it has been, since our generation certainly contained many of the built-in gender inequalities which have occupied the women's movement throughout most of it. In her recent book, Elizabeth Fox-Genevese suggests that feminist writers must include some autobiography in their work.[1] I'm not quite sure what exactly she means, yet I do feel the need to accompany a selection of my published work with some survey of my own life during the years in which it was being written.

Being married to a major historian has affected my own work in a number of ways. For example, although I should have preferred to publish under my unmarried name, by the time my first book was ready for the press *The Making of the English Working Class* had made the name Thompson a strong selling point and the editor and

1

publisher of the series insisted I use it. So only one small article appeared over my own name. In some situations I – as well as my publishers – have probably benefited from this. In others it has not helped. It was incidentally a feminist publishing house which insisted on including Edward's name in the blurb in spite of my objections, none of my other publishers has ever done so. Other problems which our relationship has produced have varied from an accusation that I have been exploited by Edward to the assumption that joint appointments have been set up as a way of paying Edward enormous fees as visiting professor.

Recently some feminist writers have taken Edward to task for exploiting the relationship between historians in a marriage in order to privilege his own work. In order to examine these criticisms I perhaps ought to say something about the way we have seen this relationship and its problems, since the question is one that faces many relationships in which both partners are committed to creative work, and one to which there are no easy answers.

Our backgrounds were not very similar; Edward came from a middle-class professional family, mine was more artisanal. One of my grandfathers was a shoemaker, the other a merchant seaman. Both my parents were professional musicians, but by the time of my birth in 1923 my father had gone into business and was running the first of a series of music shops which later took on records, gramophones and radios and television as well as musical instruments. My mother gave recitals, taught music and occasionally worked as accompanist for ballet school rehearsals or singing teachers. She was a gifted pianist and a very able accompanist. It was recognized in the family that she was a more talented and accomplished musician than my father, and the only arguments that I can remember from my childhood about work were the occasions on which my father felt that she was wasting her talents teaching mainly children when she could be making more use of her abilities. As the only girl among the four children, I can remember no occasion on which it was suggested that I was less likely to have a career or should receive an inferior education to that of my brothers. Outside school most of my education came from my mother and from my widowed grandmother who spent part of every year with us and with whom I sometimes spent the summer in her Gloucestershire village. She came from a family of East End silk-weavers of Huguenot origin. I was born in London, in Greenwich, being that rare phenomenon, a third-generation

Londoner, but we moved out into Kent when I was a baby and lived until I was about eight in the village of Keston. Our neighbours there were mainly farm labourers whose children went to the village school. Because we lived in a cottage we were not accepted as pupils in the local private school, so I and my brother used to go by bus into Bromley, a few miles away, to a small private school run by a lady whose brother had been a fellow-student of my parents at the Royal Academy of Music. She was prepared to overlook the fact that my father was now 'in trade', though we were warned not to mention the shop to any of the other children. We were certainly poorer than most of the other children but we were all good at school things – lessons, music, acting, painting – and didn't feel any particular sense of inferiority. Later we moved into Bromley and my mother started her own small preparatory school. Our former headmistress warned her: 'Don't expect other people's children to be like yours.' Perhaps attending a suburban school while living in a country village gave me an interest in outsiders very early in life. My brothers and I had very little in common with the children at our first school, and I remember thinking then, as I still do, that the villagers and the gypsies on the common were more interesting and lively than the people at school and their parents.

When we were old enough, my brothers went as day boys to a South London public school and I went to the local Girls' County, later to be the grammar school. I got the better education. The 1930s were years in which the teachers in this sort of school were women with first-class degrees from Oxford and Cambridge, and in which most of the pupils left school either at fourteen, when attendance ceased to be compulsory, or at sixteen, after the first round of examinations when they could enter the civil service or take a variety of office jobs. A small number stayed in the sixth form to enter the civil service at a higher grade after Higher Certificate examinations, or to enter teacher training college. Only a handful of girls had any ambition to go on to university education. These were years in which women like those who taught us in school and at college were actively concerned to establish a female presence in public life. Most of them were scholars of high quality and in our all-girls' school as later at my all-women's college we were encouraged to take part in educational and political activity of all kinds. Women like Maud Royden presented the prizes and addressed us on speech day, we were given *A Room of One's Own* as essential reading in the sixth form and the history of the women's suffrage movement and the struggles for the admission of women to higher education and the professions was taught in the classroom and illustrated by visiting speakers, many of whom had personal reminiscences. We were clearly intended to further these causes, particularly those of us whose families were prepared to allow us to go on to higher education. This is not the place to examine the complexity of the problems created by the fact that the role-models with whom we were presented were powerful, impressive women but almost all unmarried and childless. In some ways the very fact of their strong personalities and unusual lives may have added to the persuasions of families in encouraging most of the brightest of the schoolgirls to leave school early and go into jobs which were viewed as having no other purpose than filling in time and providing a means of earning some money before they got married. For those of us who did want to go on, however, the way was open.

This kind of educational background almost inevitably produced a profile of the history of women in which the highest achievement was entry into the 'public' spheres of politics or scholarship. We looked for traces of these ambitions in women of earlier periods and found many heroines to admire. Women politicians like Eleanor Rathbone and Ellen Wilkinson were making careers in politics and not simply in 'women's politics'. The more daring among us began to envisage the possibility of a woman becoming prime minister in our lifetime. Those of us who aimed at careers got every encouragement and on the whole a pretty good education. I was one of a group of four studying history, two doing French, two Latin and was the only person in the school doing Greek and sixth-form German. The English class numbered about half a dozen. A wide range of school societies and out of school activities was available. I was the leader of rather a good school orchestra, designed the costumes for choral and dramatic productions and organized a lively programme of lunch-time meetings through the International Society. Had I been less idle and less interested in London first nights and teenage milk-bar culture, I should have got better exam results than I did, but I was able eventually to go to the college of my choice, Girton, as an exhibitioner in 1942.

I had progressed through school two years faster than the average and my original idea, to which my parents subscribed with enthusiasm, had been to spend this extra time at a European school or college, and then to go on to study modern languages. My mother had many childhood associations with France and we spent many pre-war summers there. We were there when the war started, and came back on a crowded boat the day before war was actually declared. After a brief attempt to settle into a country district as evacuees – I refused to go to the grammar school in the Forest of Dean where I could not do Greek – I came back to Bromley and finished my schooling in the years of the phoney war and the Battle of Britain.

History excited my interest then as being at the interface between literature, politics and family traditions. Growing up in a family of non-believers I was always intrigued by the thought of Huguenot ancestors who had adhered so strongly to their own religious sect that they had been prepared to leave their homes and settle in poverty in an alien environment. There were stories in the family which I later tried to sort out – my great-grandmother remembered the weavers and their velvet looms, and told me that the family had come over at 'the Reformation'. Later I realized that a brief national school education had conflated the word in her mind with family references to 'the revocation'. I was only seven when she died and most of her stories came to me through other family members. They taught me, when I came to reconsider them much later, to treat so-called 'oral history' with care. As stories and anecdotes they were lively and interesting, as were the stories passed on by other branches of the family – stories of seafaring under sail and of the theatre and music hall. But as factual or descriptive accounts they lost and gained much in the telling. My great-grandmother used to describe the emergence of the French prisoners from the Fleet prison after the end of the French wars. She gave me a little tortoise-shell box which had been made by these prisoners. When they were let free, she said, they ran into the streets cheering and grabbed the local girls and kissed them. But my great-grandmother had been born twelve years after the end of the French wars, so could never have seen the events she described so vividly. Perhaps her mother's memory had joined up with hers, or I have misremembered the attribution she gave. But the little box and the other artifacts that I used to look at in the Horniman museum remind me of the prisoners of two hundred years ago.

My older brother, a talented painter and designer, had joined the air force just before the war in order to avoid conscription and choose the service he wanted. By the time I went to Cambridge he was a wireless operator rear gunner in bomber command. I had by then been in the Young Communist League for three years.

After two years at college we were conscripted and I chose to be trained to work in industry rather than go into the forces. I trained as an industrial draughtswoman, learning in a crash course the rudiments of the machinery and processes in most departments of an engineering works, and got a job in Buckingham Gate, in central London. The firm was working as a subsidiary of Royal Dutch Shell, making oil plant for the reinstatement of the Dutch oil industry in anticipation of the reclaiming of the Far Eastern fields. I was the first draughtswoman they had ever employed and the only woman in any of the drawing offices, though there were women in the tracing room and in the administrative office.

By the time we first began to live together – in 1945 – both Edward and I were already strongly committed to political action. We were both members of the British Communist Party. I had been in the communist movement since 1939, and many of my friends from school and college were left-wingers of one kind or another. I was already involved in socialist and communist seminars concerned with working-class history and with examination and criticism of the existing Cambridge syllabus. Edward had served in Africa and Italy and had rejoined the Communist Party when he left the army. At Cambridge we shared political and academic interests, and in fact this is how we met. Neither of us had any idea of working within the academic establishment.

We decided that we wanted to live in the north country before we decided what sort of work we wanted to do, although adult education soon began to seem the obvious choice. For seventeen years we lived in Halifax and worked in adult education, Edward full-time as an extra-mural tutor and I part-time as a tutor and later in other part-time work for various university departments. In those years we were both active politically, in the Communist Party, the New Left, the Labour Party and the Nuclear Disarmament Movement. We took part in running several publications for the dissident communists, the New Left and the peace movement. We also had three children and, since we were both the only surviving children in our families, some responsibility for parents and other elderly relatives. We had a large house which was often the base for political activity, was the editorial and distribution centre for a national journal, the *New Reasoner*, and was constantly visited by people of all kinds from Britain and abroad. Of course we lived in a shambles, house and garden were rarely far away from complete chaos, one project only ever got completed by putting off something

6

equally important and what money we had tended to get absorbed into political activities instead of into clothes, furniture or re-decoration of the house. But in those years *William Morris* and *The Making of the English Working Class* were published, as well as journalism, reviews, etc. from both of us.

This is not an autobiography, so the whole story of those years is not relevant. What I am trying to explain is how a partnership of historians worked under those conditions. The first thing is that, although we had very little money (Edward's starting salary in 1948 was £425 a year), some of it always went to a bit of help in the house and paying for laundry, etc. We have always had some domestic help, and this has come before new clothes or outside enter-tainment. One thing about adult education work is that there are very few evenings available for theatre visits or dinner parties anyway, and when we were both teaching in the evenings part of my earnings would have to be used for child-sitters. Although we did not earn a great deal, we both had supportive families and were never in a situation in which lack of money could have been an absolute disaster. Family presents certainly helped with the chil-dren's clothes, toys and holidays.

Another vital element to me was the support and friendship of fellow political activists and of other adult education workers and historians. As a member of the Communist Party Historians' Group (until 1956) I made very many friends and took part in group work and group research. The Leeds University extra-mural department always invited me to academic conferences. I was a member of the Society for the Study of Labour History from its foundation in 1960, and, as well as attending conferences and serving on the committee, was encouraged to publish in the *Bulletin*. Although my time was usually pretty fully occupied with the house and the children, Edward always took over for a couple of weeks each year so that I could attend conferences or work in the London archives. By modern standards it could be said that I had a very limited space for my own work, but that space was always made. Edward and other colleagues also helped me to keep up to date with publications in my fields of interest. During those years we began to put together our collection of publications connected with nineteenth-century social history. Old bound copies of journals, trial reports and shabby editions of nineteenth-century memoirs and local studies could still be picked up for coppers or shillings, and we formed the basis of our library in this way. This meant that there was almost always raw material in the house for research and writing.

Like many women, I suppose, before I had any children I thought that the main problem in keeping one's intellect and work alive would be to find good systems of child-minding. But for me, this did not become the major problem. I never felt happy about handing the children over to a state agency in their pre-school years for any but short stretches of time. This was, however, a personal choice and I believed then, as I believe now, that all women should have a genuine choice in this matter. One of the first political campaigns that I organized in the West Riding was to prevent the closure of the day nurseries in the district, a campaign in which we succeeded, at least for a time. Many women need to work while their children are small, others would like to if good child care were available. Even those parents of either sex who prefer to work part-time or to stay at home with young children should have access to good facilities so that they have some time of their own to provide release from the isolation of domestic child care, especially since the 'traditional' support of old-style extended families is no longer available. In our case, since the part-time teaching I did was evening work, we usually only left the children regularly when they were asleep. Even when they were all at school it did not seem possible to take a full-time appointment, although we were fortunate in that Edward's work was in the evenings so that he was available to meet them from school or see them off in the mornings if I was away on day-time work. But I don't think I would ever have had the emotional or physical energy to take on a full-time position which involved anything more than a nine-to-five commitment while the children were young. Part-time teaching and working as an interviewer on various sociological inquiries were absorbing jobs but both allowed for flexibility of working hours and neither involved overall responsibility for the projects of which they were part.

We moved into internal academic work partly because we felt the need of a change but also because as the children got older we needed more conventional social hours to stay in touch with them. Edward had always intended to work as a freelance writer, so that once we had moved south and the children were teenagers, I began to look for a full-time job. Here again I was very lucky. The last work I did part time was to write a school textbook. In order to do that I read an enormous amount of recent secondary work outside my own immediate fields of history. By the time I was looking for jobs I had a textbook in print and several articles and a document collection either in print or ready for publication. I obtained a fellowship at the University of Birmingham which was turned into a full-time lectureship after two years. Edward meanwhile resigned from Warwick in order to write full time. We have actually never both been engaged in full-time work outside the home except in more recent years when we have taken joint teaching appointments in other countries.

This story explains why my output has been small for a career covering more than forty years. In a working partnership exact equality is seldom achieved, and I have had less time and space for my work than Edward has. However, I don't think that I resent this at all, since the quality of his work is its own justification. If I did not respect his work I might feel differently, since I don't suffer from undue modesty. If our work is set side by side there is no doubt which is the more important and interesting. But of course there are marginal matters in the relationship which can be irritating.

Dale Spender and Marion Glastonbury have come, unasked, to my defence and claimed that my name should be on the cover of some of Edward's work.[2] This is not so. The way academic partnerships exist in our generation is that each of us does his or her own work and has to be judged by it. In the last generation of historians there were a number – outstandingly the Hammonds and the Webbs – who worked as a team and presented themselves as joint authors. In an earlier period the wife would not expect to be named – Dorothea would hardly have expected her name to appear with Casaubon's, though she was prepared to dedicate her life to helping him with his work. In our generation we are individuals and expect to be judged as such. Edward's acknowledgement of my help in the preface to *The Making* is, *pace* Ms Glastonbury, handsome. It is also intended seriously. But it has become so much the custom for formal acknowledgements to be made by men writers to their wives that it has usually been taken by other historians to be merely another one of these. We did discuss the presentation of the book together, there are ideas in it which I recognize as having started with me (as I am sure there are ideas in my books that Edward recognizes, though everyone assumes that this will be so). When one of a couple publishes first, there will be joint ideas that come out in the first publication. I am not making any claims here to support the Spender/Glastonbury line – 'borrowings' from my notebooks were just that; historians' notebooks are full of notes on primary sources not sublime thoughts, and we have both always shared and passed on discoveries with each other as we have done also with many friends and students.

It has become something of a cliché that people of our generation who lived through the war were optimists about the possibilities of social and political change. We had defended the Beveridge Report which many people now seem to assume was accepted without question when it was first published. Edward, who was a junior officer when it appeared, was told by his commanding officer to talk to the men about it and to get hold of a copy 'because you can't attack it without reading it first'. In Cambridge a meeting of support was attacked and shouted down with more vigour by right-wing undergraduates than any other political meeting I remember. In the 1945 election I voted for the first time and also cast proxy votes for my brother and others in the armed forces. I have never experienced an election in which people were so anxious not to miss their chance to vote and the massive support for Labour and its programme of social reform surprised everyone, including the leaders of the Communist Party, who were proposing a post-war coalition to include all shades from Churchill to Gallagher. Several of my friends who stood for Labour as a gesture in safe Conservative seats found themselves elected to Parliament and pushed into political careers in spite of themselves. There certainly was an eagerness for change and an optimism about political and social improvement based on the twin Beveridge prerequisites of full employment and universal free health services. There was also, inevitably, a degree of conservatism even amongst the young and optimistic. The war had evoked a renewed interest in our own history. Movements for colonial freedom brought into high profile the conflicts within metropolitan countries in Europe between imperialist and anti-imperialist political programmes, while the stories of the resistance to the Nazi occupation in Europe focused attention on the patriotism of the common people. Young people who were interested in history turned from the stories of high politics and international diplomacy to the history of labour and of their own ancestors among the common people of the world.

The first models for the new interests were historians like G.D.H. Cole and H.L. Beales, radicals from the 1930s who helped to found the Society for the Study of Labour History, and who encouraged the great burst of research work which took off after the war. For Edward and me probably the greatest influence at this time was Dona Torr. Dona was a life-long communist who had worked for the party in many parts of the world. Her scholarship included academic training in music as well as in history and literature. She was a linguist with an interest in modern and classical languages. The boundaries of academic disciplines for her were never conventionally set, but this did not mean that she was ever sloppy or undisciplined in her work. Her great fault as a scholar was her generosity. She would always set aside her own work to give a close reading to work of other writers, often spending days in the libraries before she made her final comments. Her letters were full of information and sparkling with ideas, and her conversation was full of wit and insight – on at least one occasion I became so involved in discussion with her that we missed our stop on the underground and had returned to central London before we realized that we had been to Stanmore and back.

The Communist Party Historians' Group was one of the organizations which I attended more often than Edward. With a young family we could rarely both attend, but for me the meetings and the work of the duplicated sheet *Our History* kept me in touch and working at a time when I had very limited time and space for independent work. Some of the friendships we made in the group have remained, though a few fractured completely in 1956 – but that is another story.

The events of 1956, beginning with the secret speech of Khrushchev and continuing through the conflicts within all the European Communist Parties during the next two years or so, have been well documented. Perhaps there is room for a more reflective study by some of those who took part, in the light of the most recent developments in the former Soviet Union and Eastern Europe. Edward and I were part of a group within the British Communist Party who believed it would be possible to develop democratic processes and expand the discussion of socialist ideas and programmes within the party. We were publishing a duplicated 'journal', *The Reasoner* (the title borrowed from the nineteenth-century rationalist publication), of which several of the contributors were in the Historians' Group. Feelings in the party were running high; on the day on which I attended the annual meeting of the Historians' Group Edward was at the meeting of the Yorkshire District Committee, of which he was a member. Until that day neither of us had considered leaving the party. The evening before the group meeting my friend James Klugman, the national party education officer, who was to speak at the meeting, telephoned me at my parents' house in London to ask what he should speak about: 'Surely the historians don't want to talk about all this Joe business?' I told him that I thought we did, but I was amazed at the extent to which he had totally under-estimated the effect of the Khrushchev speech on people in the party. It was at the meeting of the Yorkshire District Committee that same weekend that Mick Jenkins casually let drop the information that the party's programme, *The British Road to Socialism*, had partly been written by Stalin's 'own fair hand'. There are many more stories that can be told about the almost complete lack of understanding among the officials of the CPGB of the impact of the revelations and later of the Hungarian rising on the British membership. These two incidents which led Edward and me both to say publicly that we were likely to find it impossible to stay in the party are small illustrations. The people who left the party then and over the next two years were the activists who had, in the peace movement and in some trade unions, worked with activists outside the party and who were appalled both by the admissions from the Soviet Union but even more by the response to them of the leaders of the British Communists. It is an odd coincidence that we both reached the same point in our relations with the party simultaneously – I must admit that I was very relieved to find when we telephoned that evening that we were in agreement.

I had been in the Communist Party for seventeen years. In that time I had had several rows with party officials and had always been uneasy about aspects of discipline and the demands made on active members. In many ways leaving was a great liberation. Nevertheless there were many positive sides to party membership – very able people from different classes were united in a movement that respected achievement and organizing ability. Women were respected and allowed to choose their own fields of work, specific 'women's work' was sometimes done, but the men members took an interest and sometimes a part in it and many women did other kinds of work. Wives who were not party supporters often had rather a bad time, I suppose, but then so did husbands in the same position. The commitment of party activists was often of a religious intensity, just as many of the thought processes of conventional Marxism are closer to religious dogma than to rational inquiry. But the experience of membership of a closed church has some positive features. Membership of an out-group disliked or distrusted by most of the rest of society is a useful counter to certain kinds of ambition, and perhaps leads to a better understanding of minority cultures of all kinds. Such membership may lead to exclusion from some kinds of social activity, but it is also an automatic passport when travelling in Britain or throughout the world. Servicemen serving overseas made immediate friends in Europe and in the East, whilst friendships we made with US communists and radicals stationed in Britain have in some cases lasted for the rest of our lives.

The first wave of nuclear disarmament agitation owed a great deal in Britain to ex-communists. The CP itself remained to the bitter end the advocate of peace agitation as the instrument of Soviet foreign policy. There have been times at which any sane person would have accepted the logic of Soviet policy, and support by the world peace movements was logical enough. But by the time that the Soviet Union became a nuclear power and the military could be seen to have gained increasing control, not only was Soviet nuclear weaponry equal at least in danger to that of the other nuclear powers, but the lack of any kind of possibility of anti-government pressure by the citizens on their authorities removed even the degree of pressure which could be exerted in the West. While citizens in the USA significantly retarded the development of nuclear power if not of weapons, the Soviet regime allowed nuclear disasters on a scale which has still to be fully assessed. The lack of elementary citizens' rights in the Soviet Union and most East European states under its suzerainty had always concerned socialists in the rest of the world, but there were people in the peace movement, chiefly the communists but also some of the pacifist and religious groups, who insisted that the issue of world peace must be considered quite separately from that of democracy and citizens' rights within the nuclear powers. The peace movement of the 1980s brought the two issues of peace and freedom together. It aimed at the restriction of nuclear weapons throughout the world but had also inevitably to concern itself with citizens' rights and democratic control in the countries concerned. Many of the courageous dissidents in Central and Eastern Europe and the Soviet Union reached out for international support by aligning themselves with the European and world movements for the limitation of nuclear weapons.

As an introduction to a book of essays this account seems to be going out of control. However, in attempting to offer a profile of the work it is relevant briefly to set it in the context of the politics of the period in which it was being written. The strong and deep movements for political and social change which had begun between the wars but which had surfaced with an assumption of possible success in the war and the immediate post-war years led to an awakening of interest in the history of the majority of the people of Britain and of the movements which in the past had embodied some of the same beliefs and values. From the women teachers at school and college I had learned the history of the movement for women's education and admission to public life and the professions. In the CP we were encouraged to study the history of earlier socialist movements – albeit often by way of the immensely condescending judgements of Marx and Engels. In the peace movement the experience of 'single-issue' campaigning and its ability to draw together energy and aspirations from many sources illuminated the power of a slogan or a prophecy to release bursts of energy and commitment far exceeding those usually involved in party political campaigning.

My first interest, started while I was at school, was in Chartism and in the agitation for political rights for working people and for women. As I hope the essays illustrate, this rather narrow politically directed framework of research soon began to seem inadequate.

When it came to the past history of women of the lower classes, the main accounts of the Chartist movement had very little to say. The mainstream histories seemed to show only one reference to women, one that is still reproduced in secondary accounts – William Lovett's assertion that the inclusion of women's suffrage as one of the points of the Charter, which he supported, was over-ruled by those who thought the idea too extreme and likely to alienate many reformers. I have shown elsewhere the extent to which he had in any case misremembered the matter, but one of the first things I found when I went back to the research in the documents and publications of the Chartist period was a very considerable presence of women in the movement. But, disappointingly, they rarely seemed to be pressing for the suffrage or for the right to work or for access to higher education. I noted their presence and their behaviour, but to begin with found them difficult to write into the picture. It was a chance remark in a colleague's paper at a conference which set me reconsidering these women. My colleague spoke of Chartists in the later 1840s and 1850s organizing tea parties to which they could 'bring their wives'. The idea of the women whom I had encountered in the movement being 'brought' by husbands from somewhere outside the movement did not fit with my picture of these Chartist women. I went back to my notes and found them there, often the source of their sons' and other family members' radical ideas – W.E. Adams's Chartist grandmother and aunts reading Chartist papers and hanging John Frost's portrait on the wall of the room in which they earned their living as washerwomen, and hundreds taking part in crowd activity, whether shouting abuse at the soldiers at times of high tension or singing hymns on the way home from mass camp meetings. Looking afresh at what the women were actually doing and not at what I would have liked them to be doing brought them into focus and threw new light for me on the nature of the movement and on the communities in which it flourished. There weren't enough Chartist women asking for the vote, though there were certainly many more than most standard histories allowed. But if they weren't asking for the vote what were they doing? For as soon as one goes back to the archives and reads press and police reports, the women tumble into the picture. In fact without the support of a good many women the kind of community involvement which was clearly there in the Chartist period would have been impossible.

There are many other places in which changes in the contemporary world or in my own circumstances have led me to reconsider my version of the past. This is part of the experience of all scholars who are not simply antiquarians. Our awareness of the fragility of the physical environment has made us look again at one of history's major teleological assumptions – the measurement of 'progress' in terms of economic growth and the exploitation of natural resources. That other teleology which saw history as the inevitable and predictable movement from one mode of production to another in which each produced greater material wealth and increasingly egalitarian liberating social formations made possible by greater material resources, whilst not identical with the first, nevertheless underlay much social and historical theory which was by no means Marxist in origin. Various versions of enlightenment thought which envisaged the gradual replacement of superstition, bigotry and prejudice by tolerance, scepticism and free inquiry have received heavy punishment in an age which has seen the revival of nationalism and passionate adhesion to religions and sects which have over-ridden loyalties to class, gender or other assumed transnational loyalties.

Nevertheless, there is at least an equal danger in automatically reading contemporary tensions back into history – even though we have to admit the need to re-examine some of our past work to see how much our desire to see such phenomena as ephemeral may have led us to miss essential signs.

The main theme of this collection is the radicalism of the 1830s and 1840s and those who turned its programmes into political action, including hitherto under-estimated sections like the women and the Irish. The final piece, which arose out of the work I did for a book on Queen Victoria, may seem a bit tangential, but it is a brief attempt to look at some of the ways in which the gender of the monarch defused the republicanism of the radicals of the period. Republicanism was always an element in popular radicalism, but after the advent of Victoria it assumed a lower profile. Most Chartists, rightly or wrongly, saw the monarchy as an anchronism rather than as a source of power and oppression. Whereas in most of the rest of Europe republicanism was a leading component of movements for radical political reform, in the British Isles it remained, even in Ireland, of primary importance only to a small minority.

Historians of the crowd or of the non-propertied classes in general have always faced particular problems in terms of sources. The wealthy and educated insiders have left many records. Not only in the mass of material concerned with government and high politics, but in literature, in the records of legal cases, property transactions, in personal journals and correspondence and in every kind of document from wills to laundry lists. The poor had no muniment rooms and seldom entered any records on their own terms. They appear as servants, criminals, recipients of charity or as turbulent or obedient subjects. If Marxists have tended to attribute general sensations of class to whole populations on the basis of a sometimes limited amount of organized labour activity, some recent tendencies have succeeded, by consulting alternative narratives, in producing a picture of working people based on the lowest common denominator of a trivialized, reductionist and largely commercial reading of 'popular culture', particularly in the late nineteenth century. If labour historians put too much weight on organization and rhetoric which indicated a class consciousness which con- formed to an over-simplified view of economic class as the only true determinant of positive action, a swing seems now to be taking place towards a patronizing and reductionist view of working people's identity. Working people in the nineteenth century, we are told, adopted 'the cult of the parlour'. Fancy working men and women wanting a place in their miserable dwellings free from the clutter of children and the clobber of working clothes and equipment. Some of them even bought pianos! Such behaviour was clearly an attempt to become middle class and to desert the genuine culture of the working class. The genuine working man was to be found in the pub or at the football match. In these historical narratives the trade unionist or independent labour politician of either gender is replaced by the stage Irishman, the stage Lancastrian or the 'dialect poet' who trivialized local tradition for a metropolitan readership.

I have argued elsewhere that nineteenth-century British history cannot be written without great regard to the idea of class. It was present in relationships in the home and in the workplace; speech, eating habits, dress, location of homes and of children's education all defined the status of the individual in the hierarchies of class society. If earlier definitions of class can now be seen to have been over-simplified and inadequate to describe all kinds of social tension, then we need different definitions. Gender, regional and national loyalties, religious and ethnic divisions have been neglected as divisive factors, just as monarchism, an over-arching 'British' form of patriotism and a generalized adhesion to Christian principles have been under-estimated as forces of national cohesion. The hidden or overt teleologies of class, nation and gender have often led us to ignore or suppress movements or occasions in history which don't fit in. The concept – hidden or enunciated – of true' and 'false' forms of consciousness has too often led to judgemental and teleological forms of history. But in re-examining the difficult source material to gain greater understanding of the majority of the population, let us not be drawn into another form of over-simplification and reductionism. The music halls, at the height of their popularity with the urban populations in the late nineteenth and early twentieth centuries, were governed by rules of censorship and of commerce. The chapels and churches relied for their income and support on the propertied members of their congregations. Among the music hall audiences and the Christian congregations were people who also attended Labour Party or suffragette meetings. The Irishman laughing at 'Paddy McGinty's Goat' probably supported the Fenians. The audience cannot be conflated with the providers of mass culture. The politics of the first quarter of the twentieth century sees class representation emerge under the protection of the ballot in spite of the counter-propaganda of churches, music halls and popular press. No one who has studied the history of Britain during the First World War could possibly ignore the enormous power of class distinction nor under-estimate its influence on the post-war elections.

Two of the essays here deal with matters of consciousness which appear to be more powerful than class. The mass movement of the Irish under O'Connell for the repeal of the union called on all members of both churches and none and on people of all classes to rally in support of national liberation. I suggest that one of the reasons for its failure was distrust of the class-based programme of the British dissidents. In a brief consideration of the role of a female monarch in defeating republicanism in Britain, I look at the way in which a female figure was seen as less threatening to political liberty than alternative male candidates, and was later to epitomize a non-political, familial and moral ambience which could call forth loyalty from families in all classes. There are other aspects of the monarchy which call on deep-seated superstitions and myths, and which provide a bonding force in a society in which the ethnic, religious and linguistic uniformities which characterize many other nation states do not exist. For all the flippancy and irreverence with which the public speaks of royalty, there is no political party which would dare to puts its abolition on the programme.

Working people of both genders were outside the pale of the constitution for most of the nineteenth century. Not only were women politically and legally outsiders, but historical definitions of class and community have too often been so dominantly male that they have failed to see the women, and they have remained outside the main historical narratives. The Irish have been surprisingly under-studied in the context of British working-class history, where they have all too often been treated as a single out-group with little awareness of the divisions and complexities of their own politics. Excellent work is now being done to remedy these oversights. I hope that my writing and teaching have made some contribution to this work.

Notes

1. Elizabeth Fox-Genevese, *Feminism Without Illusions*, Chapel Hill and London 1991, p. 246.
2. Dale Spender, *The Writing or the Sex?*, New York, Oxford, Beijing, Frankfurt, São Paulo, Sidney 1989, p. 142. Glastonbury in ibid.

1

Chartism and the Historians

Chartism was a movement which involved considerable sections of
the working people of Britain in the years between 1838 and 1858.
At three high points during those years massive national campaigns
were held to collect signatures to a national petition, and the
petition was three times presented to Parliament. It asked, in
constitutional language, for the extension of the suffrage to all adult
males, with the safeguard of a secret ballot; the abolition of
property qualifications for members of Parliament and the payment
of such members; the division of the country into electoral districts
of the same size; and the annual election of Parliaments. The
campaigns which accompanied the presentation of the petitions saw
almost every form of political action employed, legal and illegal.
Huge outdoor demonstrations were held with speakers, banners
and music at which resolutions were passed, money collected and
delegates elected to national gatherings. Indoor meetings included
educational activity of all kinds, children's schools, adult literacy
classes, women's groups and lectures. The National Charter Association, with national and local elected officials and local branches
throughout the country, was perhaps the first political body of its
kind in the world, and challenged the existing law on corresponding
societies. The national paper, the *Northern Star*, had for a time the
largest circulation of any provincial weekly, and many other
shorter-lived newspapers and journals as well as pamphlets, handbills, posters and prints testified to the enthusiasm and literacy of
the movement's supporters. Local riots occurred as well as attempted risings, whose leaders were punished with sentences varying
from imprisonment to transportation for life. Chartists were arrested and imprisoned by the hundred for seditious utterance, seditious
libel, incitement, drilling, conspiracy and other charges. Their trials

19

and the government's responses to their actions helped to form the law on many of these issues.

Chartism left its mark on a whole range of the country's institutions. It inspired or speeded up the establishment of a national network of police forces and the provision of a morally acceptable system of schools in the manufacturing districts. It affected areas of philanthropy and welfare provision and undoubtedly contributed to the passing of the Ten Hours Act, the repeal of the Corn Laws and the modification in practice of the working of the Poor Law Amendment Act. These were not by any means all achievements at which the Chartists aimed. But the interaction of the movement with the moral concerns of the period can be examined in a range of writings – journalism, essays and novels – some of which deal specifically with Chartism, others which concern themselves with crowd action in a way which clearly indicates the effect of Chartism on educated opinion.

The fascination of the movement for contemporaries has been paralleled in subsequent generations. The nineteenth and twentieth centuries have witnessed movements in most parts of the world of subject classes and subject peoples seeking access to political power and to a degree of social and political control over their lives. In turn, working men, subject national and ethnic minority groups and women have organized to gain citizen rights or to overthrow or reorganize existing structures of power. Chartism's claim to have been the first large-scale national movement to embody the demand for universal male citizen rights has lent it an especial interest as a movement which tackled at an early stage many of the complex questions which were later to face modern labour movements. Many of these were seen to have been presaged in the Chartist period, either explicitly in the political programme of the movement or in the many debates, discussions and activities which accompanied the main agitation. Those who have written about the movement, whether as participants or as historians, have usually been guided by political commitments of their own, looking back for the ancestry of their own reforming principles or a testing-ground for their own historical theories.

A review of the history of Chartism is, therefore, both a study in historiography and part of the study of labour history. The present controversies surrounding the interpretation of Chartism are closely connected with events in the modern world, particularly perhaps with the changes taking place in Eastern Europe. In looking back at the way history has been written it is possible to see how the language used to describe popular politics has changed over the years, and how the changes have affected the assessment of Chartism and of its influence.

Until very recently few writers have questioned the definition of Chartism as a class movement. The nineteenth century was imbued with the concept of class, and all its earlier historians saw the social divisions within British society as the main motivations of the Chartist movement. Some historians have questioned Frederick Engels's description of Chartism as 'the compact form of their [the proletarians'] opposition to the bourgeoisie',[1] but their objections until recently tended to stress the influence of middle-class thought and leadership on the movement's programme and policy rather than to dismiss the concept of class altogether. In recent times, however, the very omnipresence of the word and the concept 'class' and its frequent use without precise definition has suggested to some writers that the term is of no value as a historical category.[2] The same objection could, however, be made to many other categories, including those of 'race' and 'nation'. To write modern European history without using these terms, employed so often by the actors being described, would seem wilfully to ignore the strong element of self-identity which they embody. In an age in which the adoption of 'working-class' clothes – Feargus O'Connor's fustian suit or William Morris's reefer jacket – could send out an immediate message to an audience, or when almost every gesture from the way of holding a fork to the order in which tea and milk were added to the teacup could be taken as an indication of social class, the term has to be used descriptively if not analytically. This is not to deny that Chartists and their historians have undoubtedly used terms like 'class' and 'nation' differently in different contexts, and changes in the meanings attached have been part of the story of Chartist history.

The language of class is to be found in all three of the main kinds of historical writing about Chartism. These were accounts by participants, accounts by mainstream historians and accounts by historians and publicists involved in the labour movement.

The first published history of the Chartist movement was that issued originally in serial parts in 1854 by R.G. Gammage, himself an active participant in the later years of the movement.[3] The revised edition produced in 1894 included some corrections and comments from other actors in the movement, and was taken rather uncritically as an objective account by a participator until John Saville pointed out some of its distortions in his work on Ernest Jones.[4] Gammage's book remains a valuable source, but one to be read with the caution brought to any other contemporary account.

The widespread nature of Chartism and the interest it aroused can be seen from the large number of contemporary accounts which have survived. These include full-scale autobiographies, local reminiscences, letters to local and national newspapers, obituaries of former Chartists and a considerable number of fictional recreations of Chartists and Chartism.[5] Many of these contemporary accounts, like that of Gammage, lay stress on the political nature of the movement, showing the turn by the working classes towards political reform in the wake of the middle-class victory of the 1832 Reform Act. Looking back from the 1860s, George Eliot described the 1830s and 1840s, the age in which she placed her radical hero Felix Holt, as a time when 'faith in the efficacy of political change was at fever-heat in ardent reformers'.[6] Disraeli, the foremost English political novelist of the nineteenth century, gave what was in many ways a surprisingly sympathetic account of Chartism as a political movement in *Sybil or the Two Nations*, particularly in the famous speech by the Chartist leader who enunciates the concept of the two nations

> between whom there is no intercourse and no sympathy; who are as ignorant of each other's habits, thoughts and feelings as if they were dwellers in different zones, or inhabitants of different planets; who are formed by a different breeding, are fed by a different food, are ordered by different manners, and are not governed by the same laws.... The rich and the poor.[7]

Alongside the political view of Chartism was the view stressed in most of the other middle-class novels on the subject and enunciated by Thomas Carlyle in his pamphlet of 1839, which saw Chartism as the expression of social misery, whose motivation was not, in reality, political reform but the improvement of social conditions. For Carlyle and for those who followed his analysis, Chartism was an inarticulate cry for the establishment of a more humane dialogue between the poor and their social superiors. He spoke of the need for

> a genuine understanding by the upper classes of society of what it is that the underclasses intrinsically mean; a clear interpretation of the thought which at heart torments these wild inarticulate souls, struggling there,

with inarticulate uproar, like dumb creatures in pain, unable to speak what is in them![8]

The so-called 'condition-of-England novelists' – the name comes of course from Carlyle – including Dickens, Eliot, Gaskell and Kingsley, largely accepted his interpretation. Many of their readers, including some Chartists and ex-Chartists, considered these authors, particularly Charles Kingsley and Elizabeth Gaskell, to be sympathetic to the movement. Both these writers created specifically Chartist characters whom they depicted as serious and articulate. But neither writer had any sympathy either with the leaders of the movement or with its political aims. Mrs Gaskell offered a more Christian version of Carlyle's analysis when she wrote that

> The actions of the uneducated seem to me typified in those of Frankenstein, that monster of many human qualities, ungifted with a soul, a knowledge of the difference between good and evil.... The people rise up to life; they irritate us, they terrify us, and we become their enemies. Then, in the sorrowful moment of our triumphant power, their eyes gaze on us with mute reproach. Why have we made them what they are; a powerful monster, yet without the inner means for peace and happiness.[9]

Charles Kingsley's *Alton Locke* is the story of a gifted young working man misled by his experience of poverty and misery into seeking political solutions to what are essentially moral problems, and to following the leadership of scheming and corrupt demagogues. As G.J. Holyoake, himself a Chartist in his early years, pointed out, Kingsley's picture of the events of 10 April 1848, in which O'Connor appears as a coward and the whole movement collapses into ridicule and despair, became the accepted picture for historians in the later nineteenth century, and seriously distorted the history of the movement.[10]

By the later years of the nineteenth century most British academic historians had begun to combine a political with a social interpretation of Chartism. The dominant historical philosophy by this time was some version of the 'Whig interpretation of history', which saw British political history as the gradual development of representative parliamentary institutions under a benign constitutional monarchy. In this interpretation the political aims of the Chartists were not so much evil and misguided as premature. The second half of the century had seen the spread of popular education and the expansion of the economy, and working men of regular habits and settled dwellings were gradually being admitted within the pale of the constitution. Historians of this view considered that the Chartists were wrong to demand political rights, and mistaken in the methods they adopted to attain them, but they were usually prepared to accept that conditions among the working people had been very bad in the first half of the century. Liberals among them were even inclined to justify the responses of the Chartists and to stress the evils of the 'hungry forties' in order to illustrate the enormous benefits that had eventuated from the repeal of the Corn Laws in 1846 and the subsequent moves towards world freedom of trade. Some were even prepared to recognize the steadying force of a political programme:

> the working classes, maddened by sufferings which their ignorance often led them to impute to wrong causes, committed many deplorable and guilty actions. At the direct incentive of the Trades-Unions, the factory-hands sent threatening letters to the masters, fired the mills, made murderous attacks on such of their fellow-workmen as were willing to serve for lower wages, destroyed valuable machinery, and kept a large part of England, Scotland and Ireland in perpetual terror. Chartism, by its assertion of political principles, whether right or wrong, did a certain amount of good, by giving another direction to all this turbulent socialism.[11]

The writer's use of the word 'socialism' to describe the turbulent and irrational elements in working-class protest indicates a profound change which had occurred in the writing of the history of popular movements since the mid century. During the Chartist period the word had been used mainly to describe the cooperative and communitarian ideas of Owen and his contemporaries, the 'Ricardian Socialists', and had even been later used by the conservative group which included Kingsley, Ludlow and Maurice who advocated cooperative ventures for working men under the name of 'Christian Socialism'. In the years following the publication of the *Communist Manifesto* of 1848, however, the development of socialist movements in Britain and Europe had changed the whole ambience surrounding the word. It had come to be seen as a philosophy which raised the profile of class conflict and advocated the violent overthrow of existing social and political institutions and their replacement by institutions controlled by and for the working class.

Labour historians, Marxist and non-Marxist, began to look in

Chartism for the ancestry of the labour organizations that were arising all over Europe in the last quarter of the nineteenth century. The old Chartists themselves divided between those, like Harney, who adopted some form of Marx's analysis and those, like Benjamin Wilson of Halifax, who saw Gladstonian Liberalism as the logical successor to Chartism. 'It might now be said', wrote Wilson after having admitted to buying a gun in 1847, 'that we were fools, but I answer young people now have no idea of what we had to endure.' He spoke of a friend who had been moulding bullets in his cellar in the same year, who

> had a wife and children dependent on him, but was unable to get work, trade being so bad. Since then, however, under the blessings of free trade and by dint of perseverance, he has succeeded in saving a considerable sum and is now living retired from business.[12]

Wilson had no time for the Independent Labour Party which had begun in his later years, but, like his hero Ernest Jones, he believed that liberal democracy could be extended and used to achieve the social aims of the Chartist movement.[13] Brian Harrison and Patricia Hollis have pointed out the considerable continuities between Chartism and Gladstonian Liberalism in their study of Robert Lowery. Lowery was one of the few Chartists – Henry Vincent was another – who made the transition during the Chartist period.[14] At the time such men were seen as apostates from a radical tradition which stressed its opposition to both established parties. This tradition is described in the obituary notice of the old Huddersfield Chartist Thomas Vevers in the *Northern Star* in 1843:

> For half a century [he] had known what it was to 'brave the battle of the breeze'. He had been a Jacobin in the days of Church and King mobs, a reformer in the days of Horne Tooke and Hardy, a radical in the days of Hunt and Cobbett, and a Chartist in the present day of Whig and Tory persecution, of stern and stubborn principle.[15]

By 1891 the Liberal politician John Taylor was recalling the life of Ernest Jones, one of the last Chartist leaders:

> He was one of the chief pioneers in obtaining for the labouring classes non-conformists and others the freedom and privileges they now enjoy. In him the classes who were suffering under unjust laws had a bold, honest, straightforward and upright advocate.[16]

The early labour historians, like many of the Chartists and their contemporaries, did not make a clear distinction between political and social aims in the Chartist period. The Whig historian Macaulay had seen universal suffrage as threatening civilization itself.[17] Karl Marx's view of the consequences of political emancipation was not dissimilar. He wrote in 1852

> Universal Suffrage is the equivalent of political power for the working classes of England, where the proletariat forms the large majority of the population, where, in a long though underground civil war, it has gained a clear consciousness of its position as a class.... The carrying of Universal Suffrage in England would, therefore, be a far more socialistic measure than anything which has been honoured with that name on the Continent. Its inevitable result, here, is the political supremacy of the working class.[18]

Both Marx and Engels had heard the language of class among the Chartists in England in the 1840s. Marx's definition, however, which marginalized or excluded the artisan and the peasant from the mainstream of the proletariat, led many later Marxist historians to question the class nature of Chartism. The presence of many Irish among the leadership, concerned with problems of landholding, religion and national identity, as well as the high profile of the outworkers and the lower- and middle-range artisans in the movement rendered its definition as a proletarian movement problematic, whilst the insistence on a political programme which did not substantially differ from that of middle-class radicals of the eighteenth and early nineteenth century presented similar problems. Surely a truly proletarian movement should have been demanding the expropriation of the expropriators and the transformation of the economic rather than the political system?

The earliest academic historians of Chartism wrote at a time when the struggling British labour movement was sensitive to accusations that socialism was a doctrine of violence imported from abroad. As the onset of depression and the revelations of the desperate poverty of British cities in the late 1880s and 1890s revealed the inadequacy of free trade as a panacea, new movements began which combined political and social programmes and rejected the optimistic free-market dogmas of traditional liberalism. Two major traditions emerged which may be roughly divided into the Fabian – a Benthamite, positivist restatement of traditional liberalism, initially aimed at converting liberals to a degree of interventionism – and the Marxist – aiming at the revolutionary transformation of society by the transfer to a democratic government of all the means of production, distribution and exchange, the establishment of working-class power and the recognition of the international community of interest between workers in all parts of the world. The two concepts overlapped at some points and have been the subject of much learned and enlightened consideration during the present century. The two approaches, however, each tended to inform a different interpretation of the history of Chartism. The Webbs's *History of Trade Unionism* (1894) and Graham Wallas's *Life of Place* (1898) were scholarly Fabian works which gave Chartism a place of dignity and importance. The many references to the Chartists in the writings of Marx and Engels ensured that Marxist historians would pay the movement serious attention. H.M. Hyndman, one of the intellectual leaders of the socialist movement in Britain, wrote to Marx after the publication of *Capital* in 1881 suggesting that it was time to create a new organization to 'revive Chartism'. Both trends in the British labour movement looked to Chartism for an intellectual ancestry.

The first scholarly history of Chartism in English was Mark Hovell's *The Chartist Movement*, published, after the author's early death, in 1918.[19] Based to a large extent on the Place Manuscripts in the British Library, Hovell followed Place's London-centred, liberal interpretation of events. Himself an orthodox liberal in economics and a Fabian in politics, Hovell put forward a number of propositions which formed the shape of Chartist historiography and its representation in history textbooks until some years after the Second World War. He saw Chartism as beginning with the drawing up in 1838 of the People's Charter by a group of admirable rational London artisans supported by a group of enlightened Members of Parliament. Led by the London Working Men's Association (LWMA), these men began a peaceful agitation for their political aims, but the agitation was snatched from their hands by Feargus O'Connor, who was incapable of thinking up his own radical programme, and was taken by him into the provinces. Here it was shown to the 'illiterate and semi-barbaric' working people. These 'half-starved weavers, factory operatives and semi-barbarous colliers of the North of England' were not capable of rational behaviour. But neither were many of the writers and leaders, who were either 'maniacs' like Barnard and Attwood or 'cranks' of 'ill-balanced mind' like Davenport or Beaumont. When the London Working Men's Association reluctantly admitted the provincial radicals, 'violent, unorganized and undisciplined as they were' they sacrificed for ever the chance of achieving a working-class parliamentary party which 'should rival and ultimately overthrow ... the two historic Capitalist parties'. By combining even with the immigrant Irish, these misguided men (there are no women in Hovell's account) frightened the middle classes away from the programme and prevented Parliament from acceding to their petition, thus destroying all hope of success for the movement. In 1839 the petition was rejected, 'slain by the violence of its supporters, the tactlessness of its chief advocates, the inertia of conservatism, and its own inner contradictions'.

This dichotomy between London as the source of ideas, and of intelligent, skilled, informed artisan leadership, and the provinces, the source of inchoate energy, brutal, illiterate, stupid and impatient, has bedevilled much of the subsequent history of Chartism. It derives from the massive manuscript and press-cutting collection of Francis Place, who had acted as adviser to the LWMA partly to deflect radical working-class action away from opposition to the Poor Law Amendment Act. Place was an interesting figure, with a long involvement in radical politics, dating from the 1790s. By the Chartist period, however, he was firmly attached to the *Westminster Review* circle and their Benthamite views, and his designation of the provincial radicals and their leaders as 'wicked and designing men' informed his own accounts and those of the historians who based their work mainly on his collection. His influence is to be found as late as 1940 in the seminal work of G.D.H. Cole, whose analysis in *Chartist Portraits* implies the same division between rational Chartism and 'hunger Chartism'. This interpretation puts both elements within the working class and sees the movement as being destroyed by divisions within the class between better-off artisans and unskilled factory or out-workers. Yet the division along these lines is not to be found in the record. When Henry Vincent, signatory of the Charter and a missionary from the LWMA, went to speak in Lancashire and the West Riding of Yorkshire in 1838, he was overwhelmed by the scale of the movement there for universal suffrage. He wrote back to London saying that the metropolis and the rest of the country were at last beginning to catch up with the northern provinces.[20] The movement in 1838 and 1839 had its strength both in organization and in publications in the manufacturing districts, and it was not until after 1840 that it took on anything like a mass character in London and then among the lower artisan trades rather than among the top level of skilled and organized trades. The history of trade unions and of other forms of popular organization demonstrates a decade of provincial activity before the Charter. Trade unionism, general unionism, the demand for the suffrage and for factory reform and organized hostility to the Irish Coercion Act of 1833 and the Poor Law Amendment Act of 1834 followed the short-lived triumph of the 1832 Reform Act. The lack of response of the reformed Parliament and the hostility shown by the new electors to the demands and grievances of the unenfranchised led to the break-up of the reform alliance between middle- and working-class radicals throughout the country. The Charter gained its nation-wide support precisely because it was issued after nearly a decade of agitation had demonstrated the powerlessness of the non-electors and the inefficacy of local or limited agitation.[21]

The advocacy of suffrage extension to non-property-owners was, after 1832, almost entirely confined to politicians and political journalists who looked to a working-class constituency for support. Apart from the short and rather lonely excursion into complete suffrage by Joseph Sturge and a few associates in 1842, the middle and upper classes held firmly aloof. The Chartists did indeed appeal on many occasions for support for their programme to members of the higher classes, on grounds of natural justice or of enlightened self-interest, but support in the House of Commons even for hearing their arguments never rose above 50 votes; on the single occasion when a motion to implement the six points was presented it was defeated by 224 votes to 15, and only one Chartist MP was ever returned by a post-1832 borough electorate. The hundreds of thousands who signed the petition and turned out at their meetings and rallies were overwhelmingly voteless men, women and young people. There is little in the record to support Mark Hovell's belief that a rationally argued case for suffrage extension, had it not been accompanied by violent language and threatening behaviour, might well have converted enough electors to gain the Charter.

In the years between Hovell's departure for active service, which was to lead to his death in 1916, and the publication of his book, several works appeared on the subject of Chartism. These included the three Columbia studies published in 1916,[22] and the first book devoted entirely to the subject, *Le Chartism* of Edouard Dolleans, published in 1914. These were all serious works which remain necessary reading for scholars. All, however, make the same distinction between the 'moral force' doctrines of the LWMA, and the violence of the provincial leaders, although Rosenblatt in particular is more aware of the ambiguities of that position than

Hovell, and all stress the social nature of the discontent which fuelled Chartism's apparently political programme.

Chartism's next historian, Julius West, was also to die in his twenties and his book, too, was published posthumously. Appearing in 1920, his *History of Chartism* is also based on the Place papers. It is richer and fuller than Hovell's work and is especially good on the later years of the movement which Hovell did not reach. It shares the radical-Fabian outlook, although with a rather more generous spirit. A one-time employee of the Fabian Society, West compares the LWMA and its tactics with those of the Fabians, praising the slow, rational, educational approach to politics above the turbulent and rhetorical. Although not nearly as hostile to all things Irish and to Feargus O'Connor in particular as Mark Hovell, he was still inclined to see O'Connor as a would-be dictator and dominator of the movement.

In the years after the Russian Revolution of 1917, the gap in the British labour movement between the politics of gradualism and those of the advocates of armed revolution widened. The 1930s in particular saw several attempts to claim the Chartist movement as part of a revolutionary tradition rather than a gradualist one. Foremost among the Marxist revisions of Chartism was T.A. Rothstein's *From Chartism to Labourism*, published in 1929, but including essays dating from considerably earlier.[23] As the title implies, the essays that make up this work argue that the Chartist period and some of the Chartist writers, in particular James Bronterre O'Brien, had a clearer understanding of the nature of class and a greater awareness of the need for the total overthrow of bourgeois institutions than the later, more 'opportunist' leaders and institutions of the British labour movement. Rothstein was the archetypal committed Marxist. For him Harney was the first '(one might almost call him) Bolshevik', the Christian Socialists were 'sinister', whilst Bronterre O'Brien appeared as a John the Baptist, crying in the wilderness to prepare the way of the Lord, Karl Marx (usually referred to by Rothstein as 'our master' or 'our great teacher'). The tone throughout is that of an interpreter of the scriptures, reading the earlier prophets in the light of the greater truth to come; nevertheless, aspects of the book, in particular the close study of O'Brien's writing, although mainly based on his pre-Chartist work, and of groups such as the Fraternal Democrats and other Chartist supporters of European revolutions, were a valuable corrective to the over-simple Whig version of the Fabians. What it illustrated above all was the intensity of the class feeling which existed in the Chartist movement, although as a Marxist Rothstein had problems reconciling high levels of Chartist activity with areas in which production was carried out by artisans and small masters rather than by the pure proletarians of the factories.

For the Fabians, Hovell in particular, Chartism had been destroyed by the flamboyant and violent rhetoric of Feargus O'Connor. For the Marxists, Feargus was also the villain of the movement, not, however, for his violence but for his lack of revolutionary leadership. Reg Groves, in his book *But We Shall Rise Again* – the title taken from a poem by Marx's friend Ernest Jones – wrote that O'Connor

> personified and voiced the demands, not of those in the Movement drawn from the new proletarian elements, but of the handloom weavers and of the enormous and growing number of immigrants from the Irish countryside, who wanted to be led, not to the collective, Socialist society, but back to the days of pre-industrialism, back to the land and life of their fathers.... Essentially they were reactionary in outlook, adding numbers to the movement, but confusing its aims and destroying its hope of victory.[24]

Whereas for the Fabians O'Connor and his leadership had prevented the peaceful development of a rational movement which could have convinced the authorities of the desirability of a working-class franchise, for the Marxists O'Connor destroyed the movement by his opposition to socialism and his refusal to put himself at the head of a revolutionary proletarian force which could have overthrown capitalism.

The arguments about the class nature of Chartism have continued over many decades. Underlying them have been certain assumptions. Most historians, Marxist and non-Marxist, have assumed a meaning for the word class which derives from the Marxist definition, that is, that classes derive their economic definition from the relationship in which their members stand to the means of production. Marxist political formations derived their power and their social and political dynamic from the realization of common interest between all those who share this relationship. Since those who own or control the means of production and look to that ownership as the source of their wealth are bound to have different interests from those who own no property but the labour which they hire out to the owners, the very process of production is imbued with conflict. The conflict of interest between owning and non-owning classes is a constant fact of the capitalist mode of production. The historical role of the labour movement is the elevation of this conflict into an ideological or political form and the resolution of the struggle between the two classes which will lead to the overthrow of the dominant minority and its replacement by a higher mode of production in which the conflicts between owner-ship and work have been overcome and all work is done for the benefit of the whole of society. There have been many arguments within this tradition as to the extent to which this sharp class differentiation was unique to the nineteenth century and the extent to which the non-owners and working members of society did in fact recognize a community of interest, that is, on the timing of the emergence of a 'mature' working class. The Chartist movement undoubtedly comprised many strata of the wage-dependent poor, all of whom spoke of themselves as 'working people' but not all of whom fitted tidily into a single economic or social category. Francis Place, small-scale master breeches-maker, complained that mem-bers of the higher classes tended to write as though the working people – the great majority of the population – were one undiffer-entiated mass, and many historians have gone to some lengths to illustrate the conflicts of interests within the working classes – conflicts between skilled and unskilled, between regions, between ethnic groups, between the genders and between the 'rough' and 'respectable', irrespective of income, skill or ethnicity. A case has been made for all these divisions being of greater influence than those of class.

In the last fifty years Chartism has become a major focus for the study of aspects of popular history and for the elucidation of the concept of class. G.D.H. Cole, in his *Chartist Portraits* published in 1940, offered an analysis of the movement based on a series of studies of figures each of whom represented a trend within the movement. In the same year appeared David Williams's biography of the Welsh leader, John Frost, the first major biographical study of a Chartist. In 1958 the influential series of studies edited by Asa Briggs[25] changed the focus from the leaders to the localities and offered a series of sociologically oriented studies of the Chartist movement in different parts of the British Isles. In the years since its publication there have been a number of first-class biographical and regional studies, including the recent authoritative study of the Newport rising by D.J.V. Jones which revises the judgement of David Williams on the Newport events and presents a model of close analysis of regional events as a key to the interpretation of the movement as a whole. Jones shows South Wales as a society deeply divided by perceptions of class, and the rising as motivated by strong class feeling.[26] A study of the same events by Ivor Wilks also emphasizes the power of class motivations in the rising, although his suggestion that nationalism played an important part is not convincingly demonstrated.[27]

Writing about Chartism, then, has come from different theoretical traditions and has included varying judgements of the movement and its leaders. Until very recently, however, there has been little argument about the description of Chartism as a working-class movement. Differences have been on the tactics pursued by the leaders and the extent to which these represented the best interest of the working class. D.J. Rowe, for example, considered that the framers of the Charter had gone to the middle class for their programme,[28] whilst others have suggested that the working classes of the Chartist period accepted what was essentially a Tory (and therefore upper-class?) programme in preference to the Whig reforming programme which would have brought them better returns.[29] The failure of the Chartists to achieve an alliance with the enlightened middle class, illustrated above all by the rejection of Sturge's Complete Suffrage Union by the overwhelming majority of the Chartists, has been described as a serious error of judgement, but it has usually been recognized that the conflict of loyalties which led William Lovett to combine with his great rival Feargus O'Connor to insist on the retention of the name of the Charter represented a form of class solidarity operating at a deeper level than political programme-making. It is only in recent years that historians of various philosophical outlooks have begun to question the idea of Chartism as a working-class movement. These arguments rest either on the dismissal of class as a useful historical concept or on the assertion that the Chartist programme was not a class programme.

The current arguments have for the most part taken place in articles and discussion papers rather than in works of new research.[30] In a trenchant attack upon some recent writing, Norman McCord complains of the use of the term 'class' without a clear and acceptable definition, and suggests that history would be clearer if the concept were to be avoided altogether. The fact that the word was in constant use in the years under discussion does not, he suggests, justify its use without a clear definition; it is not necessarily the case that 'because a past society generally believed something to be true we should accept its reality'. Chartism's historians, like its participants, have been so much involved with the language of class that they have avoided a sharp definition. Another argument has been the suggestion that historians have been mistaken in thinking that the Chartists understood the meaning of class, or that the programme they offered was one that could properly be called a working-class programme. This argument contends that the working class was not 'made' by the Chartist period because the movement had either not discovered, or indeed may have turned its back on, the true nature of class exploitation. Those among the Chartists who did ponder on the economic ideas of the early socialists were led astray by them into thinking that 'A fundamental change in the ownership of capital and land could be secured by creating the necessary conditions for equitable exchange rather than by recourse to forcible appropriation and redistribution.' This misreading of the economics of capitalism 'assuredly pointed in the direction of an insipid non-theoretical labourism which demanded a fair day's pay for a fair day's work'.[31] This argument lies also behind the surprisingly influential essay by Gareth Stedman Jones, 'Re-thinking Chartism'.[32] Like the Marxist historians of the 1920s and 1930s, Noel Thompson and Stedman Jones assume a progression from a political consciousness which made the simple demand for equality before the law or a trade union consciousness which demanded bargaining rights for labour within a capitalist mode of production, both of which could be seen as partial forms of class consciousness, to a mature consciousness which would demand a total restructuring of the economic system by the forcible appropriation of all private property in land and industrial and financial capital and its administration by a state controlled by the working class. Such an appropriation would end the conflict of interest between owners and workers and would lead to a classless society in which production would be for the good of all rather than for the profit of a few. Although Chartist rhetoric abounds with statements which could be taken to presage the more mature outlook, these, it is argued, have been misread by later historians. The language of class used by the Chartists represented, in this argument, a form of false consciousness, an 'experience' of class which was not expressed in the form of the mature or correct demands which were historically necessary. Rothstein had seen a regression in the post-Chartist years from class consciousness to a narrower trade union consciousness. Others have suggested that the post-Chartist period saw the opening up of divisions within the working class, and the buying off of the skilled workers by the distribution of the spoils of imperialism. Proponents of various versions of the 'aristocracy of labour' theory have seen this buying off of the skilled workers as a reason for a general decline of class consciousness in the second half of the nineteenth century. Noel Thompson and Gareth Stedman Jones argue, on the contrary, that the class consciousness of the Chartists has always been over-stated and that the Chartist programme, through its emphasis on a limited concept of political freedom, prepared the way for a more general buying off by limited political concessions. 'If this was the case', writes Stedman Jones, 'there is then little need to introduce ambitious sociological explanations, such as the emergence of a labour aristocracy, co-option by the middle class or the invention of subtle means of social control, in order to explain the disappearance of Chartism.'[33]

These arguments all have in common a basic definition of class which derives from Marx, and which in the end rests upon conflicts of interest at the level of production. Some feminist writers have questioned aspects of this definition, which places the most basic human motivations in areas largely occupied by men. The idea that 'human' behaviour takes place in the workshop and 'animal' in the home is not one which women find readily acceptable, although there are women who see their oppression as mainly arising from their exclusion from the most important sectors of the production process. Nevertheless, a historical explanation which places the important conflicts at the point of production necessarily presents women as followers or encumberers – the 'impedimenta' of history.

The discussion, therefore, of the class nature of Chartism ranges from the suggestion that other divisive motivations were greater than those of class – that, for example, the Irish in Britain were excluded from the movement by ethnic divisions within the working population, women by gender differences, chapel and church-goers by sectarian divisions and workers by the different experience and programme of skilled and unskilled, factory and out-worker, rural and urban – through the suggestion that there was not a 'made' or 'mature' working class at that period (this was to come later) to the abandonment of the concept entirely. Norman McCord seems to suggest that there was no difference of outlook or behaviour between the propertied and the unpropertied, whilst F.M.L. Thompson asserts that differences *within* social classes between the 'rough' and the 'respectable' were greater during the whole of the

35

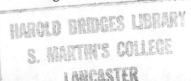

nineteenth century than any differences *between* classes.[34]

I find it difficult to believe that anyone who has worked in the archives and has studied the published and unpublished language of the Chartists can fail to see that the idea that above all united them into a nation-wide movement was the belief that there was a profound unity of interest between working people of all kinds. The concept of universal suffrage – even in its all-male form, and many Chartists also believed in women's suffrage – flies in the face of the view that the skilled feared the unskilled more than they feared the rich. William Lovett, who later in life did come to accept the idea of some kind of educational qualification for the suffrage, was fully convinced that the disadvantages of the unskilled were related to their political exclusion. Although the original demand for the suffrage included all men 'untainted by crime', Lovett was prepared to qualify even this. 'While, for instance, we agree with most reformers that felony should lead to the deprivation of political rights, we think the law which makes it a felony for a boy to steal an apple, or to kill a wild animal which crosses his path, is as cruel as it is unjust.'[35] If the divisions within the workforce were so great, it is difficult to see why so many skilled workmen were prepared to face imprisonment and even death alongside their unskilled brethren for the cause of general political emancipation. What is astonishing, in the light of later developments, is the extent to which the movement was able to incorporate people of different regional and ethnic origins, different genders and different occupations into a national campaign involving millions. The unifying factors were primarily a sense of class, a unifying leadership and a nationally distributed journal. Marx himself was impressed by the language of class, and defined it theoretically in terms of relationship to the means of production. His definition or some version of it has tended to be that taken by historians. The Chartists themselves, however, did not have the benefit of Marx's definition. Norman McCord is right to suggest that those of us who have used class in the strict Marxist sense have left many questions about the Chartist period unanswered. One might perhaps look at the cruder definition put forward by Edward Baines in the run-up to the 1832 Reform Bill. Writing to Lord John Russell in support of the proposed £10 householder franchise, he advocated it on the grounds that in his own town of Leeds, 'in the parts occupied by the working classes, not one householder in fifty would have a vote.... Out of about a hundred householders in the employment of Messers Taylor and

Wordsworth, machine-makers – the highest class of mechanic, – *only one* has a vote....'[36] The Reform Act, with its £10 urban householder and 40/- rural freeholder franchises, drew a line across the population between the propertied and the unpropertied. Of course there were a few higher-paid workmen, particularly in districts in which property was expensive, who spilled into the franchise from time to time, though such people might, by moving house, sink below the line again. Of course there were garret-masters who lived in lower-valued property than skilled artisans, but, as Baines had shown, the line had been deliberately drawn to exclude all rural and urban labourers and most artisans and skilled workmen.

Chartist speakers and writers did not use the term 'class' in the same way on all occasions. Sometimes it meant only waged workers, sometimes it included 'good' employers. The latter were defined as those who paid fair wages, who negotiated with workers' organizations and who obeyed the laws relating to the age and gender of employees. Such a definition included the 'useful' classes, that is, those engaged in the production of goods and services, as against those who gained their wealth from rents or usury. Feargus O'Connor often pointed out that small landlords and shopkeepers would benefit from the emancipation of the working people, since they depended on regular wages for their income. Bronterre O'Brien articulated the conflicts of interest between employers and workers and between producers and middlemen in a theoretical way which in many ways presaged Marx's analysis, and his writings were very widely read among the Chartists. Others, including the republicans W.J. Linton and W.E. Adams, foresaw the dangers of socialist forms which put control of labour into the hands of the state or of a centralized bureaucracy. For them the republic was a society informed by moral and ethical values rather than by a restructured economic system. All these and many other strands of thought were united in the campaign for the rights of citizenship, seen not as abstract desiderata but as the only means of access to the laws which governed the lives of the working people. The apparent success of the electoral influence of the employing classes in the post-1832 legislation undoubtedly helped to convince them of the need for the vote, just as the reform campaign itself and the campaign for Catholic Emancipation which preceded it encouraged them to believe in the efficacy of mass crowd action.

The underlying teleology of a Marxist interpretation of history suggests that class consciousness, once achieved, becomes the driving force of popular politics, and increasingly takes precedence over more limited forms of consciousness such as those pertaining to region, ethnicity or nationality. Historians have therefore tended to become concerned to account for the apparent retreat in the post-Chartist period. They have either read back ethnic conflict which did not in fact occur on a significant scale during the Chartist period, or have looked for economic or socio-economic explanations. It has usually been acknowledged that the late 1840s and early 1850s saw an improvement in trade and the rapid decline of a few of the most distressed trades, particularly the wool-combers, combined with a considerable emigration from the manufacturing districts. This, together with the natural exhaustion after ten years of energetic involvement, is sufficient to account for the decline of Chartism after the end of 1848, although this decline was not as rapid in all areas as has sometimes been suggested.[37] It does not, however, account for the lack of a political revival during the next period of distress in the mid-1850s.

It is not my purpose here to rewrite the history of Chartism. I have suggested elsewhere my view of the reasons for the decline of a working-class political movement, but there are some points in the question which especially relate to questions of historiography. As I have indicated, almost all historians have laid the blame for the failed revolution or the failed democratic conversion on the leadership, particularly that of Feargus O'Connor. In attempting to question this judgement I have been accused of writing 'O'Connor hagiography'.[38] Far be it from me to consider any politician saintly, and Feargus was very far from perfection. Nevertheless, to speak as though he was only one among a variety of possible leaders of the movement seems to me to be a misreading of the story. Indeed, had the name Chartism not been adopted, the movement would almost undoubtedly have been called after O'Connor in much the same way as the earlier reform movement is associated with Henry Hunt. O'Connor held the movement together, by his personality and through the *Northern Star*. Remove either from the picture and the movement crumbles into regional and sectarian agitations. The paper continually reported and described activity at all levels. Feargus held together a political and journalistic group of quarrelsome and talented individuals. The *Star* provided an income for local activists and a forum for discussion and description. Many other papers appeared before the *Star* and contemporaneously with it, but none provided anything like the same unifying and leadership qualities. It is possible to devise a 'better' leader or a 'better' paper, but it is not possible to point one out in history. As Harney wrote to Engels, who had suggested that he, Harney, would make a better leader for the movement, no one else, least of all himself, had the personality, the constitution, the physical presence, the eloquence or the physical courage for the position. Even in the knowledge of arms and military science, Harney believed, 'Was O'Connor thrown overboard, we might go further and fare worse'.[39] The leader of a failed movement rarely gets much praise from his associates, and the memoirs of Lovett and Cooper lay much blame at O'Connor's door, though Cooper admits to having been caught up in the general enthusiasm for his leadership during his Chartist days. In the recollections of those lower down the scale, who had no aspirations themselves to national leadership, however, O'Connor, 'that noble but unfortunate Irishman',[40] is remembered with respect and affection. For good or ill, he was an essential element in the movement, and it is not an exercise in hagiography to recognize this.[41]

Feargus O'Connor's politics were based on the need for independent working-class political action. He was certainly not above accepting political or financial help from other members of the higher classes who sympathized with his advocacy of working-class action, but his philosophy of universal suffrage was founded on the belief that every member of society should have an equal voice in making the laws by which it was governed. There were advocates of universal suffrage who believed that 'the people', given a voice, would follow their 'natural' leaders, usually enlightened aristocrats with a proper sense of social duty. For the Chartists, however, the suffrage was the road by which all members of society could take part in the political process. They certainly envisaged a working-class presence in the House of Commons, and envisaged a law-making system which would protect the extra-parliamentary institutions of the workers, their trade societies, cooperative ventures and educational institutions. Theirs was a political movement which did not, as Stedman Jones has pointed out, for the most part see the oppression of the working people as beginning in the productive process. In the Chartist period it was the liberal political economists and the growing socialist movement who moved their emphasis away from politics towards an emphasis on the nineteenth-century science of economics. Socialists increasingly tended to see economic change as the necessary precursor to political and cultural change. The Charter lost its power as a panacea for the cure of all social ills, to be replaced in some socialist vocabularies by the Revolution. The failure of ten years' agitation to effect an expansion of the suffrage, combined with the apparent cooption of universal suffrage by the powers of reactionary Bonapartism in France, turned workers in all parts of Britain towards more limited and local activity. In the years of greater economic stability and expansion space was made for the development of trade unions, cooperative societies, friendly societies and other organizations of protection for the regularly employed and thrifty. In the changed atmosphere of the second half of the century, ideology, expanding trade and industrial production, the control of local communities by police and renewed educational and propagandist activity all helped to divide the urban working class so that the better-off or more regularly employed developed social mores and social institutions which differed from those of the unskilled labourers and migrant workers with whom they had made common cause in the Chartist period. The institutions of the working people were not built without conflict and sacrifice. The trade unions of the skilled workers were often involved in bitter conflicts with employers and a rhetoric of class conflict can always be found in the journals and speeches of the union leaders. When towards the end of the century the unskilled workers began to organize in a new kind of trade union, it was from amongst the skilled trade unionists that much of their early support came. Nevertheless, as working men gradually came to be included in the political process, it was under the wing of the Liberal Party for many years, rather than as part of a declared working men's organization like the National Charter Association.

The Russian Revolution of 1917 saw the first attempt to overthrow the power of private property and replace it by a workers' state. Belief in the primacy of economic over political forces led many democrats to believe that whatever the short-comings of the political system which accompanied the Revolution, the basis had been laid for a society which would be both more productive and eventually freer and more egalitarian. Byzantine communism may have seemed a long way from the just society envisaged by the Painites and the Chartists, but the basis had been laid in the expropriation of private property and the social control of production. The end of the Soviet system and the socialist states of Eastern Europe has called this basic assumption into question, and may perhaps result in the return to a greater interest in the political concepts of democratic reforming movements than in the presence or absence in their programmes of alternative economic structures.

I have argued elsewhere that the Chartist period was remarkable for the low level of ethnic conflict among the working people. The Chartists included the repeal of the union with Ireland in their programme and campaigned actively against Irish coercion.[42] They also formed organizations for solidarity with Poland and Hungary and with other European movements for political reform or national liberation. Like class consciousness, internationalism has often been seen as a once and for all achievement. Once prejudice and false consciousness has been cast off, it can surely never return? The experience of the 1980s and 1990s has demonstrated the enormous power of ethnic, nationalist, religious and sectarian loyalties to cut across class and regional loyalties. What had often been seen, especially by Marxists, as superficial and spurious divisions invented to assist imperialists and exploiters have re-arisen to fuel conflicts which uproot families and communities and lead to fratricide and destruction. Perhaps this makes all the more remarkable the apparent lack of such conflicts among the working people in early industrial Britain, when Chartist leaders could include several Irishmen – some Protestant, some Catholic, some neither – at least one black West Indian and one Eurasian, all of them trusted and popular figures whose ethnicity emerges only from police records or hostile press comments.

Women's historians of the modern variety have shown little interest in Chartism because it was a movement for manhood suffrage. The fact that many women took part was not seen as significant, since they took part in a movement whose agenda was written by men, and since they never combined as women for specifically women's issues. That the women of the manufacturing districts were active in the movement would not now be denied, but they were not – at least not all – demanding votes for women, or the right of women to work. In fact they tended to demand the right not to work but to care for their homes and children. Some writers have seen the main oppression of women as the attempt by men of all classes to confine them to the home. By this interpretation the demand that a man's wage should allow him to support his family without his wife or children working is seen as a reactionary, male-dominant demand. Without entering this argument, which will no doubt continue among historians of women, I think it is worth

41

noting that none of the various ways of writing the history of Chartism have so far included the women. For Gammage and for the earlier labour historians of all complexions, the presence of women in a serious political movement was an embarrassment. They were either a decoration or a trivialization, when they were there a meeting became a fair or a tea party. The fact that many of the leading figures in the movement, including James Watson, Thomas Frost, W.E. Adams and a number of others, recorded that they had obtained their political ideas from their mothers or from other female relatives did not affect the argument, neither did the fact that many of the radical groups to which the original Charter was circulated wanted to add women's suffrage. But even the women in the movement seem rarely to have put women's suffrage above manhood suffrage. Again class loyalties took precedence, as they were to do among some women in the labour movement later in the century. The inclusion of these working women and working men's wives in the definition of class may again illustrate the need for a broader definition of class. The values of a community are not formed only in the workplace, and if, as I think we must, we keep the concept of class to describe the motivation of the Chartists, it must be a concept which sees the educational role of the working-class family and its importance as a locus of resistance to exploitation – by shopkeepers, parsons and school boards as well as by employers.

A discussion of the history of Chartism, therefore, involves us in a discussion of theories of class, nation and gender as well as of political and social theory. Theoreticians by their nature look for a quick answer to questions of definition, historians too often find that the record is obscure or contradictory, and hesitate to generalize too broadly. The history of Chartism reminds us that the division between 'economic' and 'political' is an arbitrary one made for the convenience of historians, not necessarily obvious to the actors in history. Movements for the maximization of liberty have taken place on many different fronts and the results have rarely been those aimed at. The Chartists combined to gain access for the working classes to the political system of the country. They did not achieve it, but they did put the question firmly on to the agenda.

Notes

This is not a bibliographical essay and will in the main only cite works actually quoted. In 1978 I produced, jointly with John Harrison, a *Bibliography of the Chartist Movement* which goes up to 1976. The text had some shortcomings as it was set from an unrevised manuscript, and contains a number of unnecessary errors. Although the location of many items is missing, the full titles and place of publication are in the main correct. Work on a corrected and updated version is now in progress and this should be published within the next year or so.

1. F. Engels, *The Condition of the Working Class in England in 1844* (Leipzig 1845), first English edn, tr. Wischnewetzky, London 1982, p. 228.

2. Norman McCord, 'Adding a Touch of Class', *History*, vol. 70, no. 230, October 1985. All references and quotations below to McCord are to this article. See also F.M.L. Thompson, 'Kind Hearts versus Coronets', *Times Literary Supplement*, 16 August 1991.

3. R.G. Gammage, *The History of the Chartist Movement, from Its Commencement Down to the Present Time*, 1st edn, London 1855; 2nd edn, Newcastle 1894.

4. John Saville (ed.), *Ernest Jones: Chartist*, London 1952.

5. A valuable collection and analysis of many of these accounts is in Christopher Godfrey, 'Chartist Lives', Ph.D. thesis, Harvard University 1978.

6. George Eliot, *Felix Holt, the Radical* (1866), Cabinet edn, London and Edinburgh n.d. [1890], p. 162.

7. Benjamin Disraeli, *Sybil or the Two Nations* (1845), Penguin edn, Harmondsworth 1980, Book II, Chapter 5, p. 96.

8. Thomas Carlyle, *Chartism*, London 1839.

9. Elizabeth Gaskell, *Mary Barton* (1848), Oxford Classics pub edn, Oxford 1987, p. 199.

10. George Jacob Holyoake, *Bygones Worth Remembering* London 1905, vol. 1, chapter 7 passim. For an up-to-date account of 10 April see John Belchem, 'Feargus O'Connor and the Collapse of the Mass Platform', in James Epstein and Thompson (eds), *The Chartist Experience: Studies in Working-Class Radicalism and Culture 1830–1860*, London 1982.

11. Robert Wilson, *The Life and Times of Queen Victoria*, London 1900, p. 59.

12. Benjamin Wilson, *The Struggles of an Old Chartist*, Halifax 1887, p. 13.

13. Even those Chartists who did join forces with Gladstonian Liberalism in the 1860s often found certain subjects on which they were unable to reconcile their Chartist views with those of their new allies. In particular their attitudes to Ireland, to women's suffrage and to questions of trade union action usually left them well to the left of most Liberals. See Anthony David Taylor, 'Ernest Jones, His Later Career and the Structure of Manchester Politics', unpub. MA thesis, University of Birmingham 1984, and Owen R. Ashton, *W.E. Adams, Chartist, Radical and Journalist*, Whitley Bay 1991.

14. Brian Harrison and Patricia Hollis, 'Chartism, Liberalism and the Life of Robert Lowery', *English Historical Review*, vol. lxxxii, July 1967. William Dorling, *Henry Vincent: A Biographical Sketch*, London 1879.

15. *Northern Star*, 27 May 1843.

16. *Halifax Courier*, 19 February 1891.

17. Hansard, 3rd Series, vol. lxiii, 3 May 1842.

18. Karl Marx, 'The Chartists', *New York Daily Tribune*, 25 August 1852.

19. Mark Hovell, *The Chartist Movement*, Manchester 1918 – all quotations in the following paragraph are from this work.

20. Letters from Henry Vincent to John Minikin, 1838–39, in Minikin–Vincent papers, Museum of Labour History, Manchester.

21. See E.P. Thompson, *The Making of the English Working Class*, London 1963,

James Epstein, *The Lion of Freedom: Feargus O'Connor and the Chartist Movement, 1832–1842*, London 1982, and John Belchem, *Orator Hunt*, Oxford 1987, for provincial pre-Chartist radicalism.

22. H.U. Faulkner, *Chartism and the Churches*, F.F. Rosenblatt, *The Chartist Movement in Its Social and Economic Aspects*, P.W. Slosson, *The Decline of the Chartist Movement*, all published New York 1916.

23. Theodore Rothstein, *From Chartism to Labourism*, London 1929, from which all quotations in the following paragraph are taken.

24. Reg Groves, *But We Shall Rise Again: A Narrative History of Chartism*, London 1939, p. 27.

25. Asa Briggs (ed.), *Chartist Studies*, London 1959.

26. D.J.V. Jones, *The Last Rising*, Oxford 1985.

27. Ivor Wilks, *South Wales and the Rising of 1839*, Chicago 1984.

28. D.J. Rowe, 'The London Working Men's Association and the People's Charter', *Past and Present*, no. 36, April 1967.

29. R.N. Soffer, 'Attitudes and Allegiances in the Unskilled North 1830–1850', *International Review of Social History*, vol. x, pt 1, 1965.

30. For a discussion of the issues involved and a full bibliography of recent work on the question of class, see Neville Kirk, 'In Defence of Class', *International Review of Social History*, vol. xxxii, pt 1, 1987.

31. Noel W. Thompson, *The People's Science*, Cambridge 1984.

32. Gareth Stedman Jones 'Re-thinking Chartism' in his *Languages of Class*, Cambridge 1983 – a fuller version of the paper published as 'The Language of Chartism' in Epstein and Thompson.

33. Stedman Jones, 'The Language of Chartism', p. 15.

34. F.M.L. Thompson, 'Kind Hearts versus Coronets', and see the same author's *Rise of Respectable Society*, London 1988.

35. William Lovett, *Life and Struggles of William Lovett in His pursuit of Bread, Knowledge and Freedom*, London 1876, reprinted New York 1986, p. 170.

36. Edward Baines, *Life of Edward Baines* (1851), pp. 157–9, cited in E.P. Thompson, p. 818. (Italics in the original.)

37. See, for example, George Barnsby, *The Working Class Movement in the Black Country*, Wolverhampton 1977, and Kate Tiller, 'Late Chartism, Halifax 1847–58' in Epstein and Thompson.

38. McCord, p. 411.

39. Letter, G.J. Harney to Engels, 30 May 1846, in Frank Gees Black and R.M. Black (eds), *The Harney Papers*, Assen 1969, p. 241.

40. Adam Rushton, *My Life as Farmer's Boy, Factory Lad, Teacher and Preacher*, Manchester 1909.

41. For a serious analysis of O'Connor's radical and early Chartist career, see Epstein. For the later period, see Belchem, 'Feargus O'Connor and the Collapse of the Mass Platform'.

42. See below, p. 103, and John Belchem, 'English Working-Class Radicalism and the Irish,' in Roger Swift and Sheridan Gilley (eds), *The Irish in the Victorian City, 1815–1850* London 1985.

2

The Early Chartists

At one level, Chartism is one of the most richly self-documented subjects in British social history. Coming at a time when the press was comparatively free and cheap, and being essentially a movement of people to whom the printed word was important and accessible, Chartism has left behind an enormous number of printed documents, newspapers, journals, pamphlets, broadsides, handbills and posters. The extent to which these have survived depends partly on the obvious accidents of history. Journals survive better than pamphlets, both are more likely to have been bound and preserved than the more ephemeral broadside or poster, which may only have survived among the papers of a lord lieutenant or Home Secretary to whom it had been sent by an indignant or alarmed citizen. Handbills urging exclusive dealing or violent action are least likely to have survived, since their circulation enters an area of semi-legality or outright illegality, with all the precautions that that involves.

Apart from the publications of the Chartists themselves, there is a great volume of contemporary published material relating to Chartism. Parliamentary debates, newspaper reports, and descriptions and discussions by novelists, journalists and moralists abound all through the years in which the movement was a major political and social force in Britain. The value of this material as a source of information, both about Chartism and even more about the reactions to it of other classes in the country, is considerable.

The press in Britain was in a period of change and growth in the late 1830s. The provincial press was expanding rapidly, but not uniformly. Some papers were becoming genuine provincially based newspapers, produced in the local centres, and providing local news gathered by their own staff. Thus for some localities there is a coverage of Chartist activity which earlier radical movements outside London seldom received. But many provincial papers were still run on an older model, employing very small reporting staffs, and still concerned mainly to copy items of news and interest from the London and major provincial journals. The absence of reports of local Chartist activities from such newspapers does not mean the absence of such activity in the locality. Even in the case of areas served by more modern papers, hostility to Chartism could apparently show itself by the non-reporting of events as well as by hostile reports. In the rather rare cases of provincial papers such as the Tory *Halifax Guardian* or the Liberal *Birmingham Journal* which show some editorial sympathy towards the Chartists, this sympathy may itself dictate the aspects of the movement which get the widest coverage. The *Guardian* was particularly sympathetic to the Oastlerite kind of social protest, and tended to give full reports of meetings and demonstrations in support of this end of the movement, in particular to anything discreditable to the non-conformist manufacturing interest, whilst the *Journal*, like some other early provincial papers, was of a strongly radical aspect, and tended to report favourably the local spokesmen who expressed the sort of political radicalism which brought Chartism nearest to the views of the local middle class. It would be wrong to assume from this bias in the reporting that other kinds of activity did not occur in the districts concerned.

The novels which concern themselves with Chartism, and there are a number of them, are fairly easily accessible; indeed, it may well be that the availability and readability of *Alton Locke*, *Sybil* and *Mary Barton*, the three most frequently reprinted, formed the main picture which existed of Chartism until it began to be studied seriously by historians. Their value as sources of evidence need not be considered here, except to suggest that the one thing which all the 'Chartist' novels have in common – whatever the motivation of their authors – is the acceptance of the fact that the Chartist case is an articulate one, and one which demands a reasoned reply.

An obvious source of information about any period is the memoirs of those who lived through it. Most published Chartist reminiscences are those of men who lived on until late in the century, and who had entered the movement late, during the 1840s rather than the 1830s. The reason for this is probably that it was in the ambience of Gladstonian Liberalism that Chartism finally achieved an aura of respectability. In that period, Chartists could be viewed as Liberal reformers, ahead of their time. As Benjamin Wilson wrote in 1887:

> what they wanted was a voice in making the laws they were called upon to obey; they believed that taxation without representation was tyranny, and ought to be resisted; they took a leading part in agitating in favour of the ten hours question, the repeal of the taxes on knowledge, education, co-operation, civil and religious liberty and the land question, for they were the true pioneers of all the great movements of their time.[1]

The Liberal *Halifax Courier*, which published Wilson's reminiscences, further accented the point when it reported on a meeting of old Chartists in 1885:

> At the time of the Chartist agitation they were all working men earning low wages, not the least interesting part of the speeches therefore was their account of the hardships the working classes had to endure within living memory, enabling young politicians to make a useful and instructive contrast.[2]

But whatever the motives for the rediscovery of a tamed Chartism by late-century Liberals, the memoirs themselves sometimes break out of the frame of their premature Gladstonianism, as when Thomas Frost describes the various communitarian experiments towards which he looked for a more satisfying way of life, or when Ben Wilson himself admits to having joined the 'physical force' Chartists.[3] Here a different, illiberal Chartism can be briefly glimpsed, a breadth of aspiration, a passion of protest and an intensity of resolve which had no place in the politics of Liberalism.

For the early years of the movement few coherent reminiscences exist. The outstanding exception is, of course, William Lovett's *Life and Struggles*. Invaluable alike for its picture of the making of a radical artisan, and for its detailed documentation of the activities of the London Working Men's Association and of the first Chartist Convention, this book is now easily available in more than one edition. But London in the years 1838–40 is less important in Chartist history than many provincial centres, and indeed than London itself was to become in the later years of the movement.[4] The mainsprings of action were outside the metropolis, and unfortunately no provincial centre had its Lovett, recording memories and preserving documents. The autobiography of Robert Lowery gives some picture of the making of a provincial Chartist, although it is written partly as a temperance tract, and bears some of the marks of this.[5] John Frost never committed his memories to paper,[6] and R.G. Gammage, whose personal experience illuminates part of his rather badly written history of the movement, did not become an active participant until after 1840. For personal memories of the first years we have to rely mainly on fragments, often produced to illustrate arguments in a quite different context, such as the letters of Matthew Fletcher, published in 1852, or Alexander Somerville and David Urquhart's apologias, also published in the 1850s. An interesting series of letters on events in Newcastle in 1839 was published in 1889–90 in the *Newcastle Weekly Chronicle*. These were occasioned by the publication of one of the few books which do contain personal reminiscences of this period: Thomas Ainge Devyr's *Odd Book of the Nineteenth Century*, published in New York in 1882. Perhaps because the general tone of Devyr is so different from the mellow Liberalism of most English ex-Chartists, his book has not generally been taken very seriously as a source of information. Allowing, however, for discrepancies of detail which might be expected after so many years (and which are to be found equally in all the books of memoirs), the picture which he paints of Newcastle Chartism does fit in very well with that given by other sources, including the Home Office Papers. The discussions evoked by his book, and by his visits to Newcastle as an old man, suggest that his memory of events coincided with that of some of his surviving contemporaries of the days 'before the introduction of salad oil'.[7]

Unpublished material about the early years of Chartism comes mainly from official sources. Lovett preserved the papers of the first Convention which are in the MSS room at the British Museum. Both the Place collection in the British Museum and the Lovett Collection in Birmingham Central Reference Library contain a certain number of manuscript letters. But by far the richest sources of unpublished material are the Home Office and the Treasury Solicitor's Papers. Magistrates' letters, spies' reports, depositions, etc. throw light on aspects of Chartism. But since the material is so patchy, each must be taken to illustrate a limited area only. There was no uniformity in the police system during these years. The Rural Police Act was not passed until August 1839, and the reform in the boroughs was in its earliest stages. The main instruments of detection were still informers, and their use, and that of agents or spies, depended very much on the initiative of local magistrates. The extent to which even the most able and efficient magistrates were able to find out about the activities of the Chartists varied enormously from place to place. In Birmingham, where the magistrates included former members of the Political Union, and one of the original delegates to the Convention, and where police spies were regularly employed, it seems likely that the authorities were fairly well-informed about the local Chartists. But in most manufacturing districts the magistrates had little access to the activities and opinions of the labouring people, and their reports were based on hearsay and guesses. Letters to the Home Office, therefore, vary from the panic-stricken to the calm and self-confident, depending more on the personality of the writer than on the objective total situation. Since in most cases reports on a given locality came to the Home Office from only one source, it is clear that the assessments contained in them cannot be taken as objective. Even if the whole body of reports from magistrates, informers, police, and the reports of the military commanders on special duty are taken together, they give only a fragmentary idea of what was going on. Working-class communities in the industrial townships which were the main centres of Chartism were opaque communities, rarely accessible to parson, policeman or magistrate. The authorities were on the whole ill-informed as well as excluded.

Nothing would be further from the truth than to see Chartism as a sudden eruption into the political scene. Radicalism of the various kinds that came together in Chartism had been gathering momentum fairly steadily since the beginning of the 1830s. Most of the delegates to the first National Convention had taken part in the agitation for the Reform Bill of 1832, and many of them, like Peter Bussey of Bradford or Matthew Fletcher of Bury, had organized at the time of the passing of the Bill considerable campaigns for the extension of its terms. Bussey had collected six thousand signatures to a petition for manhood suffrage immediately after the passing of the Bill, and Fletcher had helped to sponsor a candidate in the first election after the Reform Bill who stood on the platform of universal suffrage and the ballot.[8] In the years that followed, both men, and others like them all over the country, had emerged as town radicals, taking the lead in various radical campaigns, which increasingly appeared as campaigns of resistance to the actions of the reformed Parliament. In 1834, Bussey is described as demanding of a parliamentary candidate, in front of a hustings crowd of five thousand people, whether if elected, he would vote for the abolition of tithes, the entire abolition of church rates, the abolition of punishment by death in all cases; for triennial parliaments, the abolition of flogging in the army, the reduction of the army estimates, the emancipation of the Jews so as to place them on the same footing as himself; for the ballot, for the throwing open of the universities to all classes of His Majesty's subjects of whatever sect; for corporate reform; for household suffrage; for the abolition of the stamp duty on newspapers; for the repeal of the Corn Laws; for a careful revision of the pension list; for the abolition of the taxes on industry and for the repeal of the Game Laws.[9] This was the programme of working-class political radicalism, soon to be absorbed into the wider movement of Chartism. A few miles away, in Ripponden in the Ryburn Valley, another kind of organized radicalism was to be found. Here the Cooperative Society, founded in 1832 with a membership of twenty-four, had, by 1834, reached a membership of forty-five. The fundamental principles of the society declared:

> First.   – That labour is the source of all wealth; consequently the working classes have created all wealth.
> Secondly.   – That the working classes, although the producers of wealth, instead of being the richest, are the poorest of the community; hence, they cannot be receiving a just recompense for their labour.[10]

Both Bradford and Ripponden were to become centres of Chartism. The movement brought together political radicals like Bussey and Fletcher with the Owenite weavers of the Calder Valley.

The years between 1834 and 1838 saw a continuous series of radical campaigns, in which groups from various backgrounds and various traditions were increasingly involved. The New Poor Law, introduced in the same year that saw the prosecution of the Dorchester Labourers, isolated in Parliament the handful of independent radical members who expressed in any degree whatever the opinions of the articulate working people in the country. William Cobbett opposed the new law in the short time that remained to him, whilst Thomas Wakley and Thomas Duncombe, members for Finsbury, and John Fielden, member for Oldham, always made it clear that they considered that they had a responsibility to represent the views of the working people as well as the views of those who had actually elected them. In a famous speech in support of an amendment to the first speech from the throne of Queen Victoria in 1837, Thomas Wakley described himself as the representative of

Labour in the House of Commons, whilst Fielden, in the election address at Oldham in 1833, declared that 'nothing but an anxious solicitude to see the people restored to their just rights, and especially the labouring portion of society greatly improved could have induced him' to enter Parliament.[11] These three men remained strong supporters of the social programme of Chartism, as well as of its political points, throughout the first ten years of the agitation, and were to be the main spokesmen in Parliament for the petitions and against the ill-treatment of imprisoned Chartists.

In the main, the Chartists received little support from the members of the House of Commons. Middle-class radicalism seemed in many cases to be acting against the interests of the working people in the years immediately following the 1832 Bill. Even the Municipal Reform Act of 1835, which on the face of it was an attempt to fulfil a long-standing Radical demand, the reform of the corrupt borough corporations, appeared in the event as simply a further strengthening of the powers of the middle class, a postscript to the 1832 Act. Thomas Cooper wrote of the 1835 Act:

> how the scale has turned, since the greater share of boroughs where the poor and labouring classes threw up their hats at 'municipal reform' – and now mutter discontent at the pride of upstarts become insolent oppressors – or openly curse, as in the poverty-stricken and hunger-bitten manufacturing districts, at the relentless and grinding tyrannies of the recreant middle classes whom municipal honours have drawn off from their hot-blooded radicalism, and converted into cold, unfeeling wielders of magisterial or other local power.[12]

The prosecution of trade unionists which took place in the 1830s was seen by working-class radicals as part of the same oppressive policy as the exclusion of working men from the franchise or the punishment of poverty by the proposals of the Poor Law Amendment Act. This interconnection of activity persisted throughout the Chartist period, although the emphasis laid on the achievement of the suffrage usually stressed its priority over other issues, as the primary means of obtaining reform in other fields. But, as Challinor and Ripley have shown in their study of the Miners' Association,[13] the Chartists were usually prepared to take any opportunity which presented itself to encourage the development of trade union organization. Many of the leading Chartists, in the south as well as in the industrial north, had gained their first experience of radical activity as members of trade unions. William Cuffay, for example, son of a West Indian slave, leading London Chartist, who was to end his days in Australia as a transported convict after the Orange Tree conspiracy of 1848, entered politics after he had taken part in the tailors' strike of 1834.[14] The London radicals who organized the great demonstration in support of the Dorchester Labourers on 21 April 1834 included the organizers of the cooperative societies, the unstamped press, the Owenite bazaars, as well as the National Union of the Working Classes and the Grand National Consolidated Trades Union. The prosecution and transportation of the Glasgow cotton-spinners in 1837 provoked a nation-wide campaign against the Whig government and in support of the convicted men. One of the men who took the lead in the collection of signatures and money to assist the convicted men was Lawrence Pitkethly, of Huddersfield, local leader of radical politics, and in particular of the campaign against the Poor Law and of the movement for factory reform. Pitkethly was later to become a leading West Riding Chartist.[15] In Barnsley two of the leaders of the linen-weavers – both of whom were to become prominent Chartists – had been transported for their part in industrial disturbances in the 1820s. In 1838, when Chartism began, one of them, William Ashton, had returned from Australia, his fare having been collected by a public subscription in Barnsley, and the other, Frank Mirfield, was awaiting repatriation.[16] The concern with trade unionism was one of the issues which divided the Chartists from the middle-class radicals, many of whom, like Daniel O'Connell, were bitterly hostile to the idea of trade unionism.

Radicalism in the early 1830s had been given an increasingly national character by the activities of the cheap press. The unstamped press, produced in defiance of the government regulations, canalized metropolitan radicalism, and spread out into the provinces, where the sellers found themselves part of a national movement, taking part in a campaign of direct opposition to the law which won widespread respect and support among the lower orders of society. In spite of the limited gains actually conceded by the act of 1836, it is impossible not to see the story of the 'unstamped' as one of a triumph for radicalism, a David-and-Goliath confrontation in which the honours went to the irreverent upstarts, giving them new confidence as well as the journalistic and organizational experience of producing newspapers.[17] But the metropolitan papers produced after the 1836 newspaper act – the *London Despatch*, the *London Mercury*, and the smaller sheets, including *Bronterre's National Reformer*, in which many of the ideas of the Chartists first appeared, did not meet the needs of the radical movement in the late 1830s. It is with the foundation of the *Northern Star* in Leeds in November 1837 that the new era of radical journalism begins.[18] The Chartist period sustained a great number of journals and periodicals, but the *Northern Star* was by far the most widely read. Its circulation waxed and waned with the movement. Its staff, editorial, reporting and distributing, included many of the ablest men in the movement. Its columns contained the widest reporting of radical activity ever made – covering a range which went beyond the Chartist movement itself. Feargus O'Connor, as owner of the *Northern Star*, was, of course, in a position of great strength to influence the readership. But his exercise of his power seems, in the main, to have been very reasonable. His editorial staff, who often had interests and emphases which differed from his own, were allowed a great deal of freedom, and the paper never became a purely personal vehicle – a fact which undoubtedly helps to account for its immense lead over all other Chartist and radical journals of the period.[19] Of course the owner was the final arbiter, the *Star* was the journal of the O'Connorites, if not of Feargus as an individual, and many Chartists were unfairly treated in its columns. It must never be used as the only source of information, particularly at periods of controversy. But it does provide a quite unequalled continuous record for the years of its publication of a kind which was never available for earlier radical movements. It also leads into a new kind of popular journalism which developed in the second half of the nineteenth century, for which the bridge with Chartism is the work of former Chartist journalists like G.W.M. Reynolds, Edward Lloyd and W.E. Adams. But this again belongs to a later period of the movement.

The early numbers of the *Northern Star*, taken with the *London Despatch* of the same period, show some of the questions which were concerning radicals immediately before the beginning of the Chartist agitation. As well as the questions already mentioned, it is interesting to notice the intense interest which was taken in the revolution in Canada.[20] Ireland was continually to the fore, although the hostility between O'Connor and O'Connell meant that many of the latter's working-class followers kept clear of Chartism.[21] Not that O'Connor's differences with the 'Liberator' were of a purely personal nature, as is sometimes suggested. As Devyr shows, there were always a number of Irishmen who were in agreement with the sophisticated radicalism of O'Connor rather than with the popular Catholic nationalism of O'Connell.[22] But the period in which there was the closest cooperation between the Irish repealers and the Chartists came after the death of O'Connell, in the later days of Chartism.

A question on which the working-class radicals found common cause with many middle-class reformers and even some Tories was the hostility to the Whig–Radical policies of centralization. At its most hated this policy was attacked in the New Poor Law, but it was also fought in the debates about the Rural Police Bill. The twin dangers of the breakdown of traditional community responsibilities, and the setting up of a continental-type state administration were very widely feared. This fear accounts for a great deal of the division amongst the authorities, for the hesitancy of some magistrates in the face of insurrectionary threats, and above all for the intense hostility towards the metropolitan police when these were introduced into provincial centres. The Calthorpe Street affair, in which a jury of London tradesmen had returned a verdict of 'justifiable homicide' at the inquest on a policeman stabbed to death whilst helping to clear a radical meeting from a London street, had occurred as recently as 1833.[23] It is a paradox that Chartism, one of whose motive forces was the fear of the introduction of a centralized police system, should have helped substantially to clear the way for such a system by arousing in the respectable classes a fear of popular disturbance which over-rode their suspicion of centralized administration.[24]

Popular radicalism can thus be seen in the 1830s as a diverse but increasingly coherent force. It was the response to changing social and economic conditions which were becoming felt over wider sections of the country. It was no new experience for large sections of the working people of Britain to feel hungry. What is of interest in the late 1830s is why the British workers responded to hunger by forming a nation-wide movement around a political programme instead of by more traditional means of protest like food rioting, arson, begging, poaching or praying.

New methods and techniques of production, new relationships between employers, merchants and workers, the breakdown of traditional institutions and traditional relationships, the growing dependence on an increasing but fluctuating world market – all these were affecting the major industries of Britain, and affecting above all the many branches of its textile industries, still by far the most important manufacturing industries. Although there is still a great deal to be learnt about the occupational distribution of Chartism, and a great number of generalizations to be tested about the participation of different sectors of the labour force, nevertheless it is clear that the textile centres in general were strongholds of the movement throughout most of its active period. Chartism was the response to economic and social change of an urban working class, and it was in the manufacturing districts that it was always strongest. This is not, of course, to suggest that there were not important Chartist activities in the cities and in the villages. Local research seems to be providing an increasing number of illustrations of such activity. But it was above all in the groups of industrial townships which were the typical manufacturing centres of the nineteenth century, areas such as the West Riding of Yorkshire, Lancashire, Nottinghamshire, Staffordshire and South Wales, that the movement had most continuity, and that its tone was largely set. Within those areas it seems likely that the division which has sometimes been made between the factory workers and the domestic workers will not stand up to examination. Apart from the obvious fact that many factory operatives were women and children,[25] the occupations of arrested Chartists would suggest that cotton-spinners, powerloom-overlookers and other male factory operatives were often amongst the active local leaders, even before the Plug Riots of 1842. That the handloom weavers in particular seem to stand out as local speakers and organizers may be due to the traditional participation of these men in the chapel and other social and cultural activities of their communities, rather than to their numerical superiority in the movement as a whole.[26]

It is an important part of the definition of Chartism to see it as the response of a literate and sophisticated working class. It is the response of a labour force faced not with the timeless custom of traditional work patterns and social structures, or with the vagaries of weather or harvest, but with a set of articulate postulations, the arguments of the philosophical radicals and the political economists. Much of the Chartist propaganda took the form of argument, a dialogue with the middle classes. Although clearly not all Chartists were able to read (classes at which members were taught appear in the programme of some localities) and although the level of literacy even amongst those who could nominally read and write must often have been low, nevertheless written and printed material was an essential part of the lives of them all. Newspapers and pamphlets were available in even very small communities, at beer-houses, inns, coffee-shops and at the homes of newsagents. In bigger centres the agents often provided both distribution centres for journals and collection points for money and signatures. Sometimes the local newsagent also ran a coffee-shop, as Thomas Cooper did for a time in Leicester, and here, and in each other's houses, journals were read and discussed, to an extent which represented a new dimension in radical politics. One writer reports that at Todmorden, on the day that the *Northern Star* was due, the people used to line the roadside waiting for its arrival 'which was paramount to everything else for the time being'.[27] The language of Chartism, in spite of the bitterness and hostility towards the ruling classes, both middle and upper, nevertheless contains a degree of rationality, even of optimism, which it would be difficult to define in earlier protest movements. The desperation which characterized the agricultural disturbances of the early 1830s is very little in evidence. The machinery of the law and the constitution is invoked to resist the self-interest of the industrialist or the greed of the monopolist. Where force is invoked or threatened, it is the organized force of an excluded class, not the sporadic violence of desperate individuals or small groups. It will not do to over-simplify this question, or to describe every aspect of Chartism as being entirely rational and articulate. But a comparison of surviving Luddite letters, or the letters from the 'Captain Swing' agitation,[28] with the closing sentences of the appeal by the strikers at Ashton-under-Lyne against wage-cuts in 1842 will illustrate the point. The appeal ends:

> Whether we succeed or not, we shall have the satisfaction of knowing that we have asked for nothing unreasonable or unjust. We want a uniform price for the whole of the manufacturing districts, and it is in the interests of the masters to have it, in order that one man cannot undersell another in the market. Much is said about over production, and about the market being glutted. In order to obviate the past, let us all work ten hours per day, and we are sure it will lessen the amount of goods in the market. The home consumption will also be considerably increased by increasing the wages of the labourer.
>
> The operatives of Ashton-under-Lyne[29]

In the Chartist publications this element of rationality predominates. But obviously the motivation behind the actual movement operated at a different level. The impetus which sent people out in tens of thousands to demonstrate against the New Poor Law, or to take part in marches or listen to speeches, many of which were of a more violent tone altogether than was usually to be found in the published material, operated at another level of compulsion. Chartism was pervaded by a sense of class – both a positive sense of identification and a negative hostility to superior classes – which was stronger than perhaps existed at any other point in the nineteenth century. It has often been suggested that this class feeling was misdirected, and that the Chartists were badly misled in seeing their chief enemies as the manufacturing middle class. It has also been argued that they were used by upper-class interests, which also feared the increasing power of the middle classes, or even that the Chartists themselves were deferential towards the old landowning ruling class, and therefore failed to see that their own interests were in reality bound up with those of the non-conformist manufacturers.[30] The intense class bitterness, which it would be exceedingly difficult not to discern in almost every statement of the Chartists at all stages of the agitation, is seen as mistaken – mistaken in its main target, the manufacturing and employing class, or indeed in its whole tone. It is argued that the minority of leaders who, like Vincent and Lowery, turned away from the mainstream of Chartism after 1840 and who were disavowed by most of their fellow Chartists were, in fact, pursuing the truest interests of the working class by helping to oppose monopoly and privilege in association with the radical part of the Liberal Party, which they themselves helped to radicalize.

This is a serious argument which developed to some extent within Chartism itself in the later stages of the movement. There can be little doubt that the turning towards Liberal politics by former Chartists encouraged the development of popular Liberalism with its emphasis on parliamentary reform and muted opposition to imperialism. But in turning towards the Liberal Party after the end of Chartism the former Chartists were to a large extent abandoning the social programme which had been such an essential part of the movement, and reverting to the political questions alone, which had not been essentially different from the radical demands which had always had the support of a considerable group in Parliament. It was the social content of Chartism which had made cooperation with this group impossible, and it was not until the revival of independent working-class politics towards the end of the nineteenth century that this submerged social programme again became a part of British politics. The Liberal Party did not in fact long survive the growth of this kind of radicalism, since it was not possible to contain both traditional nineteenth-century Liberalism and a dynamic policy of social reform within the same party. The Chartists certainly rejected the possibility of combining middle-class and working-class reform programmes within the same party; but to put the question in this way is to show its absurdity even in an academic sense in the years 1838–40, when the mutual hostility between the classes was at its height. The leaders of the Anti-Corn Law League may have wished to encourage working-class demonstrations against the Corn Laws, but they had no desire to see working men on the councils of the League, least of all leaders of the trade unions or short-time committees. Lord Ashley was for them less an object of hatred in his capacity as a Tory landowner than he was in that of a factory reformer. Amongst the working classes and the extreme radicals the actions of the reformed Parliament had bred a suspicion against the middle classes and their upper-class allies which included the fear of a dramatic increase in repressive government. Chartism in 1838–40 is pervaded by the possibility of a government terror, evident in the manifesto of the Convention as well as in the *London Democrat*.

Chartism in its early years was held together by these various factors. First there was the breadth of the opposition of those who had been excluded from the franchise in 1832 to the activities of the government, secondly the strong sense of class engendered partly by the property definitions established by the 1832 Act, and partly by the increasing cohesion and stability of the merchant and employing classes in the industrial districts, thirdly the fear of strong government action, the establishment of a centralized state with a powerful punitive force at its disposal, and finally the example of 1832, in which determined political action backed by demonstrations and the threat of force in the country had succeeded in forcing a radical change on an unrepresentative legislature. These factors gave the movement a unity and a cohesion which it was never to achieve again after 1840, although the very divisions which existed in the later years sometimes made for the more sophisticated articulation of alternative programmes.

The unity of the movement centred on the programme of the collection of money and signatures to the first national petition, and the organization of the General Convention of the Industrious Classes which had been called for January 1839. The months of activity leading up to the Convention were informed with a sense of purpose and a discipline which is particularly surprising in areas such as the West Riding and East Lancashire with their recent history of violent opposition to the Poor Law. There was talk of violence, of arming, and of 'ulterior measures' to be adopted if the petition should be rejected. But both the talk of violence and the actual arming were contained and controlled, and the enormous meetings which were held in preparation for the Convention took place without clashes with authority or the destruction of property.

A question which arises in these early months – the winter of 1838 and the early part of 1839 – is how far there was a genuine intention to resort to violence if peaceful methods failed to achieve the Charter. The whole question of Chartist violence, in fact, must be examined from the very beginning.

Given that Chartism was a popular movement, rooted in the communities of the working people, an interesting phenomenon is the rarity of what might be called 'folk violence'. The manifestations of violent protest which were most common in villages and townships – the pillorying of unpopular individuals by effigy-burning or rough music, sporadic outbreaks of arson, machine-breaking or cattle-houghing directed against unpopular employers or magistrates were almost unknown amongst the Chartists. Although such occurrences were probably becoming rarer in the nineteenth century, they certainly occurred in this period in the agricultural districts, and recur again in popular demonstrations against the Cobdenite Liberals during the Crimean War and the 'pro-Boers' in the Boer War. In Chartist times, however, when tension was extremely high, there are almost no examples of their use by the Chartists. The few riots which did take place before the Newport outbreak did not follow the general pattern of popular rioting which had taken place even as recently as the Reform Bill crisis of 1831–32.

At Llanidloes, where the Chartists were provoked by the use of special constables from an unpopular neighbouring district, and where representatives of the hated metropolitan police were brought down to the district, the Chartists began by attacking the inn in which the policemen were lodged, but although doors and window-frames were torn out and furniture destroyed, the cellar was not invaded, and no ale or spirits were taken.[31] In general, the extent to which discipline was maintained at a high level when thousands of people, many of them armed, were gathering regularly together, was novel and remarkable.

The movement against the Poor Law had contained a considerable element of lawlessness and direct action. Oastler believed that the Chartist movement had been deliberately started by London middle-class radicals to channel the violence and discontent in the manufacturing districts into the safe and predictable stream of an unrealizable political campaign. He was not alone in this view. Matthew Fletcher, a member of the Convention and a firm believer in universal suffrage, repeats the idea in his account of the origin of the Charter:

> When ... honest and humane men of every political opinion which has regard for the ancient principles of the constitution, and for the ordinary rights of humanity, were banded in determined opposition to it; when the mandates of the commissioners were defied and their pretended authority set at nought; some of these people set to work to devise means of drawing off the attention of the 'masses' and depriving the anti-poor-law agitators of their support ... after some quiet but futile attempts to get up a movement, a negotiation was set on foot, in 1838, between the Working Men's Association of London and the Political Union of Birmingham. A great movement was decided upon; the radicals of the North of England and Scotland were communicated with, and all agreed to join it. In this neighbourhood we had our doubts, and they were not concealed, as to the source and motives of the agitation, but it was deemed most advisable to join it. We did so, and made it our own. It was obvious we were in earnest, and both the London and Birmingham men wished to back out of it. We would not let them, and for a time they were obliged 'to get into harness and do a little work'.[32]

In its early days the anti-Poor Law men were amongst Chartism's most violent speakers. Fletcher, Stephens, Oastler and a host of local leaders had advocated opposition to the Law, and had carried out forms of direct action varying from mass meetings of protest and attacks on the commissioners in Huddersfield to the closing by the Fieldens of their factories in Todmorden and the throwing of all their employees simultaneously onto the poor rates. They brought the concept of the direct defiance of the law with them into the Chartist movement. Yet most of the prominent anti-Poor Law agitators were amongst the leaders who dropped out of the movement after 1840. The violence which developed within Chartism, and which came to a climax in the Newport rising and the events immediately following it, was of a different kind from that of the local resistance to the Poor Law.[33]

One of the most difficult tasks in describing Chartism is to distinguish between the different kinds of violence within it, from the largely verbal bellicosity of Harney or O'Connor to the undoubtedly insurrectionary plans of Holberry or the Bradford Chartists. The attitude of the authorities varied from time to time, but on the whole they seemed to be fairly undisturbed by spoken or written threats by national figures until late in 1839, with the notable exception of the Stephens case.[34] Before Newport a certain amount of threatening language appeared to be expected and tolerated. After the arrests of Frost, Williams and Jones the atmosphere changed, the violence became less generalized and more related to the circumstances of the trial and transportation of the Welsh leaders, and arrests for sedition increased dramatically.

Much of the violent language of the Chartist leaders was a style of speech – a rhetorical device which both their followers and the authorities recognized to be a form of bluff. It was of two kinds, one provincial, coming from the anti-Poor Law movement and harking back as well to the armed demonstrations of the Reform Bill period. Certain phrases occur again and again in the speeches of the provincial leaders all over the country. The Whigs are reminded of their own bellicose posturings in the past, and Englishmen are reminded of their right and duty to defend the constitution. In Cornwall a clerical magistrate was horrified to hear Lowery declare that a musket was an essential article of furniture in every Englishman's home.[35] But this expression was part of the stock-in-trade of most of the Chartist leaders. Thus Peter Bussey, replying to a toast at a dinner in his honour at Halifax in January 1839, is reported as saying:

> now he recommended that every man before him should be in possession of a musket, which was a necessary article that ought to provide part of the furniture of every man's house. And every man ought to know well the use of it, that he may use it effectively when the time arrives that requires him to put it into operation.[36]

This type of rhetoric, summarized by the slogan 'Peaceably if we may, forcibly if we must', runs through almost all of the speeches made by Chartist leaders in the year before the Newport rising.

Rather different is the revolutionary vocabulary used by Harney and a small group of mainly London leaders who took their expressions much more directly from the first French Revolution. It is in Harney's *London Democrat* that 'the sacred right of insurrection' is appealed to, and a different kind of rhetoric appears. The *Democrat* and Harney himself in many of his speeches suggest not a people arming to protect themselves against a violent and repressive government, but a revolutionary people, prepared to rise in support of their demands. Of the two kinds of rhetoric, the second is apparently the more revolutionary in tone, and has led some historians to suggest that Harney might have been expected to lead any rising that was being contemplated in these years.[37] The Home Office was never very worried by either Harney or the *London Democrat*, however. The real threat to authority in these years was in the community-rooted organizations of the provincial Chartists, less articulate though this leadership may have been than the French-inspired rhetoric of Harney or Taylor. When the two came together briefly in Newcastle and the north-east in the late summer of 1839, Harney's role was highly ambiguous. His speeches obviously appealed to the Tynesiders, and his popularity in New-castle and district was obviously great. But how far he was in fact involved in insurrectionary activities – the manufacture of pikes, drilling, the collecting of arms and money – is not clear. It seems as though he was not in any way a leader of this kind of activity, which remained in the hands of the local people. Harney's recollections were only published in snippets in his later years, but one letter, published in the *Newcastle Weekly Chronicle* in 1890, suggests that he was very much borne along by the tide of popular feeling at this time. Referring to the events of autumn 1839, he wrote:

> One marked feature of the proceedings had been the consensus of opinion that force would have to be resorted to to obtain justice and the acknowledgement of right. This opinion has been placed to the account of certain names, at the head of which stands Feargus O'Connor; but I venture to affirm that, if any reader of these remarks has the opportunity to turn to the Newcastle papers of the time, he will find in their reports that it was not only Dr Taylor and others in unison with his views who referred to the probable employment of force, but also those who, at least later, acquired a character for moderation, who held the same view and expressed themselves in like terms. The opinion expressed and the terms of its expression may have been unwise; that I am not discussing; but the opinion was general. It was, so to speak 'in the air'. The fact is curious and suggestive of reflection.[38]

Harney was quite correct in his recollection of the tone of Chartist speeches at the time. There is scarcely a single leader who remained prominent in 1838 and 1839 in whose speeches and writings there appears no suggestion of a recourse to arms. The May Manifesto of the Convention in 1839 was signed by William Lovett and Bailie Hugh Craig, one of the extremely moderate Scottish delegates, who withdrew soon afterwards from Chartist activity. It included among the eight questions put to the people 'Whether, according to their old constitutional right – a right which modern legislators would fain annihilate – they have prepared themselves *with the arms of freemen to defend the laws and constitutional privileges their ancestors bequeathed to them?*'[39] After the Birmingham Bull Ring affray, Lovett and Collins were arrested for seditious libel for attacking the behaviour of the magistrates and police, and Henry Hetherington, always on the moderate constitutional wing of the movement, announced that he would henceforth advocate going armed to meetings.[40] The line between the advocacy of violence and the expectation of provocative violence by the authorities was always very fine. Advocates of the 'Sacred Month' – the general strike for the Charter – included some who, like Thomas Attwood, believed it to be a totally peaceful method of persuasion, and others who, like Bronterre O'Brien, considered that once it was embarked upon it would amount to a declaration of war against authority which must inevitably lead to a violent confrontation.

Since most of the Chartist leaders in the early months used to some extent the rhetoric of violence, it is difficult to assess which of them might have been expected to put themselves at the head of an insurrectionary movement after the rejection of the Charter. In the event the only national leader to find himself on trial for his life for levying arms against the Queen was John Frost. Frost was a middle-aged man, a life-long radical whose activity in politics had mostly been in the local government of the borough of Newport, Monmouthshire, where he was a magistrate and a respected local leader. He was removed from the bench as the result of his Chartist activity, but continued to speak and to write for the Chartist press. Although his radicalism went back to the days of the English Jacobins, he was very much in the mainstream of British provincial radicals, and was never of the Harney or O'Brien type of revolutionary. He belonged to the category of men like Fletcher, Richardson and Bussey, who tended to drop out of activity after 1840. The logic of Frost's position as a leader of the Welsh radicals forced him to the head of the columns which marched on Newport on the night of 4 November 1839. Had the revolt succeeded, and had it been followed by other outbreaks at this time, it is almost certainly men of his sort throughout the country, men who had strong and long-standing links with their local communities, who would have been at the head of them.

The evidence for the widespread belief that the Newport events were only a part of a wider national conspiracy has not yet been fully assembled and examined. The difficulties in assessing it now are, of course, very considerable. Had the Newport rising itself never taken place, it seems highly unlikely from the information which survives in official sources that the scale of the arming and preparation which must have gone into it would ever have been guessed at. There is no real suggestion in the reports from South Wales that in the month or so before the rising the arming and drilling being carried on in the locality was more than sporadic. The Home office had no more reason from the information available to it to suspect an outbreak there than in Lancashire, the West Riding or Newcastle. On the other hand, there was obviously a very widespread belief that a conspiracy was in existence. Napier certainly believed it,[41] and later evidence exists from the pens of Dr Taylor, William Ashton, Thomas Devyr and other Chartists, as well as from possibly more suspect witnesses such as David Urquhart and Alexander Somerville.[42] Certain stories, such as the story of the defection of Peter Bussey, who should have led the West Riding outbreak, appear in different forms in the writings of contemporaries. The details may vary and make reliance on their absolute veracity impossible, but the fact that both Benjamin Wilson and Frank Peel,[43] who were personally acquainted with many of the leading West Riding Chartists, repeat versions of the story of Bussey's defection makes it seem likely that there was some basis for it. In general, however, the ferreting out of the details of the 'underground' Chartist organization is bound to be a complicated task. Information has been obscured by so many factors. At the time both fear of government action and the desire to justify flight – as in the case of Devyr – may have led to a denial or an exaggeration of the conspiracy. Later the record will have been obscured by the motives of men who had become active in different kinds of politics. The very fact that the death sentences on the Welsh leaders were commuted, and that the government terror did not materialize on the scale which it threatened, led many ex-Chartists to regret their adhesion to the idea of forcible resistance, and to suppress this part of their past. Thus one of the most fascinating questions about the early years of Chartism remains, by definition, the least well documented.[44]

A straightforward military rising aimed at the overthrow of the government and the taking-over of the strategic points throughout the country was not, however, the most likely way for a clash to have occurred between the Chartists and the authorities. In such a confrontation, even had the Chartists had better organization and better weather than the Newport contingent, it is impossible to imagine that the military and tactical advantages could ever have been other than with the government. Two other main possibilities were present in the situation. One, which has not been taken very seriously by later historians, was that the proposed 'national holiday' should have been called in August 1839. It is quite impossible to predict how such an action might have developed, but it is at least possible that the tensions which were undoubtedly present throughout the manufacturing districts might have been increased to the point of civil war by strike action on a large scale, as Harney indeed prophesied would happen. In the atmosphere of 1839 such action would have had a different effect from the strikes of 1842. The national holiday was, however, rejected by the committee of the Convention which was set up to examine the question, and this possible collision was averted. The other, and in some ways the most likely, way in which hostilities might have broken out was by the use of force against a Chartist demonstration. Such provocative action was always anticipated by the Chartists, and a Peterloo-type action by the military forces would have certainly sparked off a reaction throughout the country.

The fear of repressive action against the movement was, as has already been said, present throughout the first two years of the movement. The Manifesto of the Convention already referred to makes continual reference to the possibility of such attacks:

> The mask of *constitutional liberty* is thrown aside, and the form of *despotism* stands hideously before us. Shall it be said, fellow-country-men, that four millions of men, capable of bearing arms, and defending their country against every foreign assailant, allowed a few domestic oppressors to enslave and degrade them? ... If you longer continue passive slaves, *the fate of unhappy Ireland will soon be yours*, and that of Ireland more degraded still ... we trust you will not *commence* the conflict. We have resolved to obtain our rights, 'peaceably if we may, forcibly if we must'; but woe to those who begin the warfare with the millions, or who forcibly restrain their peaceful agitation for justice – at one signal they will be enlightened to their error, and in one brief contest their power will be destroyed.

But the authorities did not provoke a clash during the vital period.

The only armed confrontation was initiated at Newport, by the Chartists themselves.

The avoidance of provocation was obviously an important part of the policy of Lord John Russell, who as Home Secretary had the main responsibility of dealing with the Chartist crisis. It was also an essential element in the plans of Sir Charles Napier, who was appointed in February 1839 to command the army in the north. In the circumstances the appointment of Napier was a brilliant one, although it was by no means universally approved.[45] He had been without an appointment for eight years, partly no doubt because of his well-known radical views. Both he and his brother William, to whom he wrote many of the letters which give a picture of his work in the Chartist period, had made no secret of their political views. William had, indeed, been invited by the Chartists of Bath to be their delegate to the National Convention, and had declined for two reasons, one the republicanism of some of the local Chartists, and the other the currency theories of Thomas Attwood, which he could not support, being himself a staunch supporter of the views of William Cobbett.[46] Charles Napier shared his views, although he subsequently declared that

> Conscience should not wear a red coat. When I undertook the command of the Northern District under Lord John Russell, I put all my Radical opinions in my blue coat-pocket, and locked the coat in a portmanteau which I left behind me. I told Lord John this when I went to see him on taking the command.[47]

His journal and his letters to William show, however, that he retained a considerable degree of sympathy for the aspirations of the Chartists.

They also show that he made more than one attempt to propose political measures, in the form of major concessions to the demands of the Chartists, as well as the enforcement of order.[48] He had, as the result of his experiences in Ireland during the rebellion of the United Irishmen,[49] a horror of civil war, and a particular sensitivity to the position of a military commander who, as his father had done in that period, had sympathies with both sides in the conflict. The extracts from his journal and the letters which were published in *The Life and Opinions of General Sir Charles James Napier*, edited by his brother William in 1857, reveal various changes in his attitudes and his views of the activities of the Chartists in the north during 1839. But all through is a constant determination to prevent bloodshed, and above all to restrain the magistrates, whose hasty invocation of armed force might at any time have sparked off a conflict. 'At Manchester', he wrote to William in July,

> I found the magistrates reasonable, yet several were for stopping the meeting by force, and would have done so without any encouragement; but I swore if they attempted it not a soldier should quit the barracks till both constables' and magistrates' heads were broken. This was bravado, for I dare not refuse to obey their orders.[50]

Before the Kersall Moor meeting earlier in the year, he is reported as having called a secret meeting of Chartist leaders and told them:

> I understand you are to have a great meeting on Kersall Moor, with a view to laying your grievances before parliament: You are quite right to do so and I will take care that neither soldier or policeman shall be within sight to disturb you. But meet peaceably, for if there is the least disturbance I shall be amongst you and at the sacrifice of my life, if necessary, do my duty. Now go and do yours![51]

He attended the meeting himself, and reported to one of his officers that there were 'twenty-five thousand very innocent people, and ten thousand women and children' present. 'The remainder might have been Chartists, expressing orderly, legal political opinions, pretty much – don't tell this! very like my own.'[52] His radical sympathies were not merely political, but were informed by a very deep humanity which shows continually amongst the military and political comments in his journal. He wrote from Nottingham in September:

> There is among the manufacturing poor a stern look of discontent, of hatred to all who are rich, a total absence of merry faces: a sallow tinge and dirty skins tell of suffering and brooding over change. Yet often have I talked with scowling-visaged fellows till the ruffian went from their faces, making them smile and at ease: this tells me their looks of sad and deep thought are not natural. Poor fellows![53]

His concern to prevent a clash with the Chartists and his abhorrence of civil war did not prevent an occasional flash of sympathy in his journal even for the 'physical force' Chartists. On 8 April 1840 he summed up the position in the northern district:

> This meeting of delegates has not produced any sensation, the physical force heroes are cowed for the present: they started too sharply and are obliged to pull up: they had zeal, good-will and arms, but were deficient in arrangement, in union, in leaders, in money, all of which are necessaries of life to a rebellion![54]

In July 1841 Napier relinquished the northern command to take up an appointment in India. His brother, writing his memoir in 1857, briefly summarized the subsequent history of the movement, ending with the opinion 'Chartism is, however not dead, it only sleeps to awaken with an improved judgement.'[55]

During the summer of 1839, particularly in the months after the rejection of the petition, there were undoubtedly wide-spread preparations amongst the Chartists for insurrection, and a continual fear of government attack and the provocation of open conflict. That such conflict did not occur was due to the discipline and restraint which existed among the Chartists, to the policy of the home secretary in restraining local action by the authorities, other than the precautionary swearing-in of special constables, and to the determination of Napier and his juniors to avoid provocative action. The two major clashes which did occur in those months, at Birmingham and Llanidloes, although they roused very great local feeling, and resulted in heavy punishment for some of those arrested, nevertheless remained local incidents. They may have strengthened the Chartist conviction that a clash with the government was inevitable, but neither of them occurred in a context in which they sparked off other incidents. The Newport rising of 4 November was the occasion chosen by the Chartists themselves for the challenging of the authority of the government.

The reasons for the failure of the Newport attempt have been discussed many times, and will be discussed again.[56] Apart from the local misfortunes and failures of organization, the basic reasons why an insurrection had little chance of success are clear enough. The British government was secure in the support of the upper and middle classes, the army was loyal, no foreign forces threatened – even Ireland was able to spare troops for the English manufacturing districts in 1839 and 1840.[57] But, although Chartism as an alternative government was not a possibility, it may well have been possible that skirmishes and outbreaks could have occurred which would have changed the pattern of development of British politics in the later years of the century. One event which might have led to further outbreaks and to a heightening of class feeling, which could well have embittered the political atmosphere for decades, would have been the execution of the Welsh Chartist leaders. John Frost in particular was not simply a local leader. He was a chairman of the Convention, a hero to the whole movement since his public exchange of letters with Lord John Russell,[58] and was respected by all sections of the Chartist movement. Whilst he and Zephenia Williams and William Jones were under sentence of death, there was considerable talk of risings, rescue attempts and retaliatory action of all kinds. Had the executions taken place, they might well have been the first of many. The legal query on which Frost's appeal was based allowed time for a slight cooling of the atmosphere on the side of the authorities, and for a nation-wide campaign by the Chartists in support of the three leaders.[59] The commutation of the sentences almost certainly prevented many outbreaks of violence, although there were in fact some abortive risings in January 1840, notably in Yorkshire, in the period between the trial and the commutation of the sentences.[60] The decision not to execute the Welsh leaders was undoubtedly, as Napier noted in his journal,[61] a very wise one politically, and prevented much bitterness in the later development of working-class politics.

The radicals of the older kind who had stayed with Chartism after the end of the first Convention mostly seemed to have dropped out after the Newport rising. The atmosphere had changed, and the government, having avoided a policy of terror, was able to pursue a policy of repression with the maximum of support from the respectable classes. For the radicals of the Jacobin type, who had seen Chartism as an extension of the movement for political reform which had achieved a partial success in 1832, with its threats of armed action being essentially a tactic, Newport was a watershed. They saw here a face of radicalism which they neither understood nor approved. For Matthew Fletcher, the leaders of the movement

> had contrived almost to bury the term radical, which had begun to find much favour in the political world, and conjured up a terrible 'raw head and bloody bones' called chartism, associated in the minds of old ladies with nothing but 'treasons, stratagems and spoils', and which soon died a natural death.[62]

Chartism was to remain an important political force for another ten years, but it was an almost entirely working-class movement in this period. It was carried on, as Fletcher said sneeringly, by 'miserable knots of a dozen or two in each town, meeting generally in some beer-shop, and calling themselves branches of the National Charter Association'.[63]

It was, nevertheless, these 'knots of a dozen or two' who argued out, and attempted to implement, programmes of working-class activity. The National Charter Association was founded in July

1840. O'Connor himself was an elected member of the national executive, and submitted to annual re-election with the other members. This was certainly a decisive break with the past, with the tradition by which popular leaders declared their policies and relied on a 'following' amongst the common people. The idea of, for example, Cobbett or Hunt submitting themselves for election to the leadership of a popular movement illustrates the great change that Chartism had made in the tradition of popular radicalism. O'Connor undoubtedly had many of the qualities of an old-fashioned mass leader – the messianic as well as the oratorical gifts which aroused enthusiasm and devotion in his followers. But he was also leader of a movement in which democratic control was an essential element – he had to be prepared to debate his actions and his policies with other leaders, and to submit them to the membership for final judgement.

In the years following 1840 the Chartists debated the most effective way of achieving their aims. Their publications contain discussions of socialism, republicanism and nearly all possible variations of democratic government. In practical terms they carried out experiments ranging from the presentation of working men candidates at the hustings to the establishment of Chartist land colonies. Many of the ideas which were touched on in the early years were examined and developed at greater depth in the later years of the movement. But in the years covered here certain essential definitions were established. Above all, the national scale of Chartism was something quite new in popular politics. It is not the differences in the movement in the regions which are surprising – they were to be expected, given the great regional variations in the country's industry in these years – but the very great similarity of political and social response. Essentially a provincial movement, Chartism arose at a time when the workers engaged in industry and crafts had achieved a sense of class identity, and were able to respond to a national programme and a national press, but lived still in sufficiently small and closed communities to sustain an organization with the minimum of finance and very few paid officials. The desperation of dying trades and the expansive prospects of the newer industries were contained for a time within the same movement, just as the pessimism of those who feared political reaction and the optimism of those who believed in the possibility of a breakthrough into a new phase of political democracy combined to forge a movement which seemed for a time to gain its strength from an equilibrium of threat and promise and a controlled tension between discipline and despair.

That there is a connection between large-scale protest or political action by the working people and the state of trade and the price of provisions is clear. But the correlation should not be over-simplified, nor should it be assumed that such a correlation effectively 'explains' any movement even of the complexity of a bread riot. Chartism was not, in fact, always at its strongest in areas of the greatest deprivation,[64] and it was certainly not the programme of the most deprived and oppressed sections of society. The Chartist critique of contemporary industrial society found the greatest support in the areas of Britain's key industries – textiles, mining, iron-working and light metal-working. It was here that the working man who had hitherto been able to provide for his family by practising his trade appeared to be threatened. Here the changes associated with the Industrial Revolution were beginning to be felt on a large scale during the Chartist period. They did not necessarily involve an absolute lowering of the family's standard of living, but they often seemed to involve the removal of control and decision-making from the home to a wider social context. There was, therefore, every reason to look for political solutions to problems. Hunger, exploitation and oppression might each or in combination lead a working man to react against society. To some extent the working population of Britain were constantly aware of all three, and local recessions in particular trades must often have accentuated the insecurity of working-class life without necessarily provoking a political or even a turbulent or riotous reaction. But the Chartist solutions to the three questions evoked the enormous response which they did because they appeared to be both rational and possible of achievement. Hunger and deprivation resulting from bad trade could be remedied by enlightened taxation, and by a humane system of out-relief. The extremes of exploitation could be prevented by the legal restraint of some employers by the limitation of hours of work and the protection of young children, and oppression by the defence of the rights of publication, assembly and free speech, all of which had been recently challenged and successfully defended. The working class had before them the example of the successful campaign by the middle classes for political recognition. The 1832 Bill and the subsequent Whig government had shown that it was not necessary to change the class of the representatives to have a House of Commons and a government that was sensitive to the requirements of a wider electorate. Not only were the political demands of the Chartists encouraged by the success of the middle-class campaign of a few years earlier, but they were made essential by that very success. The measures which had been passed in the interests of the middle-class voters seemed in many cases, as has been suggested earlier, to be directed against the working class.

The great interest of Chartism was that it was so much more than a movement of protest. It gave to the British working class a self-awareness and a self-confidence which, for all the short-term failure of the movement, were carried into varied forms of activity, social and political, in Britain, and in other countries overseas. The working class was established as an essential and articulate force in British politics, whose effect was to be felt increasingly throughout the second half of the century, in both local and national affairs.

Notes

1. Benjamin Wilson, *The Struggles of an Old Chartist*, Halifax, 1887.
2. *Halifax Courier*, quoted in ibid., p. 39.
3. Ibid. See p. 25 above.
4. For discussion of the importance of London as a Chartist centre, see: D.J. Rowe, 'The Failure of London Chartism', *Historical Journal*, vol. no. xi, 3, 1968; I. Prothero, 'Chartism in London', *Past and Present*, no. 44, August 1969.
5. Originally published between 12 April 1856 and 30 May 1857, in the *Weekly Record of the Temperance Movement* (not, as William Lovett mistakenly states in chapter 7 of his *Life and Struggles*, in the *Temperance Weekly Record*). Republished in Brian Harrison and Patricia Hollis (eds), *Robert Lowery, Radical and Chartist*, London 1979.
6. See the letter from Frost in W.E. Adams, *Memoirs of a Social Atom*, London 1903, vol. 1, p. 201.
7. A phrase attributed to Frederick Engels, describing the Chartist period, by Belfort Bax, *Justice*, 24 August 1895. The reliability of Devyr's account of Newcastle Chartism in 1839 is discussed briefly in Adams, *Memoirs of a Social Atom*. Adams knew Devyr later, and heard him tell the story again. He comments, 'Such is the story of my Irish friend Thomas Ainge Devyr. It is a story I have heard old Chartists dispute, and other old Chartists say they believe.'
8. Short biographical notices of delegates to the National Convention appeared weekly in *The Charter*, while the Convention was sitting. Fletcher's appeared in the issue of 31 March 1839, and Bussey's in that of 5 May 1839.
9. W. Scruton, *Pen and Pencil Pictures of Old Bradford*, Bradford, 1889.
10. J.H. Priestley, *The History of the Ripponden Cooperative Society*, Halifax 1932.
11. Joshua Holden, *History of Todmorden*, Manchester 1912.
12. Thomas Cooper, *Wise Saws and Modern Instances*, London 1845, vol. 11, pp. 23–4. Cooper goes on to describe the only Radical alderman in the old Lincoln corporation, who became a councillor and later the mayor under the new: 'The abhorrent enactments of the New Poor Law, – how he hated them! – and how

staggered he felt in his reforming faith, when the "liberal" administration urged the passing of the strange Malthusian measure! "I cannot understand it" he would exclaim, in the hearing of the numerous participants in his English hospitality; "I never thought that Reform was to make the poor more miserable and the poorest of the poor most miserable. It is a mystery to me! Surely it is a mistake in Lord Grey and Lord Brougham!"'

13. Raymond Challinor and Brian Ripley, *The Miners' Association: A Trade Union in the Age of the Chartists*, London 1968.

14. *Reynolds's Political Instructor*, 13 April 1850.

15. *Northern Star*, 16 November 1839. An interesting short account of Pitkethly is given in a series of articles on Chartism by Lloyd Jones, the Owenite Socialist, in the *Newcastle Weekly Chronicle* in 1879 (*NWC*, 27 September 1879).

16. *Northern Star*, 12 January 1839.

17. For a full account of the unstamped press agitation, see: Joel Wiener, *The War of the Unstamped: The Movement to Repeal the British Newspaper Tax, 1830–1836*, New York, 1969, Patricia Hollis, *The Pauper Press*, Oxford, 1970. See also Patricia Hollis's introduction to the Merlin Press reprint of *The Poor Man's Guardian*, London 1969.

18. For the *Northern Star*, see Eric Glasgow, 'The Establishment of the *Northern Star* Newspaper', *History*, n.s., vol. xxxix, London 1954, Donald Read, *Press and People*, 1962, and Read and Glasgow, *Feargus O'Connor, Irishman and Chartist*, London 1961. For a general description of the radical and Chartist press, see my 'La Presse de la Classe Ouvrière Anglaise 1836–1848', in Jacques Godechot (ed.), *La Presse Ouvrière 1819–1850*, Paris 1966.

19. Thus, Harney wrote to Engels, 30 March 1846, 'I must do O'C. the justice to say that he never interferes with what I write in the paper nor does he know what I write until he sees the paper': R.M. Black (eds) *The Harney Papers*, Frank Gees Black and Assen 1969, p. 241.

20. An interesting footnote to the radical support for the Canadian rebels is provided by an article by Michael Brook, 'Lawrence Pitkethly, Dr Smyles and Canadian Revolutionaries in the United States, 1842', *Ontario History*, vol. lvii, 1965. See also W.H. Maehl, 'Augustus Hardin Beaumont, *Anglo-American Radical*, 1798–1838', *International Review of Social History*, vol. xiv, 1969.

21. For some of the points at issue between O'Connor and Daniel O'Connell see *Letters from Feargus O'Connor to Daniel O'Connell*, London 1836.

22. For example, an item in the *Northern Star*, 30 January 1840: 12*s* is contributed to the Frost defence fund from Barnsley, from 'A few Bandon [Ireland] men to shew the traitor O'Connell falsified the character of Irishmen when he said the Irish in England were opposed to the Radicals.'

23. For a rather unsatisfactory account of the affair, see Gavin Thurston, *The Clerkenwell Riot*, London 1967.

24. For an account of the passing of the Rural Police Act, and a discussion of its significance, see L. Radzinowicz, *A History of English Criminal Law*, London 1968, vol. 4. For the view that the Chartist threat as a stimulus to police innovation has been overstated, see E.C. Midwinter, *Law and Order in Early Victorian Lancashire*, York 1968.

25. In Ashton-under-Lyne, one of the most active Chartist localities throughout the whole of the Chartist period, and where the very great majority of the working population were cotton factory operatives, not only was there a large Chartist organization, but there were both juvenile and female Chartist groups (*Northern Star*, 16 November 1839, 4 December 1841, and passim).

26. For a brief examination of the numerical strength of the cotton handloom weavers in the main Chartist centres, see Duncan Bythell, *The Handloom Weavers*, London 1969.

27. 'Autobiography of Samuel Fielden', in *Knights of Labour* (Chicago) 18 February 1887. Reprinted in Philip S. Foner (ed.), *The Autobiographies of the Haymarket Martyrs*, New York 1969.

28. For Luddite letters, see E.P. Thompson, *Making of the English Working Class*, London 1963, chapter 14. See also the interesting group of such letters in W.B. Crump (ed.), *The Leeds Woollen Industry*, London 1930, chapter 3. For Captain Swing letters, see Eric Hobsbawm and George Rudé, *Captain Swing*, London 1969.

29. *The Trial of Feargus O'Connor and Fifty-eight Others at Lancaster*, Manchester and London 1843.

30. Brian Harrison and Patricia Hollis, 'Chartism, Liberalism and the life of Robert Lowery', *English Historical Review*, vol. lxxxii, July 1967, and R. Soffer, 'Attitudes and Allegiances in the Unskilled North', *International Review of Social History*, vol. iii, 1965.

31. Edward Hamer, *A Brief Account of the Chartist Outbreak at Llanidloes in the Year 1839*, Llanidloes 1867, reprinted New York 1986, p. 19.

32. Matthew Fletcher, *Letters to the Inhabitants of Bury*, Bury, 1852. For an earlier expression of this view by Fletcher, see *Northern Star*, 19 October 1839.

33. Among those who withdrew their support after the events at Newport was Frances Trollope, the second volume of whose novel *Michael Armstrong* was to have described the hero's participation in legitimate radical agitation, but 'when those in whose behalf she hoped to move the sympathy of their country are found busy in scenes of outrage and lawless violence ... the author feels that it would be alike acting in violation of her own principles, and doing injury to the cause she wishes to serve, were she to ... hold up as objects of public sympathy men who have stained their righteous cause with deeds of violence and blood.' (Preface to *Michael Armstrong the Factory Boy*, London 1840).

34. Rev. Joseph Rayner Stephens was arrested in Ashton-under-Lyne in Dec 1838, and charged with attending an unlawful assembly and with inciting the people to unlawful acts. He was tried in August 1839, and sentenced to eighteen months' imprisonment.

35. Letter from Rev. H.S. Graham to Home Secretary, Lord John Russell, 16 March 1839. HO 40, Correspondence and Papers, Cornwall, Public Record Office.

36. *Northern Star*, 19 January 1839.

37. A.R. Schoyen, *The Chartist Challenge*, London 1958, examines in some detail Harney's connection with the insurrectionary side of Chartism.

38. *Newcastle Weekly Chronicle*, 5 January 1890. This letter is one of a series of reminiscent letters about 1839 in the Newcastle area. Taylor was almost certainly more deeply implicated in the plans for the north-east than Harney. See letter, John Grey of Millfield to Lord Howick, and the enclosure – a letter addressed to John Taylor by 'M.L.', and intercepted by Grey, in the Papers of the 3rd Earl Grey, Prior's Kitchen, Durham Cathedral.

39. The May Manifesto is printed in full in Lovett, *Life and Struggles of William Lovett in His Pursuit of Bread, Knowledge and Freedom*, London 1876, reprinted New York 1986, pp. 209–15.

40. *Northern Star*, 13 July 1839.

41. W. Napier (ed.), *The Life and Opinions of General Sir Charles James Napier*, London 1857, vol. 2, pp. 42–66 passim.

42. [David Urquhart], *The Chartist Correspondence* (reprinted from the *Free Press Serials*, no. xiii, 1855), Sheffield 1856. Alexander Somerville, *Cobdenic Policy, the Internal Enemy of England*, London 1854.

43. Wilson, Frank Peel, *The Risings of the Luddites, Chartists and Plug-Drawers*, Brighouse 1880, reprinted London 1968.

44. The extent to which the commutation of the death sentences on the Welsh leaders 'de-fused' Chartism of its potential violence will remain a question of debate.

Devyr reports that, when the death sentences were first announced, 'there were those on the sidewalk in front of our office who gave a bound of delight, with "Thank God! the Government has just pronounced its own death sentence. That on John Frost will never be executed!"' (*Odd Book of the Nineteenth Century*, New York 1882, p. 199.)

45. Hobhouse to Lord John Russell: 'we have no particular reason for being anxious to place a Napier in high command, quite the contrary.' George P. Gooch (ed.), *Later Correspondence of Lord John Russell*, London 930, vol. 1, p. 274.

46. H.A. Bruce, MP (ed.), *Life of General Sir William Napier, K.C.B.*, London 1864, pp. 297, 346 and passim.

47. Lord Broughton (J.C. Hobhouse), *Recollections of a Long Life*, ed. Lady Dorchester, London 1909.

48. Napier so far forgot the principles he had expounded to Hobhouse as to write to the commander-in-chief in 1839, saying he could see no way to meet the evils of the situation 'but to concede to the people their just rights, while the principle of order is at the same time vigorously upheld'. The reply was uncompromising: 'Lord Hill desires me to point out your observations and to suggest that you avoid all remarks having allusion to political questions; and I am to say without entering into the merits of the question, that neither he, as C-in-C, nor you as Major-General commanding the Northern District, can have anything to do with the matter; it is therefore better that you should confine yourselves to what is strictly your province as military men.' (Butler, *Sir Charles Napier*, London 1890, and Napier.)

49. The Napiers were first cousins to Lord Edward Fitzgerald, who died of his wounds whilst under arrest for his part as a leader of the United Irishmen in 1798.

50. Napier, vol. 2, p. 53.

51. Ibid., vol. 2, p. 40.

52. Ibid., vol. 2, p. 39.

53. Ibid., vol. 2, p. 77.

54. Ibid., vol. 2, p. 122.

55. Ibid., vol. 2, p. 154.

56. See in particular Schoyen and David Williams, *John Frost*, Cardiff 1939.

57. Napier, vol. 2, p. 60.

58. Reprinted in full in the *Annual Register*, 1839.

59. In Aberdeen, the news of the death sentence arrived on Sunday. By Monday morning the petition for a pardon was ready. It was dispatched by 3 p.m. on Wednesday, with 15,000 signatures ('John Mitchell, Aberdeen Chartist', *Aberdeen People's Journal*, 24 February 1887). This is one example, which could be matched from many other centres, of the speed and scale of the response.

60. See A.J. Peacock, *Bradford Chartism 1838–40*, York 1969, for an examination of the evidence for and the reports of the attempted risings which took place *after* Newport. He shows that much of the contradictory evidence relating to a national conspiracy arises from the confusion between activity before and at the time of Newport, and activity in December 1839 and January 1840.

61. Napier, pp. 125–6.

62. Fletcher, letter iv. Fletcher also speaks of the dropping out of the Convention of the 'timid – I should perhaps say prudent' members, soon after its beginning, and their replacement by 'what Feargus O'Connor called "new blood" ... it was after the new blood had begun to show itself that an excellent friend of mine, an Unitarian minister, suggested we had better go home while we yet had a character.' Fletcher himself, however, stayed in the movement until after Newport.

63. Ibid., letter v.

64. See, for example, Home Office reports relating to the Newcastle area (HO 40). W.H. Maehl, 'Chartism in North-Eastern England', *International Review of Social History*, vol. viii, 1963, discusses the comparative prosperity of many of the

Chartists in the area, and quotes pitmen of Whitridge as saying, in August 1839, that 'it was for their political rights they were struggling, and quite unconnected with the question of wages, respecting which they had no complaints to make.' See also letter from the Bradford (Yorkshire) magistrates to the Lord Lieutenant, 18 April 1838, reporting that muskets, pikes and pistols were being bought by 'parties of the very lowest grade.... This state of things is more to be regretted as there is plenty of Employment for the working class.' (Harewood Papers).

3

Women and Nineteenth-Century Radical Politics: A Lost Dimension

Historians of the women's emancipation movement have observed the considerable gulf that existed between the aspirations of the middle-class emancipators and those of women lower down in the social scale in Victorian society. One of the many hypocrisies of Victorian conservative thought was its typification of woman as a frail, delicate and decorative creature, and its simultaneous tolerance of, and indeed dependence on, the exploitation of vast numbers of women in every kind of arduous and degrading work, from coal-mining to prostitution. Such women, labourers and servants, had no need to fight for the right to work – society would not have survived long had they been prevented from working. Their work was low in the scale of social recognition and of payment, and stable organizations to improve or protect their standards of pay and conditions were not established until near the end of the nineteenth century. Such changes as were made by law in their conditions of work were the result of radical or humanitarian campaigns rather than of the organizations of the women themselves; these campaigns were concerned as much with the moral welfare of women operatives and with the stability of the working-class family as with the improvement of the status of women as workers.

The expansion of British manufactures and the rapid industrialization of the late eighteenth and early nineteenth centuries did not mean the introduction of women into manufacturing industry. They were already an essential part of the labour force in pre-mechanized industry. What did change in some key industries, however, was the location of work; the arrival of the independent factory worker, woman or child, working away from home, but returning to her home and still responsible to it and dependent on it, was new, certainly on the scale in which it existed in the textile manufacturing districts by the early 1830s. It is possible to exaggerate the reality of the 'independence' of women in economic terms – the wages they were paid were reckoned as a contribution to a family wage rather than as the support of an independent worker.[1] Nevertheless, 'public' work alongside other members of her own sex, and a regular wage, paid to her, even if legally the property of her husband, might have been expected to produce a more active awareness among working-class women of trade and political questions and of public matters generally. My purpose here is to show the extent to which women did take part in the early radical movement. The period is one in which working-class radicalism combined traditional forms of action – mass demonstrations, processions, open political activities involving whole families and whole communities – with early versions of the more sophisticated organizational forms which were to be the pattern of later nineteenth-century politics.

Chartism was the culmination of fifty years of political and industrial activity among the British working people. In those years the manufacturing districts responded to the changes brought about by the rapid alterations in the pace and patterns of work in various ways, some defensive, some active and assertive. A long series of strikes and turn-outs in the main manufacturing trades – wool- and linen-weaving, wool-combing, tailoring, shoemaking – resulted in the defeat of the strikers and the speeding-up of mechanization. The retention of old work-patterns, customs and methods of payment were obviously not to be achieved by action within individual trades. The working people turned therefore to political action or general unionism, seeking a more general defence of wage levels and some degree of political control over the pace of mechanization. In these years political and industrial issues can rarely be separated. Faced with new industrial techniques, the workers sought a defence against the redundancy of men skilled in the old techniques and the control of the use of women's and children's labour to replace that of men in the new factories. In the search for alternatives to the uncontrolled introduction of machinery, a number of choices were presented. For some, the arguments of Owenites and other radical and socialist thinkers suggested ways in which the new machines could be a blessing and not a threat. Other radical alternatives agreed in proposing a different organization of industry, with a more equal distribution of the new wealth which was being created, and the use of some of it for the education of children, the care of the sick and aged. They argued for a better way of life for the workers in the industries as well as for the owners and traders.

The spectrum of radical thought, by the 1830s, stretched from a generally defensive stance, in which the values of the older domestic–industry communities were upheld – the supervision by the parents of their children's upbringing and training, the status of the man as the head of the family and the main wage-earner, the value of the old unmechanized skills – through more aggressive demands for the right to organize to protect wages and working conditions, and for access to the political system by means of the suffrage, to the total rejection of private enterprise industrial capitalism in favour of a more rational organization of industry which should eschew competition in favour of cooperation. Large-scale industrial production was still a minute sector of the total of productive industry, and the possibility of taming and controlling it was not at this stage seen by many as a total impossibility.

In 1832 the Reform Bill admitted the middle classes to the franchise. The old, rigid and irrational system of representation gave way, apparently under pressure, but without an armed uprising, to a system of representation which was uniform throughout the country, and which made a place in the political world for the non-landed property-owners. The working classes in London and the provinces had formed a part of the pressure which had brought about the reform. When it became clear that the new interests were ensuring both the finality of the reform settlement and the statutory reinforcement of the middle-class demands for the more effective disciplining of labour, exemplified in the Poor Law Amendment Act and in the series of anti-trade union cases in the courts, the response from the working class was one of fear of an outright attack by the authorities on working-class institutions and standards, combined with a positive and hopeful resurgence of political activity aimed at the extension of the franchise. Chartism, for all the strongly defensive element which it contained, was basically an optimistic movement. The Chartists and their followers really believed that they would achieve the vote, and that the achievement would be followed by a far greater attention on the part of the authorities to the needs of the labouring people; they believed in the possibility of major changes in the structure of power and authority in British society which would result in a more egalitarian and humane system. In that alternative system, women would play a more equal part than they played in contemporary society.

That this optimism existed can be amply demonstrated, and the story of women's part in Chartism needs to be told to emphasize this. What is more difficult to understand, however, is why this element disappeared from radical thought and action some time in the 1840s. Working-class women seem to have retreated into the home at some time around, or a little before, the middle of the century. Up until that time there is evidence of their active participation in the politics of the working communities.

The reform agitation which was renewed after the end of the Napoleonic Wars took on a mass character in some of the manufacturing districts, in particular among the cotton workers of Lancashire. In his autobiography Samuel Bamford has left a vivid description of the experience of one local leader in these years. He claims personal responsibility for the formal admission of women into the councils of the reformers.

> At one of these meetings which took place at Lydgate, in Saddleworth, ... I, in the course of an address, insisted on the right, and the propriety also, of females who were present at such assemblages, voting by show of hands, for, or against the resolutions. This was a new idea; and the women who attended numerously on that bleak ridge, were mightily pleased with it, – and the men being nothing dissentient when the resolution was put, the women held up their hands, amid much laughter; and ever from that time women voted at radical meetings.[2]

Whatever the extent of Bamford's personal responsibility for the phenomenon, there is no doubt that the reform movement included many women, and that female political unions, with their own committees and officers, were formed. When the reformers from the weaving communities formed their columns and marched to Manchester to take part in the greatest demonstration yet held for parliamentary reform, at St Peter's Fields on 16 August 1819, many women took part, Bamford's Middleton contingent set off, with

> At our head a hundred or two of women, mostly young wives, and mine own was amongst them. A hundred or two of our handsomest girls – sweethearts to the lads who were with us – danced to the music or sang snatches of popular songs.[3]

Bamford includes, together with his own vivid account of the events of that day, the account remembered by his wife who had been separated from him in the immense crowd. Sixty-five years later when the radicals of Failsworth organized a demonstration against the House of Lords at the time of the Third Reform Bill, they took with them on the demonstration a group of ten old radicals, all of whom had been present at the Peterloo massacre, taking with them the banner which they had carried in 1819. Four of the ten were women.[4]

The women in the manufacturing districts were new to politics, as, too, were many of the men. But, like the men, many had experience of other forms of protest. There is ample evidence of women's participation in food riots and other demonstrations in the eighteenth and early nineteenth centuries. Southey recorded the great ferocity of the Worcester glovemakers:

> Three or four years ago the English ladies chose to wear long silken gloves; the demand for leathern ones immediately ceased, and the women whose business it was to make them were thrown out of employ. This was the case of many hundreds here in Worcester. In such cases, men commonly complain and submit; but women are more disposed to be mutinous; they stand less in fear of law, partly from ignorance, partly because they presume upon the privilege of their sex, and therefore in all public tumults they are foremost in violence and ferocity. Upon this occasion they carried their point within their own territories; it was dangerous to appear in silken gloves in the streets of this city; and one lady who foolishly or ignorantly ventured to walk abroad here in this forbidden fashion, is said to have been seized by the women and whipped.[5]

At about the same time 'Lady Ludd' was leading a demonstration in Nottingham against a baker who had put up the price of his flour by twopence a stone:

> Several women in Turn-calf alley [stuck] a half-penny loaf on top of a fishing rod, after having raddled it over and tied a piece of black crepe around it, to give it the appearance of a bleeding famine decked in sack-cloth. With this, and by the aid of three hand-bells, two borne by women and one by a boy, a considerable crowd of women, girls and boys soon collected together.[6]

At a less spontaneous level of activity, there are numerous examples of female friendly societies during the very early years of the nineteenth century. These provided sick and burial benefits, and also must have served as social organizations. Many had rules insisting on sober and decent behaviour, including in at least one case sanctions against any member having irregular sexual relations with the husband of a fellow-member. Little is known in detail about these societies, or about the extent to which they took on functions related to trade union activities in the periods of the illegality of the unions, as many men's societies seem to have done. But they were clearly organized and run by women, and not only unmarried women. There were also female lodges of many of the male friendly societies, Rechabites, Druids, Oddfellows and so on.[7]

In the early trade unions the women's part varied from trade to trade. In most trades the problems involved in the much lower pay rates accorded to women's work made their regular cooperation with the men difficult, although amongst the weavers there appears to have been equality of rates (which were of course piece-rates) and membership of the union was open to both sexes. When James Burland attended a meeting of striking Barnsley linen-weavers in 1829, and wanted information about one of the speakers, he turned to his neighbour, 'a tall, raw-boned masculine-looking old woman with a pipe in her mouth' to ask about the speaker and the strike.[8] In 1832 the *Leeds Mercury* reported that

> The card-setters in the neighbourhood of Scholes and Hightown, chiefly women, held a meeting to the number of 1,500, at Peep Green, at which it was determined not to set any more cards at less than a halfpenny a thousand.

It also reported the presumably tongue-in-cheek comment that

> Alarmists may view these indications of female independence as more menacing to established institutions than the 'education of the lower orders'.[9]

When in the summer of 1834 the radical and trade union movements erupted into the short-lived Grand National Consolidated Trades Union, the women were present in the lodges of Operative Bonnet Makers, Female Tailors, and simply of Women of Great Britain and Ireland.[10]

Women, then, played an important part in the work processes and in the social and public activities of the community. As the people turned towards more political forms of action in the 1830s men and women took part together in these actions. The illegal unstamped papers of the campaign against the newspaper taxes in the early 1830s were hawked around the country by women as well as men. When Brady of Sheffield was returning home after serving a term of imprisonment for selling the *Poor Man's Guardian*, he was met and escorted through Barnsley by the local radicals carrying lanterns and accompanied by a band of music. Brady was, as one account stated, 'the hero of the hour. But no less was Mrs Lingard the heroine, for she was present with an armful of unstamped papers which she cried publicly for sale, and for which, we need hardly say, she did not lack customers.'[11] Mrs Lingard was the wife of a radical Barnsley shoemaker turned newsagent, Joseph Lingard, and the mother of Thomas, later to be a leader among the Barnsley Chartists. The Lingards are an example, of which there are many, of a radical family in which both sexes and more than one generation took part in the local leadership. In Leeds in the same period Alice Mann was a leading figure in the publication, sale and distribution of unstamped journals.[12]

During the riots, disturbances and demonstrations of the 1830s the presence of women in the crowds was remarked by all observers. In the movement against the New Poor Law of 1834, for example, which swept through the manufacturing districts of the north in 1837, women and girls were to the fore, as they were in the public demonstrations of the short-time committees.[13] Writing from Yorkshire in 1838, Lawrence Pitkethly, a leader of the short-time and anti-Poor Law movements, urged his fellow radical James Broyan of Nottingham:

> I hope you will get your women to work and mob all the bastile blackguards who are in or who come to your Town – persevere and you must conquer, be tame and there is nothing but Bastiles for you.[14]

The presence of women, almost as shock troops in these violent demonstrations, is certainly well established at least up to 1842 when F.H. Grundy, describing his experience of the crowd during the Plug Riots, referred to one confrontation between the tired marchers and the troops,

> all were hungry, evening was coming on; and although a few stones were thrown, chiefly *of course*, by women, when the chief magistrate came forward to read the Riot Act, the mob dispersed for that time peaceably.[15]

By the beginning of the Chartist period, the manufacturing districts of Lancashire, Yorkshire, Nottingham, Scotland, South Wales, Newcastle, and the West Midlands had an established tradition of radical and industrial activity, more recent but perhaps more widespread than the older Jacobin traditions in the cities. By the 1830s there were in most districts radical families in which more than one generation passed on traditions, beliefs and radical folklore to the children and to political newcomers. Many Chartist reminiscences later in the century recall a childhood or youth spent in close association with this tradition. Benjamin Wilson, Halifax Chartist and later historian of the movement in his town, recalled in 1887 his upbringing in Skircoat Green 'a village that had long been noted for its radicalism'.

> The Women of this village were not far behind the men in their love of liberty, for I have heard my mother tell of their having regular meetings and lectures at the house of Thomas Washington, a shoemaker ... and they too went into mourning [at the time of Peterloo] and marched in procession, Tommy's wife carrying a cap of liberty on the top of a pole.

When Wilson moved to his uncle's house to work as a bobbin-winder and warehouse boy, it was his aunt 'a famous politician, a Chartist and a great admirer of Feargus O'Connor' who first introduced him to politics.[16] Peterloo figures prominently in the upbringing of the Yorkshire and Lancashire Chartists. Wilson was in fact born in the same year, but learned about it almost as soon as he learned to talk. Isaac Johnson, of Stockport, when imprisoned for his Chartist activities in 1839, impressed HM Inspector of Prisons as

> A shrewd man – a republican I suspect upon principle; uneducated which he explains was owing to his being turned out of school, after gaining six prizes, in consequence of his father obliging him to go to school in a white hat with crape and green riband at Peterloo time, for which he was expelled and never went anywhere afterwards.[17]

W.E. Adams, later to become editor of the *Newcastle Weekly Chronicle*, was an ardent Chartist as a young man in Cheltenham:

> Few men now living, I fancy, had an earlier introduction to Chartism than I had. My people, though there wasn't a man among them, were all Chartists, or at least interested in the Chartist movement. If they did not keep the 'sacred month' it was because they thought the suspension of labour on the part of a few poor washerwomen would have no effect on the policy of the country. But they did for a time abstain from the use of exisable commodities.[18]

Another Chartist, William Aitken, weaver, schoolmaster and life-long radical, recalled the women who introduced him to politics as a very young man in Ashton-under-Lyne, one of the most radical districts in Lancashire:

> My earliest remembrances of taking part in Radicalism are the invita-tions I used to receive to be at 'Owd Nancy Clayton's' in Charlestown, on the 16th of August to denounce the Peterloo massacre and drink in

solemn silence 'to the immortal memory of Henry Hunt.' ... This old Nancy and her husband were both at Peterloo, and, I believe, both were wounded, at all events, the old woman was. She wore on that memorable day a black petticoat, which she afterwards transformed into a black flag which on the 16th of August used to be hung out and a green cap of liberty attached thereto. In the year 1838 a new cap of liberty was made, and hung out with the black flag on the anniversary of the Peterloo massacre. These terrible and terrifying emblems of sedition alarmed the then powers that existed and our then chief constable – no lover of democracy – was ordered by a magistrate to march a host of special constables and all the civil power he could command to forcibly seize and take possession of these vile emblems of anarchy and base revolution. Off they marched ... but the women of that part of the borough heard of the contemplated raid that was likely to befall their cherished emblems, and the women drew them in from the window and hid them. Up this gallant and brave band of men went to the front door of poor old Nancy Clayton, and placed themselves in daring military array while the chief constable with a subordinate marched upstairs, and amongst the women there he found my old friend 'Riah Witty, who told the writer what follows. Imperiously and haughtily, as became the chief of so noble a band and in so righteous a cause, he demanded the black flag and the cap of liberty. My old friend 'Riah said

'What hast thou to do wi' cap o' liberty? Thou never supported liberty, not aught 'ut belongs thee?'

However, the chamber was searched and the poor black flag was found under the bed and taken prisoner ... the house was searched from top to bottom for the cap of liberty, but neither the genius of the chief or his subordinate could find the missing emblem of revolution. Off this gallant band of men marched with poor old Nancy's petticoat – the black flag never more to grace a radical banquet of potatoe pies and home-brewed ale....

The Saturday after this grand demonstration 'Riah Witty met the chief constable, and she exclaimed

'Now, thou didna find that cap o' liberty, did tha?'

'No' he said, 'I didna 'Riah, where wur it?' She said

'I knew thou couldna find it; it were where thou duratna go for it.'[19]

Female radical organizations with a continuous existence throughout the 1820s and 1830s, are rare, but the anti-Poor Law demonstrations of 1837 saw the growth or revival of female associations in a number of centres. In the small wool-manufacturing township of Elland in the West Riding of Yorkshire, the female radicals held meetings in the pre-Chartist period, with women as speakers. After one such meeting, Elizabeth Hanson was taken to task by the *Globe* newspaper for her attack on the New Poor Law, and for her lack of understanding of the laws of political economy. Her reply was spirited:

> Sir – I am surprised that your sagacity as a politician and public instructor should not comprehend my meaning with regard to the distress that I made mention of at the female public meeting at Elland. In speaking of that subject you say – 'Could not my female quickness show me that the distress was taking place under the old poor law'. I knew that, sir, as well as you. I knew at the moment I was speaking, and every one must know that has common sense, that neither the old poor law nor the new one, had anything to do with producing the distress.
>
> The distress, sir, is the effect of the bad arrangements of society; but then the poor law, which is a sure badge of those arrangements, is given for a corrector or a palliative....
>
> ... You say, extend our commerce. We have ransacked the whole habitable globe. If you can find out a way to the moon, we may, perhaps, with the aid of paper, carry on our competition a little longer; but if you want to better the condition of the working classes, let our government legislate so as to make machinery go hand in hand with hand labour, and act as an auxilliary or helpmate, not a competitor.[20]

Elizabeth Hanson seems to have been a member of another radical family, possibly the wife of Abraham Hanson, weaver and lay preacher, and the mother of Feargus O'Connor Hanson, born in 1837. The naming of children of both sexes after leading radicals was a common practice in these years. In 1849 the *Morning Chronicle* correspondent noted:

> A curious indication of the prevailing shade of radical politics in the village (Middleton, Lancs.) is afforded by the parish register, the people having a fancy for christening their children after the hero of the minute. Thus, a generation or so back, Henry Hunts were as common as blackberries – a crop of Feargus O'Connors replaced them, and latterly there have been a few green sprouts labelled Ernest Jones.[21]

The chair at the meeting at which Elizabeth Hanson spoke was taken by Mary Grassby, who was also attacked by the *Globe* for her unseemly actions. She, too, replied with a spirited defence. The Elland female radicals maintained their public activity, issuing an address in 1838 to welcome the return of the Dorchester labourers in the spring of that year. The address congratulates the men on their release, but urges them to join in the campaign to secure the pardon and release of the Glasgow cotton-spinners, who had been sentenced for conspiracy in 1837, and whose case was the second major trade-union prosecution in the immediately pre-Chartist period.[22] The Elland women were outspoken supporters of Richard Oastler and opponents of the New Poor Law, as were the women of Staleybridge, Lancashire, who were reported in February 1838 to be getting up a petition against the New Poor Law to match that of the men, which had already gathered several thousands of signatures.[23]

In June 1838, a letter appeared in the *Northern Star* addressed to the women of Scotland, and signed 'A Real Democrat'; it began:

> Fellow Countrywomen – I address you as a plain working woman – a weaver of Glasgow. You cannot expect me to be grammatical in my expressions, as I did not get an education, like many other of my fellow women that I ought to have got, and which is the right of every human being.... It is the right of every woman to have a vote in the legislation of her country, and doubly more so now that we have got a woman at the head of the government.[24]

This is one of the rare cases in these years in which the demand for the vote for women is put specifically by working women. In general their demands are more social and more general, like those of the female radicals of Rochdale, who established their society in the following year 'determined publicly to show the world that they know their rights and will maintain them'.[25]

Women appeared, then, to be assuming a radical stance in the post-Reform Bill period, either by forming their own organizations or by taking part in demonstrations and actions together with their husbands and families. As the radical movement gathered momentum in the years 1837, 1838 and 1839, there seems little doubt that the women were part of that momentum.

When Henry Vincent visited the West Riding of Yorkshire as a missionary from the London Working Men's Association, to encourage the formation of provincial associations, he was almost overwhelmed by his reception. From Huddersfield – the home of Richard Oastler and Lawrence Pitkeithly – he wrote:

> Our meeting was called for four o'clock in the afternoon, we were met at the entrance by some friends who conveyed us to an inn where we partook of tea. We were then conducted through the town amidst delightful scenes of excitement. The townspeople, cottagers and farmers, with their wives and daughters, all came out of their little houses and flocked with us to the meeting. The meeting took place in a hollow, just at the entrance of the town, which was bounded on all sides by green

hills – the men all stood in the hollow, whilst the pretty lasses and women with white aprons and caps trimmed with green, sat all around the sides of the hill. I never witnessed a more gratifying sight in my life.[26]

He toured England in 1837 and 1838, and was impressed by the fact that not only did many women attend all the public meetings at which he spoke, but at a number of places they obviously had their independent organizations. In Trowbridge (Wiltshire) the ladies presented him with a 'handsome suit of clothes', to which the weavers of Tiverton added a 'beautiful waistcoat piece, weaved by themselves'.[27] At Birmingham the vast crowd which followed Vincent and the local speakers to Holloway Head for an outdoor meeting included women as well as men – 'as far as the eye could reach was a splendid variety of male and female beauty ... there were full 50,000 women, all neatly and cleanly attired.'[28] At Hull the new hall was 'Crowded to suffocation – and the gallery delightfully ornamented with ladies.'[29] At Bath, in October 1838, he organized a meeting for the women alone.

> I signed an address late on Saturday announcing that I had obtained Larkenhall Gardens, situate about a mile from the city and invited the ladies to attend at three o'clock ... yesterday afternoon the whole road leading to the place of meeting was crowded by highly respectable females, some on foot and others in coaches and various vehicles wending their way to the place of meeting – the gardens which will hold at least 5,000 were crammed to suffocation – no males allowed within except Mr Kissock ... Mr Young ... and myself. There were hundreds outside who could not get near the place.[30]

At Blandford, in Dorset, 'the country lads and lasses were seen flocking over the fields and hills in all directions' towards the place of meeting outside the town. As the speakers arrived at the hustings they received 'the usual friendly salutations, the men cheering us and the women clapping their hands and waving their handkerchiefs'.[31]

Throughout the country, in all areas with a history of open radical activity, the women seem to have come into Chartism with the men. They often set up their own organizations, usually with some help and encouragement from the men. In Newcastle-on-Tyne the first meeting of the Female Chartist Association was chaired by James Ayr, a well-known local radical. Men were admitted to the meeting with an entrance fee of twopence, women free.[32] Other places, like Bath, had their own officials from the beginning. Mrs

Bolwell, at Bath, had chaired the meeting at which Vincent spoke, and had made, he said, a very good speech. But, like the women at Elland, and like Mrs Anna Pepper of Bradford, who addressed the female Chartists of that town on the political duties of women in December 1840, she was speaking to an all-woman audience. Women do not seem to have appeared in the chair or on platforms before mixed audiences, although men sometimes found themselves addressing an all-female audience.

'Hurrah for the women' began one report in the *Northern Star*:

> On Wednesday last Mr Reeves of Sunderland visited this place [New Durham] to get up a meeting in support of the Charter. A room having been obtained, Mr Reeves proceeded to the spot about the time announced for the meeting, but to his surprise, instead of finding a room full of men (who had not had time to get there so early, just having left work) every part of the large room, window seats and all, was occupied by the canny women of this place. This was an agreeable surprise to Mr Reeves and, whether he would or not, there was nothing left him but to address the women, for they got him into the room, locked the door, and set him upon the chair, declaring that he should not leave until he had formed a female association. This was done, and the next morning half a dozen of these patriotic women were running about the town, with a paste-pan and bills, calling another meeting for Saturday next.[33]

The female radical associations, of which more than twenty are mentioned in the *Northern Star* during the first two years of Chartism's formal existence, were concerned in a variety of activities besides public meetings. In Sheffield, under the leadership of Mrs Peter Foden, they collected names of sympathetic women and enjoined them 'to instil the principles of Chartism into their children'.[34] They attended meetings and demonstrations, prepared banners and flags, decorated the halls and the speakers' waggons. They organized and took part in social events, from the radical suppers of 'potatoe pie and home-brewed ale' of Nancy Clayton to the more ambitious soirées and musical evenings organized in other areas. They took a major part in the educational efforts which some localities made, which included Chartist and Democratic chapels, Sunday schools and even day schools. All of these required the active support of the women to succeed, as did the important form of working-class pressure, exclusive dealing. In largely working-class districts, the holders of the £10 franchise for a parliamentary vote would be mainly shopkeepers and publicans. Many of these relied on working-class custom for their livelihood, and it was possible, therefore, in the days of open voting, for considerable pressure to be brought on at least a small number of voters. Early in 1839, the Barnsley Chartists, who were collecting money for the Chartist National Rent, and for the defence fund set up to provide legal aid for the arrested leader, Joseph Rayner Stephens, resolved

> that the persons who have canvassed the shopkeepers of the town for contributions towards the national rent and Stephens' defence fund, be requested to draw up a list of those who complied with their solicitations, such list to be read each night by the chairman or secretary as a preface to the business of the meeting and an index to exclusive dealing.[35]

In Halifax, Ben Wilson recalled several tradesmen who prospered on the custom of their fellow-Chartists, such as James Haigh Hill, a butcher in the Shambles, and known as the Chartist butcher, who employed a comber called Boden, a leader in the movement and one of the best speakers in Halifax. 'I have seen crowds of people in front of his shop on a Saturday night, and on one occasion he had a band of music there.'[36] The thousands of small purchases by working households could represent a considerable financial power if it was organized. Opponents of the Chartists, or tradesmen who had given evidence against Chartist prisoners in courts, found this to their cost in more than one strong centre of Chartism.[37] Working-class purchasing power could also be used to support leaders of the movement in small businesses, as well as to embark on attempts at cooperative trading. All these activities required the agreement and active cooperation of the women in the communities, and were carried on successfully in those areas in which men and women took part together.

A form of demonstration which occurred in some centres was the peaceful occupation of the parish church by a large body of Chartists on the Sabbath. They sat in pews for which they had paid no rent, and often insisted that the incumbent preach from a text of their choosing such as 'He who does not work, neither shall he eat', or 'Go now ye rich men, weep and howl for your miseries that shall come upon you' and many others of this kind. Some clergymen used the occasion to preach an anti-Chartist sermon, and one, the Rev. Francis Close, perpetual curate of Cheltenham Parish Church, published the two sermons which he addressed to the Chartist occupations, the first to the men, the second to the female Chartists of Cheltenham.

It were bad enough [he complained] if they used their influence over their husbands, their brothers and their fathers to foment discord, to promote a spirit of sedition, and to excite instead of allaying the bad passions of those amongst whom they live: but alas in these evil days – these *foreign* days on *British* soil, not content with this, women now become politicians, they leave the distaff and the spindle to listen to the teachers of sedition; they forsake their fireside and home duties for political meetings, they neglect honest industry to read the factious newspapers! and so destitute are they of all sense of female decorum, of female modesty and diffidence, that they become themselves political agitators – female dictators – female mobs – female Chartists![38]

The politics of the early years of Chartism, although distinguished from earlier movements by their scale and extent, were nevertheless in patterns similar to traditional forms of protest and agitation. Demands, even the demand for universal suffrage, were often couched in terms which suggested the restoration of lost rights rather than the establishment of new ones. The defence of their children from the factory system, their own and their husband's jobs from increasing exploitation, of which mechanization was only one aspect, and resistance to the encroachments of a centralizing state, as exemplified by the harsh New Poor Law and the proposals for a great extension of the police, were sufficiently strong motivating forces to get the women to take an active part in Chartist politics. There were, however, some men and women who went further, and proposed fundamental changes in society; these included the Owenites, for whom the traditional institutions of marriage and the nuclear family were seen as hindrances to the development of a genuinely cooperative community. These supporters of 'the social system' mounted a regular attack on the laws relating to divorce and marriage, and delighted in producing evidence of the injustice and inhumanity of the existing arrangements – from stories of murder and violence like the case of the murder by her husband of the wife in an unhappy marriage – 'Verily the Christians may well abuse the marriage system of the Socialists for their own is without a fault!' – to more light-hearted incidents like the one in which an anti-socialist lecturer, attacking the socialists' ideas on marriage at a public meeting in Liverpool, was interrupted by his own deserted wife, who had read the announcement of the meeting and had come 'to see him and hold a little discourse with him upon certain points of importance. Such is a specimen of some of the opponents of the social system.'[39]

The Owenites included women among their lecturers, and enrolled them in their community projects. B. Warden, of the East London branch, in address to the members of the Cambridgeshire Community, made a particular appeal to the women among them:

> Sisters of the community! you who have all to gain and nothing to lose, – you who have been counted politically dead in law, – you whose rights have never been recognised except by the social system, remember, I say, you must get knowledge; on you mainly depends the character of our youths; on you depend mainly the peace and happiness of the community circle. Without you the superstructure would be unfinished; you, the chief cornerstone that the builders rejected, have become the bulwark of our peace and unity.[40]

Many of the Owenites were also Chartists, for the pure doctrine of Owenite socialism did not concern itself with day to day politics, and those who accepted Owen's general critique of competitive capitalism but nevertheless also wanted to engage in contemporary politics joined in the agitation for the suffrage.

Although women undoubtedly took part in the work of the small number of Owenite communities[41] and in the even smaller socialist groups such as the St Simonians (who advertised with each copy of *New Christianity or the Religion of St Simon* 'a coloured portrait of a St Simonian female'),[42] little evidence of such 'advanced' thought appears in the statements of the female Chartists. The women's protests are usually more or less those expressed by the Female Political Union of Newcastle-upon-Tyne in February 1839:

> We have seen that because the husband's earnings could not support his family, the wife has been compelled to leave her home neglected and, with her infant children work at a soul and body degrading toil. . . . For years we have struggled to maintain our homes in comfort, such as our hearts told us should greet our husbands after their fatiguing labours. Year after year has passed away, and even now our wishes have no prospect of being realised, our husbands are over wrought, our houses half furnished, our families ill-fed and our children uneducated.[43]

In the outbreaks of violence which occurred during the summer of 1839, men and women alike took part. At Llanidloes, where the local crowd 'rescued' a group of Chartists who had been arrested by metropolitan police brought in for the purpose, witnesses agreed on the active part taken by the women.

> Some of the women who had joined the crowd kept instigating the men to attack the hotel – one old virago vowing that she would fight until she

was knee deep in blood, sooner than the Cockneys should take their prisoners out of the town. She, with others of her sex, gathered large heaps of stones, which they subsequently used in defacing and injuring the building which contained the prisoners.[44]

The Llanidloes riot was one of the few occasions during the Chartist period in which women were arrested and sentenced for their participation. In general, the policy of the authorities seems to have been to arrest a considerable number of people, but only to send for trial a small proportion of those arrested, rarely including women in that number.

In the so-called Plug Riots of the summer of 1842, perhaps the last major example of the 'old' open politics of the working communities in the industrial districts, the presence among the strikers of great numbers of women is well attested. Frank Peel, an eye-witness of the events he described, recalled the scenes as the thousands of factory workers marched into Yorkshire from across the Pennines:

> no inconsiderable number of the insurgents were women – and strange as it may seem, the latter were really the more violent of the body....
>
> The thousands of female turn-outs were looked upon with some commiseration by the well-disposed inhabitants, as many were poorly clad and not a few marching barefoot. When the Riot Act was read, and the insurgents were ordered to disperse to their homes, a large crowd of these women, who stood in front of the magistrates and the military, loudly declared they had no homes, and dared them to kill them if they liked. They then struck up the Union Hymn –
>
> > Our little ones shall learn to bless
> > Their fathers of the union,
> > And every mother shall caress
> > Her hero of the union.
> > Our plains with plenty shall be crowned,
> > The sword shall till the fruitful ground,
> > The spear shall prune our trees around,
> > To bless a nation's union.[45]

F.H. Grundy, another eye-witness, was impressed by the fact that the crowds in Halifax who welcomed the strikers – crowds made up of local working people who were not by any means in the same straits of economic necessity as the Lancashire strikers – contained many women. One of the most violent clashes in the whole episode occurred when the Halifax crowd attempted the rescue of a number of prisoners who were being taken away under military escort. On the morning when the rescue was to take place, Grundy wrote, the road out of Halifax was

> like a road to a fair, or to the races ... I wondered much at the multitude of persons collected in the neighbourhood, talking eagerly, but all busy – women as well as men – in rushing along the various lanes ... with arms and aprons full of stones taken from the macadamized heaps of blue metals placed along the turnpike road.[46]

The stones were used to attack an ambushed group of soldiers. Grundy, and other witnesses, insisted that the ambushers were the people of the locality and not outsiders.

In the general tumult of Chartist politics, then, women took their part. They joined in protests and action against the police, the Established Church, the exploitation of employers and the encroachments of the state. They articulated their grievances sometimes in general political terms, basing their case on appeals to former laws and to natural rights, sometimes in ethical or religious terms, appealing to the Bible for the legitimation of protest. ('I know' moaned the Reverend Close 'that that sacred volume has been prostituted to all but treasonable purposes ... the old quaint perversions and accommodations of scripture language so common in the days of Oliver Cromwell have been revived ... and directed against the peaceable in the land.'[47]) In the course of the Chartist movement, however, new forms of political organization were emerging, and new political formulations. How far did these affect the women?

On the central question of the admission of women to the suffrage, the Chartist attitude was always ambiguous. '*I believe*', wrote Elizabeth Pease in 1842 'that the Chartists generally hold the doctrine of the equality of woman's rights – but I am not sure whether they do not consider that when she marries, she merges her political rights in those of her husband.'[48] R.J. Richardson, who wrote his pamphlet on *The Rights of Woman*[49] in Lancaster jail in 1840 certainly presented this point of view, partly because, like many Chartist writers, he was concerned to argue his case within the existing legal framework. He maintained, however, that the unmarried and widowed women were entitled to full political and social rights, including the vote. His case was argued from the standpoint of a north country workman, who saw the women as the educators in the family, and as workers in the industry of the locality. His support for the rights of women rests on this view. The more 'sophisticated' political arguments of some of the

London Chartists seem to rest *in fact*, on a generally lower assessment of women.

William Lovett describes in his autobiography the care which he took to explain political questions to his wife:

> In all these matters I sought to interest my wife, by reading and explaining to her the various subjects that came before us, as well as the political topics of the day. I sought also to convince her that, beyond the pleasure knowledge conferred on ourselves, we had a duty to perform in endeavouring to use it wisely for others ... in looking back upon this period how often have I found cause for satisfaction that I pursued this course, as my wife's appreciation of my humble exertions has ever been the chief hope to cheer, and best aid to sustain me, under the difficulties and trials I have encountered in my political career.[50]

It does not appear to have occurred to Lovett, however, or to his fellow-members of the London Working Men's Association, to include women in their political councils, or even to enrol them as members of any of the organizations they sponsored. Lovett was happy to allow his wife to take over his position, at half his salary, when the First London Cooperative Trading Association could no longer afford to pay him to be storekeeper. He does not, however, seem ever to have considered that she or any other woman had anything to offer the councils of the organization. The complaint which he records, of lack of interest on the part of the members' wives in shopping at the cooperative store, might have been avoided had they taken more part in the planning and policy of the stores. Lovett records that he and some other members of the committee which drew up the original People's Charter had wished to specify women's suffrage among the main points. They were over-ruled however, because 'several members thought its adoption in the Bill might retard the suffrage of men'.[51] In most Chartist statements the matter was left vague. Undoubtedly the majority of Chartists of both sexes saw the main issue as one of class. The attainment of political power by the men of the working class would bring great benefits to the whole class, and the extension of political rights, on grounds of natural justice, to women might well be expected to follow. Moreover, as with other reforms short of the suffrage, there were disadvantages to be seen in their premature achievement. In a society basically divided between the propertied and the unpropertied classes, the granting of a vote to women in the propertied class before granting it to men of the working class could be seen only as the further strengthening of the existing holders of power.

Nevertheless, the issue of the vote for women did appear from time to time in the literature. The National Association, formed by Lovett and others after his release from jail, declared in its *Gazette* that it intended to make the rights of women 'as much the object of its attention and advocacy as the rights of man'. 'In this respect at least' it declared,

> working men stand convicted of adopting the same ungenerous policy towards women, which other classes adopt towards them. The middle class will not advocate universal suffrage for fear of perilling corn law abolition or a household franchise; and the working men will not advocate the admission of women into the representation lest it should delay their own.[52]

But what did it amount to? Some women Chartists did write in to the *Gazette*. 'As one of the sex whose rights you profess to uphold', wrote one correspondent,

> you will not, I hope refuse me a corner in your paper to express my opinion upon a subject perhaps within the peculiar jurisdiction of a woman.
>
> On Monday last I followed in the train of the grand procession which bore the National Petition to the House of Commons. And whilst I was much pleased with the general demeanour of those who composed it, yet I could not help remarking what a number of dirty men and women there were about. Surely, sir, upon such an occasion every labouring man and woman, whatever their common occupation, might have made it a point of duty to come tidy and cleanly. A little soap and water must have been accessible, and though the clothing might have been ragged the face and hands need not have been grimy. I am not exaggerating when I say that I noticed hundreds who looked as though they had not performed their ablutions for a week! It made me quite uncomfortable, I assure you sir.[53]

Other female correspondents wrote in the same vein. A comparison of these women with the ragged Lancashire turn-outs of 1842, or with Mary Holberry, arrested with her husband in Sheffield in 1840 for complicity with him in armed conspiracy, though released afterwards for want of evidence; or with Mrs Adams, wife of the secretary of the Cheltenham Chartists, arrested for displaying for sale the banned free-thinking journal the *Oracle of Reason* while her husband was serving a month's imprisonment for selling it, illustrates the great variety of political experience and attitudes contained within Chartism. The wide differences of culture and outlook were as great or greater among the women as among the men.

The ten years from 1838 to 1848, in which Chartism was the main political expression of the social and industrial aspirations of the working people, saw many changes in the movement. The foundation of the National Charter Association in 1840 and of a number of lesser associations on a national scale brought more formality into the politics, while the development in the later 1840s, of more stable forms of trade union organizations and of cooperative ventures drew the energies of many local Chartists into new forms of continuous activity. The immediate sense of crisis which had been present in the early years lessened, and more varied and less defensive strategies for political action and social reconstruction were debated. This was the period in which Chartist leaders were taking part in discussions about European socialism, making contacts with advanced thinkers in Europe and America, and taking an address of welcome to the Provisional Government in Paris in 1848. It is also the period in which, except for a few areas, the women disappear from working-class politics.

A few female sections of the NCA appear from time to time in the lists published in the early 1840s. But there are no nominations from them for women members to serve on local or national committees, nor any suggestion that any women ever held office once the Chartist organizations were formalized. In the general election of 1847, when exclusive dealing was again practised in areas of Chartist strength, like Nottingham and Halifax, the women's support must be assumed from its success. Indeed, in Halifax the women were prominent in the celebrations which followed Ernest Jones's victory at the hustings (and inevitable defeat at the poll). At the tea party to present a gold watch to their candidate, they were determined that the radical colour should be well represented. Ben Wilson was present at the first sitting down 'which was largely composed of women. Some had their caps beautifully decorated with green ribbons, others had green handkerchiefs, and some even had green dresses. I have been to many a tea party in my time, but never saw one to equal this.'[54] But this was a rare occasion. In the later Chartist period it was rare for the women to be much in evidence. Benjamin Deacon declared in 1856:

> It has long been a matter of serious consideration with me why the Chartist body have not sought the cooperation of women more than they have done. If the priesthood can secure their services to keep the world in mental darkness, why should not we seek their aid to adorn our platforms in espousing the cause of liberty?[55]

Even Ernest Jones, who was always concerned with women's rights, and who belonged to organizations among the Manchester middle classes in his last years there which supported women's suffrage, has very little to say on the question in his Chartist journalism. This was certainly not because he was unaware of the question. In the foreword to a highly sensational serialized novel which he wrote in his *Notes to the People* in 1851–52, he declared,

> society counts woman as nothing in its institutions, and yet makes her bear the greatest share of sufferings inflicted by a system in which she has no voice! Brute force first imposed the law – and moral force compels her to obey it now.[56]

But almost nowhere in the journal is there any indication that Jones or any other of the Chartists at this time were seeking to involve the women of the working class in political activity to remedy their situation. The only contribution to the *Notes* which suggests that there remained any women who were interested in Chartism in an organized way came when Jones was running a campaign against the custom of Chartist groups meeting in pubs and pot-houses. A letter was published from the corresponding secretary of the Women's Rights Association of Sheffield. Jones introduced it with a welcoming note:

> the voice of woman is not sufficiently heard, and not sufficiently respected, in this country. The greatest test of enlightenment and civilisation among a people is the estimation in which woman is held, and her influence in society. Woman has an important mission in this country, and our fair friends in Sheffield shew themselves worthy of the task.

The letter, signed 'on behalf of the meeting' by Abadiah Higginbotham, welcomes Jones's article on 'Raising the Charter from the Pot-House' with a vote of thanks, and urges him to continue the campaign. It continues,

> did our brothers but admit our rights to the enjoyment of those political privileges they are striving for, they would find an accession of advocates in the female sex, who would not only raise the Charter from those dens of infamy and vice from which so many of us have to suffer, but would, with womanly pride, strive to erase that stigma which by the folly of our brothers has been cast on Chartism, not only by exercising their influence out of doors, but by teaching their children a good sound political education. This sir, will never be done while men continue to advocate or meet in pot-houses, spending their money, and debarring us from a share in their political freedom.[57]

The final sentence may indeed be a clue to one reason for the decline in women's participation. In the early years drinking does not seem to have separated the sexes to the extent that it undoubtedly did in the later nineteenth century. When the Barnsley Chartists were in prison in 1839–40, the radicals of the town had helped their families by supporting them in small businesses, and one of the leading women Chartists, Mrs Hoey, had kept a beer-shop whilst her husband Peter was in prison. A threat by the magistrates to take away her licence if she continued to allow radical meetings there suggests that this had become the custom. As the numbers of active Chartists declined, and fewer localities were able to maintain their own premises, the beer-shop offered an obvious meeting-place. If this trend coincided with the increasing influence over working-class women of the temperance movement, and with the withdrawal from work outside the home, it may well have accentuated, although it could not have caused, the move of the women away from politics.

The fact of the withdrawal from public activity by the women of the working class is incontrovertible. The reason or reasons are not by any means clear. The explanation may lie partly in the 'modernization' of working-class politics. In moving forward into mature industrial capitalist society, important sections of the working class developed relatively sophisticated organizations, trade unions, political pressure groups, cooperative societies and educational institutions. These enabled them to protect their wages and working conditions, and to claim for themselves some share in the increasing wealth of the country. By the later 1840s the rate-paying franchise for local government in the boroughs included a significant section of the higher paid workers who were able to take part in local government, and in some cases to wage a successful campaign against local corruption. In a variety of ways they were able to find means of protecting their position within an increasingly stable system. They left behind the mass politics of the earlier part of the century, which represented more of a direct challenge to the whole system of industrial capitalism at a stage in which it was far less secure and established. In doing so, the skilled workers also left behind the unskilled workers and the women, whose way of life did not allow their participation in the more structured political forms. These forms required both regularity of working times and regularity of income for participation to be possible. This cannot be the whole answer, however, since even the wives of skilled workers took little formal part in the cooperative or educational organizations which occupied their husbands. A change seems to have occurred in women's expectations and in their idea of their place in society. In the light of the hideous stories of unskilled child care and the over-working of women and children in the factory areas of the earlier part of the century the positive gains from the increasing tendency for married women with children to stay at home and care for their children do not need to be stressed. But in return for these gains, working-class women seem to have accepted an image of themselves which involved both home-centredness and inferiority. They could not, in the nature of their way of life, assume the decorative and useless role which wealthier classes imposed on women in this period, but they do seem to have accepted some of its implications. The Victorian sentimentalization of the home and the family, in which all important decisions were taken by its head, the father, and accepted with docility and obedience by the inferior members, became all-pervasive, and affected all classes. The gains of the Chartist period, in awareness and in self-confidence, the moves towards a more equal and cooperative kind of political activity by both men and women, were lost in the years just before the middle of the century. As happens from time to time in history, a period of openness and experiment, in which people seem prepared to accept a wide range of new ideas, was followed by a period of reaction, a narrowing down of expectations and demands. One of the losses of this process in the Victorian period was the potential contribution to politics and society generally of the women of the working-class communities.

Notes

1. For a discussion of this question which does rather over-state the 'independence' of working women in this period, see Neil McKendrick, 'Home Demand and Economic Growth: A New View of the Role of Women and Children in the Industrial Revolution', in N. McKendrick et al. (eds), *Historical Perspectives: Studies in English Thought and Society in Honour of J.H. Plumb*, London 1974.

2. Samuel Bamford, *Passages in the Life of a Radical* (1844), Cass reprint, London 1967, p. 164.

3. Ibid., p. 200.

4. Percival Percival, *Failsworth Folk and Failsworth Memories*, Failsworth 1901, plate.

5. Don Manuel Alvarez Espriella [R. Southey], *Letters from England*, London 1808, pp. 46–7.

6. *Nottingham Review*, 11 September 1812. For examples of women's participation in food riots in the eighteenth century and a discussion of its significance, see E.P.

Thompson, 'The Moral Economy of the English Crowd in the Eighteenth Century', *Past and Present*, no. 50, February 1971, pp. 115–18.

7. Wanda F. Neff, *Victorian Working Women*, London 1929, p. 35. For examples of women's friendly and radical societies in two industrial districts during this period, see two Birmingham University BA dissertations: K. Corfield, 'Some Social and Radical Organizations among Working-Class Women in Manchester and District 1790–1820', 1971, and E. Nicholson, 'Working-Class Women in Nineteenth-Century Nottingham 1815–1850', 1974.

8. James Burland, 'Annals of Barnsley', MS in Barnsley Public Library.

9. John Wade, *History of the Middle and Working Classes*, cited in Neff, p. 32. Card-setting was usually done by women or children, Benjamin Wilson (in *The Struggles of an Old Chartist*, Halifax 1887, p. 13) earned $\frac{1}{2}$d for every 1,500 cards he set as a young child in the 1820s.

10. 'Lodges of Industrious Females shall be instituted in every district where it may be practicable; such lodges to be considered in every respect, as part of, and belonging to, the GNCTU.' Rule XX of Rules and Regulations of the GNCTU, in S. and B. Webb, *History of Trade Unionism*, London 1920, p. 725.

11. From the obituary notice of Thomas Lingard, *Barnsley Chronicle*, 7 November 1875.

12. *Demagogue*, 5 July 1834. William Lovett, *The Life and Struggles of William Lovett in His Pursuit of Knowledge, Bread and Freedom*, London 1876, p. 50. Joel Wiener, *The War of the Unstamped: The Movement to Repeal the British Newspaper Tax, 1830–1836*, New York 1969.

13. See Cecil Driver, *Tory Radical, a Biography of Richard Oastler*, New York 1946, for the best account of both movements.

14. Pitkethly to Broyan, 28 December 1838, HO/40/47.

15. F.H. Grundy, *Pictures of the Past*, London and Edinburgh 1879, p. 98 (my italics).

16. Wilson, pp. 1–3.

17. HO/20/10.

18. W.E. Adams, *Memoirs of a Social Atom*, London 1903, p. 163. The 'Sacred Month' was a proposal for a month's general strike which was put forward in the early days of the Chartist movement. The Chartists were never in fact called upon to observe it, as the idea was abandoned by the leadership.

In his chapter on 'Working-Class Women in Britain 1890–1914' in his *Workers in the Industrial Revolution: Recent Studies of Labour in the United States and Europe*, New Brunswick, New Jersey, 1974, Peter Stearns points to the fact that few of the working-class autobiographies of the period mention the mother of the author. For the Chartist period the exact opposite is the case. The writers of autobiographies in this early part of the century nearly all seem to have been brought up by widowed mothers or other female relatives.

19. *Ashton Reporter*, 30 January 1869.

20. *London Despatch*, 1 April 1838.

21. Angus Benthune Reach, *Manchester and the Textile Districts in 1849*, ed. C. Aspin, Helmshore 1972, p. 107. In July 1848, the secretary of the Hyde branch of the Land Company, John Gaskell, registered the birth of twin daughters Mary Mitchel and Elizabeth Frost (*Northern Star*, 15 July 1848).

22. *Northern Star*, 17 March 1838 and passim.

23. Ibid., 3 February 1838.

24. Ibid., 23 June 1838.

25. Ibid., 13 April 1839.

26. Henry Vincent to John Minikin, 4 September 1837. (MS letters in Transport House collection.)

27. Henry Vincent to John Minikin, 10 June 1838

28. Henry Vincent to John Minikin, 18 June 1838.

29. Henry Vincent to John Minikin, 17 August 1837.

30. Henry Vincent to John Minikin, 2 October 1838.

31. Henry Vincent to John Minikin, 17 November 1838.

32. *Northern Liberator*, 5 January 1839.

33. *Northern Star*, 30 March 1839.

34. *Sheffield Telegraph*, 6 April 1839.

35. *Northern Star*, 3 February 1839.

36. Wilson, p. 8.

37. As, for example, the two shopkeepers in Ashton-under-Lyne who gave evidence against Joseph Rayner Stephens in 1839, and were forced out of business by the subsequent boycott of their shops.

38. Rev. F. Close AM, *A Sermon Addressed to the Female Chartists of Cheltenham*, Cheltenham 1839, p. 21.

39. *Social Pioneer*, 16 March 1839.

40. Ibid., 6 April 1839.

41. For the best account of Owenism see J.F.C. Harrison, *Robert Owen and the Owenites*, London 1969.

42. *Social Pioneer*, 30 March 1839.

43. *Northern Star*, 2 February 1839. (The whole address is reprinted in my *The Early Chartists*, London 1972.) The Chartist demand 'no women's labour, except in the home and the schoolroom' seems to have been widely accepted.

44. Edward Hamer, *A Brief Account of the Chartist Outbreak at Llanidloes in the Year 1839*, Llanidloes 1867. Reprinted in *The Early Chartists*.

45. Frank Peel, *The Risings of the Luddites, Chartists and Plug-Drawers*, Brighouse, 1880 reprinted London 1968, pp. 333–4.

46. 'Grundy', p. 100.

47. Close, p. 23.

48. MS letter Elizabeth Pease to Wendell and Ann Phillips, 29 March 1842. (In Library of Society of Friends, London.)

49. R.J. Richardson, *The Rights of Woman* (1840), reprinted in *The Early Chartists*.

50. Lovett, p. 32.

51. Ibid., p. 141n.

52. *The National Association Gazette*, 12 March 1842.

53. Ibid., 7 May 1842.

54. Wilson, pp. 9–10.

55. *People's Paper*, 29 November 1856.

56. *Notes to the People*, 1851–2, reprinted 1967, vol. II, p. 515.

57. Ibid., p. 709.

4

Ireland and the Irish in English Radicalism before 1850

Before I reached my nineteenth year (1843) my spare time was divided between three public movements – the temperance movement under Father Mathew, the repeal movement under Daniel O'Connell, and the Chartist or English movement under Feargus O'Connor. In the bewildering whirl of excitement in which I lived during those years I seemed almost wholly to forget myself. Night brought with it long journeys to meetings and late hours, though the day brought back the monotony of the sweater's den.

Robert Crowe *The Reminiscences of a Chartist Tailor*

Historians of English radicalism and Chartism differ on the place which Irish questions played in the various movements, and on the importance of the part played in English radical movements by Irish men and women. The years during which the Chartist movement dominated English radicalism were also the years of Daniel O'Connell's domination of Irish popular politics. The earlier historians of Chartism tended to see the O'Connellite repeal movement as entirely separate from Chartism, but to allow for a considerable Irish influence in Chartism nevertheless. For many of them, this influence was unfortunate. Mark Hovell, Chartism's first historian, saw O'Connor as an Irish outsider who battened on to English politics after having failed in Irish politics and quarrelled with O'Connell, and who thereby encouraged all that was worst in English popular politics – violence, brutality, and a mindless harking back to an idealized peasant past. Hovell had no time for the Irish in any form. He regarded Feargus O'Connor as the ruin of Chartism, but interestingly, although he found it difficult to find language base enough to describe Feargus, he nevertheless saw him as 'the best of a rather second-rate lot' when he entered Parliament as one of the Irish members in 1833. The Irish immigrants in Hovell's picture always 'swarm', and serve mainly as shock troops for that turbulent side of the movement for which Hovell had no sympathy or understanding.[1]

Hovell's views were challenged by some later historians, in particular by Rachel O'Higgins, who demonstrated a considerable Irish presence among the Chartist leadership, and a concern for Irish questions which could not simply be ascribed to personal interest on the part of O'Connor.[2] However, this view has in turn been questioned from a point of view more sympathetic to Irish history than Hovell's, in the work of J.H. Treble. In an influential article he has argued that the Irish immigrants in the industrial areas in Britain were actively hostile to Chartism, and held apart from the movement. In challenging the work of Rachel O'Higgins and J.A. Jackson, he suggests that the large number of Irish among the leadership has been mistakenly assumed to imply a following of Irish in the crowd:

> an untested hypothesis, no matter how plausible, does not begin to serve as a substitute for the rigorous process of historical investigation ... the view described above presents an essentially misleading picture of immigrant alignments ... despite the firm grip which individual Irishmen exercised over Chartism's destinies, the vast majority of their fellow-countrymen domiciled in Yorkshire, Cheshire and Lancashire had little contact with the movement until 1848 the 'Year of Revolutions'.[3]

In an interesting and closely argued article, he shows convincingly that the leaders of most Irish organizations in the 1830s and 1840s were actively hostile to Chartism, and discouraged their members from associating with the English movement. His evidence, however, is entirely taken from official pronouncements, and he does not in fact establish the extent to which such pronouncements influenced the ordinary Irish working man. There is no doubt that in the major cities, in particular in Liverpool and Manchester, organizations controlled by Irish politicians and by the Catholic Church had a loyal membership, articulate and organized, if never very large. But in the years before the famine, there is no proof that these organizations represented the views or commanded the loyalties of the majority of Irish working men and women in Britain, and it is certain that there was always a significant minority of articulate Irish who were not in sympathy with such pronouncements. Outside these two cities, moreover, there is far less evidence of organized conflict between even the O'Connellite Irish and the English radicals. I will return to these points. Treble's arguments have, however, been taken up and generalized by less scrupulous historians, so that a widely distributed textbook on Chartism contains such statements as that Irish questions 'did not arouse many English proletarian passions' and 'talk of working-class collaboration between English and Irish workers was to cut little ice'.[4]

An examination of the make-up of a crowd in popular demonstrations presents many well-known difficulties. All these apply in an attempt to evaluate the Irish presence in the Chartist movement. One considerable difficulty is that people do not by any means always identify themselves as Irishmen in this period. To give an example, the former secretary of the Irish Universal Suffrage Association was in Lancashire at the time of the 1842 strikes. He was arrested and tried in the great conspiracy trial in 1843. His name was Peter Brophy, and of course we know that he was Irish, but throughout the trial no reference was made to his nationality. There are many public occasions like this, and very many kinds of record in which no mention is made of birthplace or nationality. Although it is probably safe to assume that a working-class Catholic, in the north of England anyway, is likely to be Irish or from an Irish family, other information can only be obtained by the sort of digging that could take a lifetime if it were to be done for all the Chartists whose names we know. The prison inspectors' reports on those Chartists who were in prison early in 1840 are a valuable source of information. But even here, although prisoners are always questioned as to their religious beliefs, nationality or place of birth are seldom recorded. It is probably safe to assume that James Mitchell, Catholic cotton-spinner tried and sentenced at Preston in 1839 for conspiracy, was Irish. But there is no mention in the trial or the fairly extensive notes on Timothy Higgins, secretary of the Ashton-under-Lyne Working Men's Association, of the fact that he was Irish by birth. He gave as his religion 'no sect or persuasion, has his own ideas upon religion' – the type of answer usually given by unbelievers. But Higgins was Irish by birth, as the Census enumerator's return shows, and certainly on one occasion referred to himself as an Irishman in a public speech. He did not, like O'Connor or Duffy, constantly speak as an Irishman, but was best known for his leadership of the local Chartists and his work among the cotton-spinners.[5] Of the hundreds, indeed thousands, of Chartists whose names and occupations we know, the extra information about religion and birthplace is missing. Apart from the inadequate method of name-spotting, we have no way of telling what proportion even of these were Irish, whilst of the crowds we can tell even less.

My argument here is that there was a very considerable Irish presence in the Chartist movement. Whereas formal association with the leadership of those organizations set up by Daniel O'Connell was not achieved, either at local or national level, informal association in the smaller manufacturing towns and villages was common, and in any case the clear divisions made by historians and by leaders were not observed by the ordinary members. Kirby and Musson, in their biography of John Doherty, have shown how he maintained through most of his life an allegiance to radicalism and Chartism, a passionate belief in trade unionism, and yet never lost his admiration for Daniel O'Connell, in spite of the latter's attacks not only on trade unions, but also on Doherty himself. Robert Crowe, with whom this chapter opens, was an Irish tailor working in London who seemed to find no contradiction between his adhesion to the three different movements, all led by Irishmen, in the early 1840s, long before 1848. Official condemnation of Chartism by the Church is not a necessary indication of shared hostility. Chartism would not be the first movement to include the devout in spite of ecclesiastical disfavour.

The working people who took part in Chartism lived in the manufacturing districts of the British Isles. These were the districts which had seen a very rapid expansion of population since the beginning of the century. Here the Irish were not, as they may have been after the famine in some districts, a single out-group facing a stable local population. They were one such group among many. In 1839 the magistrate at Barnsley, playing the game that all local authorities played, of blaming 'outsiders' for the turbulence in the town, spoke of the most militant and unruly being 'a deluded portion of the working-classes, who consist ... of individuals who have come from Ireland, Scotland and Lancashire, and are by occupation linen-weavers'.[6] But the majority of the Barnsley working population were linen-weavers, and as an examination of the well-documented story of Barnsley radicalism shows, they worked together in their trade society and radical organizations with very little awareness of ethnic divisions.[7] Barnsley had a fairly high proportion of Irish-born work-people in 1841, compared with county and with national figures. Other places with high levels of Irish were Bradford, which had the highest (10 per cent) in the West

Riding,[8] and Ashton-under-Lyne, which also had a figure of 10 per cent.[9] Barnsley, Bradford and Ashton were probably the towns in the north of England which had the highest levels of Chartist activity throughout the whole period of the movement. There are clear indications of Irish presence among the leaders in all three towns. In Barnsley the local priest for a time was the Rev. Patrick Ryan, who became a friend of the Dublin Chartist leader Patrick O'Higgins and a member of the Irish Universal Suffrage Association (IUSA). A letter to him congratulating him on joining the IUSA was signed by over a hundred of his former parishioners, names which included some of the most outstanding Chartists of the area such as Aeneas Daly, Peter Hoey, Arthur Collins and William Ashton.[10] In Ashton Timothy Higgins, the outstanding leader of the movement in its early years, was an Irishman, as was the Bradford shoemaker John W. Smith, who was the most consistent leader of the movement there and represented the town at delegate meetings and conferences throughout the whole of the 1840s.[11] Not only was Bradford one of the earliest and strongest centres of Chartism, but also some of the areas in the city where the first radical groups were established were those of the highest Irish settlement. Sections of the Northern Union were set up in the Wapping and White Abbey districts, which later became Democratic associations and later still localities of the National Charter Association.[12] In 1848 the Commander of the North thought that half the Bradford Chartists were Irish.[13] It is hardly likely that a change of heart on the part of the leadership of the Repeal Association could have made such a sudden change in the personnel of one of the strongest centres of Chartism. It is more likely that the agreement had worked for many years in Bradford. The town was, after all, the chief base of operations of George White, wool-comber, one of the best known of the Irish Chartist leaders. He had been a leader among the combers and had been, with other Chartist wool-combers, responsible for a detailed report on the condition of the Bradford combers produced in 1845.[14]

The population of the manufacturing districts was varied and mobile. But the Irish themselves were not a single, undifferentiated mass. Within each district there could be Irish families from several periods of immigration, some that had come by way of other English or Scottish districts, some who were Protestants, some who had drifted away from the Catholic Church, some who had deliberately broken with the Church. There were people from the textile industries of Ireland which had been destroyed in the 1820s as well as people from the countryside. After the famine the Irish community was probably rather more homogeneous, and certainly the tendency for the immigrants to remain grouped around the area in which their priest lived and their church was situated increased in the second half of the century. It is also apparent that the importance of religion as a defining element in the culture of the working communities increased in the second half of the nineteenth century. The growth of education provided by the denominational bodies, the National and the British and Foreign societies increased steadily until they were absorbed into a national system after 1870. The education, denominational or non-denominational, was uniformly Protestant, and much of it determinedly Anglican. The agitation surrounding the Ecclesiastical Titles episode in 1851–52, as well as the earlier passions aroused among many Nonconformists and Anglicans by the Maynooth grant picked up and exploited a certain amount of latent anti-Catholicism among the working people as well as the middle classes. But in the 1830s and through most of the 1840s there is little evidence to suggest that religious affiliations were sufficiently divisive to override the pervasive class loyalties. There was no particular Chartist religious grouping. As far as denominational loyalties can be recovered, the picture, as with occupations, is that Chartists seemed to represent a cross-section of the localities in which they lived. Thus in Barnsley, where there was a large Irish–Catholic population, many of the Chartists were Catholics. In Lancashire there was a high level of non-religious radicalism, but there were also a number of Catholics and members of Nonconformist sects. In the West Riding the majority of the Chartists whose affiliations we know were Nonconformists of one kind or another. But the sample in all cases is small. And although, as Treble shows, examples can be found of priests warning their flocks against associating with the Chartists, such warnings may also be found with great frequency coming from the pulpits of Established and Dissenting Churches. Religion, in fact, was invoked by the Chartists themselves, including Catholic Chartists, to support their views, as well as by their superiors to condemn them. It is therefore clearly not sufficient to demonstrate the articulate hostility of the Catholic Church to Chartism to demonstrate that Catholics necessarily followed that lead.

It has been suggested that concern for Ireland and support for repeal were grafted on to British Chartism because of a personal foible of its leader, and that this did the movement little service. It has also been claimed that the Irish themselves cared nothing for Chartist politics, but on the contrary accepted the hostility to the movement articulated by Daniel O'Connell and by their Church, and kept well clear of British concerns. A third line of argument, to be found in Carlyle and in many subsequent writers, suggests that the ethnic differences of race, religion, language and behaviour that existed between the Irish and the rest of the British population themselves prevented cooperation on any considerable scale. Such analyses need to be examined in the precise context of the 1830s and 1840s.

To understand the concern felt about Ireland, several points have to be made. The first and most obvious is that Ireland, directly ruled and administered from Westminster, contained a third of the population of the British Isles.[15] Any regulation passed by the government with respect to Ireland could well be extended to other parts of the kingdom. The expression 'disturbed districts' used to describe the districts of Ireland in which martial law was to be imposed had also been used in recent times to describe parts of the manufacturing areas of England and Scotland. The number of Irish men and women necessarily included in the labour force throughout Britain meant that anything which affected them, whether legislation, decree or custom, came very close to all working people in the British Isles to an extent that has never since been as great. The way Ireland was ruled and the living conditions of its people affected the rest of Britain intimately and immediately.

Before the final achievement of the 1832 Reform Bill, the reformers had a slate of questions on which they hoped a reformed Parliament would act in a more liberal and rational way than the old administration. At the head of these questions was the government of Ireland. Since the Act of Union of 1801 Ireland had been subjected to a series of Coercion Acts, and it was hoped that a new government would end coercion, if not immediately tackling the whole question of the repeal of the union. The disillusion with the actions of the reformed Parliament and the Whig administrations, which was the starting point of the Chartist movement, began with the first session. In January 1833 the Suppression of Disturbances Act, a draconian Coercion Act for Ireland, was passed – more severe in many ways than any that had gone before.[16] Speaking of middle- and working-class cooperation which had achieved the Reform Bill, Bronterre O'Brien wrote that 'it barely survived the Irish Coercion Bill, it vanished completely with the enactment of the Starvation

Law'.[17] The association between the two acts was often made. The placard issued by the Council of the Northern Political Union calling for a general strike in 1839 included a long list of grievances against the reformed administration:

> This brings us up to the passing of the Reform Bill; that Measure, we fondly hoped, would remove our Grievances. For seven years we reposed with Confidence on the Justice and Patriotism of the Middle Classes. Let us examine the FRUITS which the Reform Bill brought forth! 'By their fruits ye shall know them.' First – The despotic and bloody Irish Coercion Bill, which gave to Military Officers the Power to transport or hang the Irish people without either Judge or Jury. Second – the hideous and accurst New Poor Law, which tears asunder the dearest and holiest Ties of the human Heart, which consigns even the Old and Infirm to FAMISH amid the Gloom and SOLITUDE of a Dungeon Work-house.[18]

Addressing a meeting in 1838, John Fielden declared that:

> If the Parliament was composed of working men, they would not have suspended the laws and constitution of the country and have passed a Coercion Bill for Ireland. If the Parliament was composed of poor men, they would not have passed the new Poor Law Amendment Act, but would have first secured to the working class fair remunerative wages.[19]

The passing of the Coercion Act provoked an immediate nation-wide response. Meetings organized to protest against it took place in centres which were soon to become Chartist strongholds, and many of those who spoke at the meetings were soon to become leaders of Chartism. At Leeds the chairman, Thomas Bottomly, and the main speaker, William Rider, were both future Chartists, Rider being a founder-member of the Leeds Working Men's Association and a West Riding delegate to the first National Convention.[20] At nearby Huddersfield the meeting to protest against the act was attended almost entirely by 'operatives' according to the local Tory newspaper.[21] In Halifax Robert Wilkinson, Thomas Cliffe, Elijah Crabtree and William Thornton, all to become leading Chartists, spoke at the meeting.[22] In Manchester a vast open-air meeting heard John Doherty, leader of the cotton-spinners' union, warn the government that '20,000 real, stout, determined Irishmen' in the Manchester district were prepared to assist their fellow-countrymen to resist the act. A petition launched at this meeting was presented soon after by Cobbett in Parliament with 14,000 names attached, calling for the withdrawal of the bill, the abolition of tithes and the introduction of Poor Laws for Ireland.[23] In Nottingham the radicals met to denounce the bill and to relate Grey's Irish policy to their own situation. The matter was, they said, 'a subject of vital importance to the people of Ireland, and scarcely less so to the constitutional liberty of every subject in the British Dominions'. The resolution which they forwarded to the House of Commons declared that: 'Should your petitioners witness these acts of injustice done to Ireland, the most fearful apprehensions will be excited in their minds, that the same odious tyranny will be perpetrated towards themselves.'[24] In Birmingham a meeting on Newhall Hill which exceeded in numbers even the pre-Reform rallies in the district was called to protest against the government's Irish policy and in particular the Coercion Act.[25] In February 1834 John Doherty was on the platform at Oldham with John Knight, veteran of Peterloo and founder of Oldham Chartism, to set up an organization in that town to promote radical reform and the repeal of the union, based on a weekly penny subscription.[26] When he toured the provinces in 1835 and 1836, setting up radical organizations which were among the immediate precursors of Chartism, Feargus O'Connor kept the subject of Irish coercion at the head of his attack on the government.[27] Indeed the *Northern Star*, founded in 1837, was deliberately named after the journal of the United Irishmen.[28] Repeal of the union and the opposition to coercion were important parts of its policy from the beginning, and helped to make it the country's leading provincial newspaper within a few months. But it was not only the northern radicals who made this kind of protest. The London Working Men's Association (LWMA) presented a 'loyal and outspoken' address to Queen Victoria on the occasion of her coronation, and pointed out that: 'The injustice which the Whig and Tory factions have for a long time past inflicted on our Irish brethren has generated and perpetuated the extremes of want and wretchedness amongst them, and calls for an immediate and radical remedy.'[29] The LWMA could never have been accused of pursuing a personal foible of O'Connor's. The British radicals feared both the extension of coercion and the extension of the low standards at which the Irish were forced to live. When the Poor Law Amendment Act of 1834 was passed, which was based on the abolitionist attitude to the Poor Law advocated by the Benthamites, Bronterre O'Brien wrote:

I have lived in Ireland, was born and bred in Ireland ... I have seen thousands of Irish who have never tasted animal food, or fish, or wheaten bread twice a year since they were born. I have seen them, whole days together, without even potatoes and salt. I have seen them clothed in rags, their heads full of vermin their legs and hands covered with scabs, their bodies broken out in sores, and their feet cut and hacked with chilblains and stone bruises until they were unable to walk ... but you ask 'are we, the wealth-producers of England, to be brought to this?' I answer YES, unless you bestir yourselves in time, there is no escaping the Irish level if the New Poor Law Act be fully carried out.[30]

Well before the publication of the Charter (in May 1838) the radicals among the working people were seriously concerned with the question of Ireland. Before O'Connor emerged as the major leader of British radicalism in the years after 1837, Irishmen were prominent in British radical leadership. John Cleave, who edited and published several of the unstamped journals of the early 1830s, and was a leading figure in the campaign against the newspaper stamp duties, was born in Ireland in the 1790s. He was a founder-member of the LWMA and a signatory of the original People's Charter. A strong advocate of temperance, he published the *English Chartist Circular and Temperance Record* between 1841 and 1843. He was the chief London agent for O'Connor's *Northern Star* during the Chartist years. Although he is generally regarded as a fairly moderate character, Hovell considered him – possibly because of his Irish nationality – as 'less refined and perhaps less able' than his fellow signatories Lovett, Hetherington and Watson.[31] George Condy, editor and part-owner of the influential radical journal the *Manchester and Salford Advertiser* came of an Irish Methodist family. He was an outstanding campaigner in print and on the platform against Irish coercion, the new Poor Law and the abuses of factory labour. He was a member, with John Doherty and Robert Owen, of the Society for National Regeneration in 1833–34, which aimed at establishing a uniform eight-hour day through industrial action. Condy was a strong believer in independent working-class political action and in universal suffrage. He welcomed Chartism initially, but withdrew his support and that of his paper because of the increasingly violent rhetoric and the Newport rising in 1839. He died in 1841.[32] Bronterre O'Brien, most gifted of the early radical journalists and a key figure in the early years of Chartism, was perhaps at his best in the years before the movement started, especially as editor of the unstamped *Poor Man's Guardian* from 1831 to 1835. He came from a small trading family in Granard,

County Longford, and was something of a child prodigy while at school in Edgeworthtown. His family were Catholic, but he soon developed more free-thinking views. At his best he had few equals as a political journalist, but he was a difficult personality who quarrelled with everyone in the movement with whom he worked. He was probably an alcoholic, and he never completed any of his writing projects, which included a short 'History of Ireland'. He got as far as the first volume of his *Life of Robespierre*, and he translated Buonarotti's *History* of the Babeuf conspiracy in 1836.[33] John Doherty has already been mentioned. Leader of the cotton-spinners, leading exponent and practitioner of the ideal of general unionism, he was probably the most important and influential trade unionist in the first half of the century. He managed to combine leadership of his union with support for radicalism of all kinds, including Owenism, and a strong loyalty to Catholicism and Irish nationalism. Apart from the question of loyalty to O'Connell, he found no contradiction in these various courses. Like Cleave, Condy and O'Brien, Doherty was also an editor and publisher, and helped to support himself by running a coffee-house cum bookshop in Manchester.[34]

These men were all nationally known radicals, active supporters of the various pre-Chartist radical campaigns, the reform of Parliament, opposition to the Poor Law, control of factory hours and wages and the battle against the newspaper stamp and paper duties. Mainstream Chartism also included the support of the trade societies and trade unions, and here, since the Irish were so often used as cheap labour or as labour for breaking strikes, more anti-Irish feeling and fewer Irish personalities might be expected. There is no doubt that Irish men and women were often deliberately imported as cheap or strike-breaking labour, as they were in the 1844 coal strike in the north-east.[35] There is clearly, however, a difference between the use of fresh immigrant labour, or of labour deliberately imported to replace or dilute a difficult labour force, and the behaviour of immigrants already a part of that force. For example, Mr Charles Scott, shipbuilder of Greenock, told the authors of the *Report on the State of the Irish Poor* in 1835 that he had recently used Irish labourers to break a sawyers' strike in his yard. But the striking sawyers, who had been earning, he claimed, between 35/- and £3 a week, included Irishmen among their number, members though 'not the ringleaders' of the union.[36] In Leeds the stuff-weavers were about two-thirds Irish in the early

1830s, and were more intransigent than the English in their struggles to protect the price lists and lengths in 1830.[37] The Glasgow cotton-spinners' strike and the prosecution of their leaders was one of the immediate precipitants of Chartism itself, and the issue which convulsed the manufacturing districts in the winter of 1837–38. Many of the Glasgow spinners were Irish and two at least of the arrested leaders had been born in Ireland.[38] It is clearly over-simple to see the use of low-paid or unskilled labour as being necessarily ethnically divisive in the pre-Chartist and Chartist period.[39] There were certainly areas of conflict. Irish migrant labourers came to England during the harvest period, looking to earn enough to carry them over the lean winter months. English agricultural workers and many urban workers also looked for extra work at harvest time, and of course there were clashes. In some agricultural districts the labourers combined to 'run the Irish'[40] at this time of year, but the radicals tried to draw the same lesson from this as from other conflicts. In August 1833 members of the Huddersfield Political Union visited Pennistone to help the local radicals set up their own union. After the official business,

> a miscellaneous conversation took place concerning the evils in the agricultural districts, particularly what injury was inflicted by the swarms of Irish who poured in at the harvest season. This, however, was done without any bitterness being manifested towards our Irish brethren, the fault was traced to the government.[41]

Cheap immigrant labour was only one method of attack by the employers and the authorities on the organizations of the working people. The radical response was not to blame the instruments, but to turn their attention to the achievement of political power which they hoped would give them the control needed to protect their jobs and their wages.

The pre-Chartist trade union movement included a number of Irishmen among its leaders. In Lancashire, apart from Doherty of the spinners, John Allison and Christopher Doyle of the powerloom weavers were Irish. The latter had already served a term of imprisonment before the publication of the Charter for his trade union activities, and told the inspector of prisons in 1840 that he had little hope of finding work when he left prison 'through being so well-known as an agitator'. The inspector reported that Doyle was 'self-educated, possessed of a mind of great astuteness' and also that he was 'still resolved to pursue the career of agitation' when he left prison.[42] In this he was correct, for Doyle remained an active and popular leader of the Chartist movement as long as it continued. Among the linen-weavers of Barnsley, Peter Hoey, who often chaired the weavers' meetings, Arthur Collins and William Ashton were leading figures in the trade actions as well as in the Chartist movement. We know, because of the unusually full documentation that has survived, that there were more than a hundred Irish–Catholic Chartists in Barnsley, among who were several prominent leaders of the weavers. They were not, however, a separately organized group, but were part of a much larger Chartist and trade union organization. It is also interesting to note that a number of the Irish Catholics did not have Celtic names, including Ashton himself, whose religious and national loyalties were inherited from his mother. Ashton had been involved in industrial action before he became a Chartist and had, with fellow-weaver Frank Mirfield, received a sentence of transportation for his part in a weavers' strike. Their return in 1838 was achieved through the money-raising efforts of the Barnsley weavers.[43]

It is among the linen-weavers, cotton-spinners and powerloom operators that most Irish trade unionists are found. This may have been because these were recently grown industries for which formal apprenticeship was no longer required, or it may have been that the Irish who entered industrial occupations, rather than labouring or such casual work as peddling and tinkering, usually came from some kind of textile work in Ireland. The 1820s saw considerable emigration of textile workers from Ireland to Great Britain, with the decay of Ireland's own industry. Doherty had worked in a mill in Ireland as a child, and it seems probable that many of those who entered the textile trades came either from industrial backgrounds, or from some of the many rural districts in which hand-weaving and other textile trades were associated with agriculture. In 1829 there had been in the region of two thousand cotton-weavers in the Bandon district, for example. By 1840 their numbers had dwindled to a mere 150.[44] Some of them had certainly arrived in Barnsley, whence a donation to the defence fund for John Frost was sent in the name of 'a few Bandon [Ireland] men to shew that the traitor O'Connell falsified the character of Irishmen when he said that the Irish in England were opposed to the Radicals'.[45] Chartist shoe-makers, tailors and building-workers were less likely to be society men, if they were Irish, as so many immigrants could enter only the lower branches of the trades. John Smith of Bradford, however, visited Ireland on behalf of the shoemakers' union in 1845.[46]

In the ten years preceding the Chartist movement, there is clear evidence of the presence of Irishmen as metropolitan radical journalists, and as important figures in the provincial trade societies, particularly in the textile industries. However, until 1837 O'Connell himself appeared to be in sympathy with the majority of the radical programme. He was a formidable orator, unpopular with all branches of the Establishment, and his achievement of Catholic Emancipation in 1829, by the lively and imaginative deployment of mass popular pressure, had made him a favourite with radicals and reformers. In 1837, however, he made a sharp break with the English radicals, and endeavoured to take the whole of the Irish movement with him. In Ireland, apart from Dublin and a few other centres, he was successful. How far did he succeed in separating the Irish from the British radicals in other parts of the British Isles?

The Glasgow cotton-spinners' case illustrated for the British radicals what the experience of the Dublin artisans had already made clear, the hostility of Daniel O'Connell to trade unionism, and his adhesion to the dogmas of conventional political economy. The London Working Men's Association had secured the support of O'Connell and a small number of other parliamentary radicals for their proposed petition to Parliament for universal manhood suffrage. Francis Place, who had helped to secure this support, had stipulated that the price should be the dropping by the LWMA of any attacks on the Poor Law Amendment Act, the beloved brainchild of the political economists. The support of O'Connell, however, soon showed itself to be conditional upon a denial of the principles of trade unionism. This was too much even for the LWMA, several of whose members were 'society men'. The London radicals were warned by the Radical Member of Parliament for Coventry that O'Connell was making use of them in a cynical way, and at the same time they found themselves under attack from provincial radicals for associating with 'Malthusians' and political economists.[47] The litmus tests of working-class radicalism were opposition to the new Poor Law and support for the trade societies. These were the issues which divided them above all from the Philosophical Radicals in Parliament, and which formed the basis for the alternative radical programme of the Chartists. O'Connell by 1837 was ambivalent about the Poor Law, and had declared his total opposition to trade unionism. When the leaders of the

Glasgow cotton-spinners were arrested on charges of conspiracy in the autumn of 1837, the whole of the labour movement of Britain rallied in their support. O'Connell, already two years into the Lichfield House compact with the governing Whig Party, dissociated himself with the Chartists and the trade unionists, and warned his followers to have nothing to do with either movement. He dubbed his former associate Feargus O'Connor a 'Tory Radical' because of his opposition to the Whig government.

The split between O'Connell and the radicals of Britain at this time was not merely a question of English politics: it was also an indication of differing traditions in Irish popular politics. Some historians have suggested that the split between O'Connor and O'Connell was personal, and that O'Connor turned to English radicalism when he was forced out of Irish politics by his quarrel with his chief. In fact the position was more complex. The division between the two men was partly one of tactics. O'Connor believed that the only function of the Irish Members of Parliament should be to achieve the repeal of the union with Britain. The first disagreement between the two positions was about the speed with which a motion for the repeal of the union should be introduced into Parliament. O'Connell was prepared to do a deal with the government in return for limited concessions, and entered into the Lichfield House compact in 1835. O'Connor insisted that the repeal issue be put at once, and that it should continue to be raised at every possible opportunity.[48] When he was unseated in 1835 on a technicality (the family income was from leasehold not freehold property) O'Connor retired from parliamentary politics and entered the arena of popular radicalism, in the belief that only universal suffrage would achieve the repeal of the union.[49]

O'Connor was the son of a leading United Irishman, the nephew of probably the most influential of their leaders. The name of his newspaper was that of the United Irish paper, and the points of the Charter were in line with the programme of the movement. When he was elected to Parliament in 1833, it was on a programme of support for universal suffrage as well as repeal, and from the beginning he pledged himself to return and offer his resignation to his constituents at the end of every session – as a kind of personal annual parliament.[50] It seems clear that many of the other Irish in the Chartist movement came from the same tradition. Thomas Ainge Devyr, editorial worker on the *Northern Liberator*, was the son of a United Irishman,[51] and William and Walsingham Martin

117

almost certainly came from the Republican wing of the nationalist movement. The inspector of prisons described William Martin in 1840 as 'a most dangerous, violent and unprincipled man, advocating physical force, destruction of property and anarchy in its worst form. He has been for years a political agitator in Ireland, Scotland and England.'[52] When Martin left prison he settled for a time in Bradford, and was put forward as a hustings candidate in the election of 1841. His proposer introduced him as a man who had been 'born within the precincts of Dublin University and had received the finishing touches to his education at three of the Whig Universities of England. The first was at York Castle, the second at Northallerton House of Correction and the third at Lancaster Castle.'[53] He was a shoemaker by trade and his religious affiliation, Major Williams noted, was to 'the Established Church, according to his own statement, but I doubt his adhesion to any religious sect'.

O'Connell was not a republican. He believed in the continued rule of Ireland by the British Crown, and the retention of control by it of imperial and defence questions. In these matters, as in his hostility to trade unions, he undoubtedly had the support of a majority of his fellow-countrymen but, particularly outside Ireland, a significant alternative existed on both issues.

In 1837 O'Connell was at issue on the question of trade unions with both the artisans of Dublin and the vast majority of English and Scottish radicals.[54] Radical journals in Britain abound with attacks on him for his attitude. In an address to the operative trade unionists of Dublin issued by the Working Men's Association of Newcastle upon Tyne in April 1838, the attack on O'Connell was associated with an appeal to the traditions of the United Irishmen:

> whilst a great proportion of your countrymen appear hopelessly chained to the chariot wheels of the apostate, you asserted the rights of labour, and vindicated them from the grasp of the insatiate capitalists – even though they have managed to enlist in their service that arch-mountebank and hireling, Daniel O'Connell.

> as the first to burst the moral bondage which the heartless apostate has flung over your lovely and much-wronged country, we tender you our ardent and heartfelt thanks for this your past service – as the descendants of men not even yet all departed from among you – who caught the fire of liberty from America and France, we demand, we calculate upon your future assistance. Can we doubt that a tribunal composed of lords and lawyers, bankers, merchants and monopolists, naval and

military cut-throats, and all those whom plunder has raised to affluence – can we for a moment doubt that such a tribunal will dispose of Trade Unions in the same manner as the drum-head tribunal disposed of your brave, and patriotic and virtuous fathers, during the bloody era of ninety-eight?[55]

A street ballad about the cotton-spinners made the same connection between the Glasgow and Dublin operatives:

> Success to our friends in Ireland, who boldly stood our cause
> In spite of O'Connell and his support of whiggish laws,
> Away with his politics, they are not worth a straw
> He's no friend to the poor of Ireland or Caledonia.
>
> Success to O'Connor who did nobly plead our cause,
> Likewise to Mr Beaumont, who abhors oppressive laws,
> But after all their efforts, justice and law,
> We are banished from our country, sweet Caledonia.
>
> Whigs and Tories are united, we see it very plain,
> To crush the poor labourer, it is their daily aim,
> The proverb now is verified, and that you all can know
> In the case of those poor spinners in Caledonia.[56]

Within Ireland itself, certainly outside Dublin, there was little overt support either for unionism or republicanism until late in the 1840s. The Chartist movement had little support, although it was not entirely absent. The Irish Universal Suffrage Association, founded soon after the National Charter Association early in 1841, had as its aim the furthering of the six points of the People's Charter and the repeal of the Legislative Union between Great Britain and Ireland 'which cannot be achieved without the aid and cooperation of the English Chartists'.[57] Based in Dublin, where its president was the long-standing radical Patrick O'Higgins, it claimed a paid-up membership of a thousand in 1841[58] and its secretary, Peter Michael Brophy, was selling four hundred copies of the *Northern Star* weekly in 1842.[59] In Belfast the members collected two thousand signatures to the second Chartist petition in 1842, and there were groups in Athboy, Drogheda, Loughrae, Newry and Sligo.[60] Little has been recorded about the activities of these Irish Chartists, although a lively pamphlet written by another secretary of the IUSA, W.H. Dyott, gives an idea of some of the problems they faced.[61]

In England, however, the republican tradition was among the

aspects of Irish politics which was greatly respected by the Chartists. Robert Emmet had been executed within the memory of many Chartists for his attempted rebellion. His name was constantly introduced into Chartist speeches, his memory toasted at radical dinners, and representations of his trial and speech from the dock were regularly presented in dramatic form in all parts of the country. In toasting his memory, Chartists were signalling a challenge to governments and to the continued occupation of Ireland in no uncertain way. R.G. Gammage, historian of Chartism, recalled his first discovery of political matters. Two pamphlets that he came across in his teens made a deep impression. One was Paine's *Commonsense*:

> The other was the speech of Robert Emmet, the eminent Irish patriot – a young gentleman with good promise of success in life, but who before he was 22 years of age led an insurrection in Ireland which proved itself a failure....
>
> So much did I admire the daring courage of the young Irish rebel that I was never weary of reading his speech. I read and re-read until every word was fixed in my ... memory.[62]

Young Robert Lowery, attacking the sentence on the Dorchester labourers at a mass meeting on Newcastle Town Moor, declared:

> They knew what tyrants could effect by law; it was by law that Sydney perished at the block; it was by law that Emmet died upon the scaffold; and it was by law that the field of Peterloo was strewn with unoffending men and women – law it might be called, but never justice (hear, and cheers).[63]

Significantly, perhaps, the editors of the excellent edition of Lowery's writing do not seem to be familiar with the drama of Emmet's court-room defence, or the horror of his hanging and decapitation, which, as one writer has said, 'recurred in Irish nightmares for three generations'.[64] Performances of the trial of Emmet were given throughout the British Isles by Chartist groups in Nottingham, the West Riding of Yorkshire and several districts in Scotland, usually touring productions to rouse enthusiasm and raise funds. Treble is surely mistaken in seeing these as unsuccessful attempts to win over the Irish repealers. He records the response made in Manchester and published in the *Freeman's Journal*: 'Although we revere and respect his memory, we view with horror the principle that brought him to an untimely end; and therefore we call on all Irishmen to refrain from attending such a meeting.'[65] It must, however, be doubted whether this was the view of Emmet held by the repeal movement. The repealers and confederates in Marylebone were organized in the Emmet Brigade between 1843 and 1848,[66] and his name was certainly remembered in the nationalist movements after 1848.

The tradition of the United Irishmen was able to have a more open expression in England than was possible in Ireland in these years. The Cheltenham Chartist printer and balladeer Thomas Willey published copies of 'The Croppy Boy' – a United Irish ballad – at a time when it could not have been published legally in Ireland.[67] Some of the many Irish who crossed to the Cheltenham races may have bought copies as well as the local Chartists. In Dublin, however, in 1844 Gavan Duffy was indicted for sedition simply for publishing a poem which started

> Who fears to speak of 'ninety-eight?
> Who blushes at the name?
> When Cowards mock the patriot's fate
> Who hangs his head for shame?[68]

Young Ireland itself had played safe until then by organizing an 'Eighty-two Club' – a very much safer date to conjure with. Outside Ireland, however, 'ninety-eight' was remembered and celebrated, with toasts to Arthur O'Connor and Lord Edward Fitzgerald included among the gallery of radical heroes.

It is probable that many of the Irish Chartist leaders and speakers up and down the country came from families with United Irish connections, although this can never now be proved. There were certainly a good sprinkling of identifiably Irish Chartists. Henry Cronin, stonemason's labourer from Bedlington in Northumberland, was dismissed from his employment for his 'outrageous conduct' as leader of the local Chartists and set up a school to which all radicals were urged to send their children.[69] In Wigan, later to be the scene of Irish–English clashes in the 1860s, an Irish handloom weaver, John Lenegan, was leader of the Chartists. Peter Doyle, Catholic building-worker from Newcastle, later recalled some of the more dramatic incidents in the Chartist period, and described the regular outdoor meetings

> I will now advert to our week-night meetings. They were generally in front of the old riding school.... We had then men of warm imagination who aspired to overthrow the tyrants who filled their blessed country with woe. We had Mr Charlton, mason, who always commenced his

121

harangues with the oft-quoted words which O'Connell recited from Byron – 'Hereditary bondsmen' etc.[70] Mr Charlton contended that Ireland had received nothing but oppression at the hands of England from the invasion of Strongbow down to the Rathcormac massacre.[71] Mr Parker, labourer, said that England called Ireland the Sister Island, but she treated her with the iron rule of a cruel step-mother.[72]

Doyle was an admirer of O'Connell, but this did not prevent him from going sufficiently far from the 'Liberator's' 'moral force' teachings as to buy a pike and to take part in the stoning of the troops which occurred when the military tried to disperse a meeting of six thousand Chartists in July of 1839.[73] He perhaps illustrates as well as anybody the danger of assuming a kind of ideological purity among the rank and file of popular movements. Leaders who gained the loyalties of the common people may have held views which were mutually incompatible – certainly it would be difficult to reconcile the ideologies represented by Robert Owen, Richard Oastler, Feargus O'Connor and Daniel O'Connell – and yet their followers seemed able to select from the conflicting ideas a radical cosmology which they found consistent. Robert Crowe, with whom this chapter opens, is a good example of this. He came from a strongly nationalist family in Ireland to work with his brother, a skilled tailor, in London. His brother, a skilled master-tailor, was also a heavy drinker, and the younger Crowe left his apprenticeship and became a slop-worker, working for a garret-master. As the quotation indicates, he gave all his spare time to the three movements, for repeal, for the Charter and for temperance. He seems to have found no inconsistency in supporting all three movements until the Young Irelanders repudiated 'O'Connell's peace at any price doctrine', when he and the rest of the London Confederates went with Young Ireland. He was arrested and tried with other London Chartists and Repealers. Cited against him at his trial was a speech he made at the Thomas Davis Club in London when false news had been received of a rising in Dublin:

> So the time has come at last – the time long dreaded by some, but by all true lovers of liberty long hoped for; the time when our own land, our dear land, Ireland, is in arms. At last we throw off the foibles which made our country infantile; scorning any longer to crouch in the attitude of slaves, we stand erect in the attitude of men, resolved to wring from the reluctant grasp of Britain those concessions which, though long delayed, she must at last accord.[74]

John West, Macclesfield silk-weaver, was one of Chartism's most popular orators, who was offered tempting fees to use his ability in the cause of more 'respectable' reform movements. He remained loyal to Chartism and repeal, however, and often reported on cooperation between the two movements in provincial districts that he visited. Like his fellow-countryman George White, West was a national and a local leader. Both served on the national executive committee of the National Charter Association, and both also acted as local lecturers and paid agents for the *Northern Star*. White ran for a short time his own journal, the *Democrat and Labour Advocate*. Both men returned to their trades after the end of Chartism, and both died in poverty.[75]

We shall, of course, never be able to measure the participation of anonymous Irish in the Chartist crowds. We know that at least seventeen Irishmen were among the three hundred-odd awaiting trial for Chartist offences in the winter of 1839–40, and we do not know the nationalities of all of those three hundred.[76] There were no Irish among those arrested after the rising at Newport – or at least none was brought to trial. But Lady Charlotte Guest's diary for the following days records:

> It is said to have been lamentable to see droves of these poor tired and defeated men returning from their ill-fated expedition, and the scene at Tredegar was equally distressing owing to the wailing of the women, among whom were many Irish, all ignorant of who had suffered, and fearful lest some of their friends should have been among the number of victims.[77]

There is no time here to examine the often-quoted punch-ups in 1841 between the Chartists in Manchester and the Irish 'supporters' of the Anti-Corn Law League. But this brief moment was specifically concerned with local electoral politics, and the Irish, it seems, participated more in the character of 'rent-a-mob' than as supporters of political principle.[78] In fact the fisticuffs of this occasion serve to illustrate the rarity, in an age of violent political confrontations, of other examples of conflict between Irish and British working men in the Chartist period.

The Tory victory in the general election of 1841 released O'Connell to an extent from his compact with the Whigs. He returned again to extra-parliamentary agitation for repeal, and founded towards the end of 1842 the Loyal National Repeal Association. O'Connell again used the tactic he had exploited so brilliantly in 1829, of a mass peaceful organization, closely allied to the Church, which was to achieve its ends by the peaceful display of enormous numbers.[79] He was determined that members of his organization should not associate with the Chartists, and there are many examples of occasions on which such cooperation was discovered and condemned. In Birmingham George White and other local Chartists had their subscriptions returned when their membership became known to the Dublin leadership. When the London repealers invited O'Brien and O'Connor to speak to them, the meetings went off without conflict. However, when the news of the meetings and of the support given by the Chartist leadership reached Dublin, a letter was immediately sent to the London societies, warning them not to associate with Chartists:

> What could have induced the wardens or Repealers to listen for one instance to the suggestions of any junction with the Chartists? They have mortified and grieved their friends very sadly ... we can countenance no connection whatever with the Chartists.

They were warned that 'if they intend to act with us and under the guidance of our august leader' they must return all subscriptions and sever all connections with the Chartists.

> The reading of the above letter – commented *The Times* – caused much astonishment, but its adoption was immediately moved and carried without a dissentient voice. It is, however, as well to observe that the document caused more of sorrow than rejoicing.[80]

This kind of 'official' discouragement, however, does not by any means show that cooperation did not occur at a lower level, and between men and women less easily identified by the leadership. Cleave published a 'memoir' of Emmet in 1843, Bronterre O'Brien's short-lived *Poor Man's Guardian and Repealer's Friend*, published in the summer of 1843, was largely concerned with repeal, and contains some of Bronterre's most interesting writing on Ireland and on Irish history. In February 1844 John West reported from Halifax that:

> The Irish repealers and the Chartists are on the best of terms. The Repealers regularly attend the Chartist meetings, and in turn the Chartists do all in their power to aid and assist them. I had a good meeting at night ... a petition of the repealers which was in the room was signed by every one present.[81]

After the failure of the Clontarf demonstration in October 1843, the Irish repealers in Britain seem to have moved even more towards the Chartists, a movement which was followed more slowly by Young

Ireland on the other side of the Irish sea. At first the Young Ireland leaders echoed O'Connell's distrust. As John Mitchel wrote in 1847, 'We desire no fraternisation between the Irish people and the Chartists, not on account of the bugbear of physical force, but simply because some of their five points are to us an abomination.'[82] W.H. Dyott of the IUSA was as suspicious of Young Ireland, whom he considered to be a 'corporation of literary adventurers':

> What they have ever done for the country beyond the production of rhythmical balderdash and one-sided accounts of historical events I know not. They have endeavoured both by writings and speeches to engender and foster a rancorous spirit of irrational animosity between the laborious classes of the two countries whose interests are identical.[83]

As the year of revolutions dawned, however, Mitchel's tone changed. By February 1848 his journal the *United Irishman* was urging the Irish not to reject Chartism: 'Every Chartist is a *Repealer*, to begin with; and all English labourers and artizans are Chartists.'[84]

The full story of 1848 in England remains to be told. All historians are agreed, however, that in that year cooperation between Chartists and repealers was close. Many of those arrested that year were Irish, and it was in those areas in which the cooperation between the two movements was closest that the authorities made the most arrests. The street balladeers like the writer of the verses about the 'gagging act' of 1848 certainly associated the two movements:

> Now you must look before you speak
> And mind what you are after,
> Tis death if you should say Repeal,
> Or, please we want the Charter.
> Sew up your mouths without delay,
> The Government proposes,
> And what the people wants to say
> Must whistle through their noses.

> ### CHORUS
> Mind what you say by night and day
> And don't speak out of season
> For everything God bless the Queen
> Is reckoned up high treason.

The chartist and repealers say,
    In spite of wind and weather,
Both day and night we'll gain our right
    By meeting all together.
We can whisper where we cannot talk
    And speak of might and reason
But they do say, good lack a day,
    That everything is treason.[85]

Hostility to the Irish on ethnic and religious grounds certainly existed among the common people, but among the Chartists a feeling of community based on common work experience and a joint feeling of oppression was always very much stronger, and in many cases seems to have produced the opposite effect – that is, a great admiration for Irish nationalism. Among the middle classes, however, hostility was much more often enunciated in ethnic terms. Charles Kingsley warned the Chartists against any association with the United Irishmen: 'What brotherhood ought *you* to have with the "United Irishman" party, who pride themselves on their hatred to your nation, and recommend schemes of murder which a North American Indian ... would account horrible?'[86] Thomas Carlyle, in a famous passage in his pamphlet on Chartism, made a savage attack on the immigrant Irish:

> this well-known fact that the Irish speak a partially intelligible dialect of English, and their fare across by steam is four-pence sterling! Crowds of miserable Irish darken our towns. The wild Milesian features, looking false ingenuity, restlessness, unreason, misery and mockery, salute you on all highways and byways. The English coachman, as he whirls past, lashes the Milesian with his whip, curses him with his tongue; the Milesian is holding out his hat to beg. He is the sorest evil this country has to strive with. In his rags and laughing savagery, he is there to undertake all work that can be done by mere strength of hand and back; for wages that will purchase him potatoes.... The Saxon man, if he cannot work on those terms, finds no work ... he has not sunk from decent manhood to squalid apehood ... the uncivilised Irishman drives out the Saxon native, takes possession of his room. There abides he, in his squalor and unreason, in his falsity and drunken violence, as the ready-made nucleus of degradation and disorder....[87]

There is plenty of evidence that Carlyle's pamphlet had a great deal of influence on those novelists who wrote about Chartism.[88] There is none that it influenced the Chartists themselves, indeed such influence would be unlikely, since the language he uses about

Chartism itself is hardly more restrained. Trade unionism, particularly, in the context in which he was writing, the trade unionism of the Glasgow cotton-spinners, is referred to as 'Glasgow thuggery', while Chartism is 'bitter discontent grown fierce and mad, the wrong condition, therefore the wrong disposition, of the Working Classes of England. It is a new name for a thing which has had many names, which will yet have many.'[89] Carlyle was writing in the language of class. His friends in the Young Ireland movement a few years later did not have 'wild Milesian faces', or if they did he was prepared to gaze at them across the teacups.[90] For the Chartists the use of this abusive language was as likely to cement them in sympathy to the Irish as to divide them, since it was a tone which was widely, if not universally, adopted towards them also in the first half of the nineteenth century. To quote a more or less random example from a contemporary local history, an account describes a Halifax beerhouse, in which:

> the incendiary and the unionist fraternise together; from hence, under the influence and excitement of their too often adulterated beverage, they turn out at midnight ... the one to fire the cornstack and the barn, the other to imbrue his hands in the blood of a fellow-workman, or peradventure the man to whom he was formerly indebted for his daily bread.[91]

The wild Milesian faces are almost mild by comparison.

In conclusion, whilst not denying that there were divisive factors in national and ethnic differences during the Chartist period, I find a much greater cohesion in the consciousness of exclusion from the constitution of both Irish and English workmen, in a sense of being under attack from government and employers, and of being misunderstood and rejected by those with political power in the country. In an age when the mass of working people who took part in political movements – clearly in absolute terms always a minority of the population, although in some areas whole communities participated – believed that their grievances could be solved by political means, the outstanding grievance of the Irish, the union, was also seen as susceptible of a political solution. For those among the Chartists who believed that an armed rising was either desirable or unavoidable, the experience of the United Irish rising of 1798 was always in their consciousness, both as illustrating the possibility of a popular rising, and as illustrating the dangers of lack of preparation and the ruthlessness of British government action. The

Chartists always expressed common cause with the Irish repealers. Those Irishmen who were prominent in British radical politics tended to be from the tradition of the United Irishmen rather than from the Catholic Emancipation movement of the late 1820s, although in districts in which support was organized for the emancipation movement, as in Leeds, radicals who took part included many who were later to become Chartists. James Duffy was secretary of the Leeds Catholic Association in 1828, was a reformer in the 1830–31 period, became a Chartist and was arrested for his part in the unsuccessful Sheffield rising in 1840. The prison inspector who interviewed him formed the opinion that Duffy had been 'a political agitator most of his life'. Duffy himself claimed at this time that he was 'an O'Connellite and repealer but no Chartist', but he nevertheless continued his Chartist activities after his release until his premature death as the result of his treatment in prison.[92] Many radicals were ambivalent in attitude to Catholic Emancipation. O'Connor saw it as a diversion from the more important emancipation represented by universal suffrage. Doherty paid tribute to the organizing power which O'Connell and the Catholic Association had displayed, but vacillated in his own attitude between admiration for the achievement and the view that it constituted a diversion.[93] It is important to remember that the six points of the Charter would have given self-determination to the Irish people, and this was a point which was often made by Chartists, particularly by Irish Chartists. It was also quite often given as a reason for opposing Chartist demands – even Thomas Attwood who came to support the main Chartist programme, dissociated himself in presenting the first Chartist petition to Parliament from the point demanding equal electoral districts, on the grounds that this would give too much weight in Parliament to the Irish.[94] By the time of the second petition in 1842 the demand for the repeal of the union had been included in the preamble.

The question of Ireland was continually brought forward by the Chartists. Neither O'Connell nor the Catholic Church accepted as strong a commitment to a complete rupture with Britain as the Chartists demanded, and later nationalist movements were to reiterate. The Irish Catholic Chartists of Barnsley must, however, have spoken for many of their countrymen in England when they wrote:

> our efforts are not directed to the benefit of any one class, creed or locality to the exclusion of another; all are included in the Charter,

without distinction of party, sect or colour ... we are all advocates of repeal of the union, but will this give the people any control over the power that oppresses them? Does Mr O'Connell imagine that a Parliament sitting in Dublin, elected by the present constituency, would extend the franchise? but it is absurd to talk about a repeal of the union ever being obtained by the vacillating means he adopts; and if it were possible, it would be a mere delusion, unless the people have control over the action of government which they cannot possibly have without the franchise.[95]

Notes

I am indebted to a number of colleagues and students for illustrations to this paper from their local research. In particular, Nick Cotton, James Epstein, Sieglinde Huxhorn, John Sanders, Jonathan Smith and Robert Sykes.

1. Mark Hovell, *The Chartist Movement*, Manchester 1918, pp. 92–3 and passim.

2. Rachel O'Higgins, 'Ireland and Chartism: A Study of the Influence of Irishmen and the Irish Question on the Chartist Movement', Ph.D. thesis, Trinity College Dublin 1959 and 'The Irish Influence in the Chartist Movement', *Past and Present*, no. 20, November 1961.

3. J.H. Treble, 'O'Connor, O'Connell and the Attitudes of Irish Immigrants towards Chartism in the North of England 1838–1848', in J. Butt and I.F. Clarke (eds), *The Victorians and Social Protest: A Symposium*, Newton Abbott 1973.

4. J.T. Ward, *Chartism*, London 1973, p. 65.

5. For Timothy Higgins's indictment and trial, see TS 11/1030/4424, and for the interview with HM Inspector of prisons, HO 20/10. For the information about his nationality I am indebted to Sieglinde Huxhorn.

6. Cited in Treble, p. 41.

7. F.J. Kaijage, 'Labouring Barnsley, 1815–1875', Ph.D. thesis, University of Warwick 1975.

8. C. Richardson, 'Irish Settlement in Mid-Nineteenth Century Bradford', *Yorkshire Bulletin of Economic and Social Research*, May 1968, pp. 40–57. This article explains some of the problems of making an assessment of the number of Irish families in the pre-1851 period.

9. Figures for Ashton town have been calculated by Sieglinde Huxhorn. See also Nicholas Cotton, 'Radicalism and Popular Religion in Ashton-under-Lyne 1815–1836', M.A. thesis, University of Birmingham 1975.

10. Address to the Rev. Patrick Ryan, parish priest of Donabate, from the Barnsley Irish Catholic Chartists, dated Sunday 3 October 1841 (Burland, MS Annals of Barnsley), pp. 186, 187, 188.

11. I am grateful for the information about the nationality of Smith (or Smyth as he was sometimes spelt) to Jonathan Smith of York University.

12. For areas of high Irish settlement, see Richardson; for Northern Union and Democratic Associations, see *Northern Star* 1838–39 passim.

13. HO 45/2410 (4) AB.

14. *Report of the Bradford Sanatory Committee. Appointed at a Public Meeting Held on Monday May 5th, 1845*. Signed by George White, Secretary.

15. Population figures in 1841 were:

	England and Wales	15,929,000
	Scotland	2,622,000
	Ireland	8,200,000

(B.R. Mitchell and P. Deane, *Abstract of British Historical Statistics* London 1962.)

16. *3 and 4 William IV cap 4* (1833). The act forbade meetings of more than a very small number, suspended the right of petitioning Parliament in designated 'Disturbed Districts' and imposed martial law, including trial by military tribunal on these districts.

17. *Twopenny Dispatch*, 10 September 1836.

18. Placard GENERAL STRIKE, issued by the Council of the Northern Political Union, 8 August 1839. Copy in HO 40/42.

19. R.G. Gammage, *The History of the Chartist Movement, From Its Commencement Down to the Present Time*, Newcastle 1894, p. 61.

20. *Leeds Times*, 14 March 1833.

21. *Halifax Guardian*, 2 September 1833.

22. Ibid., 16 March 1833 (this and the two previous references from John Sanders).

23. *Manchester Guardian*, 6 March and 6 April 1833; *Manchester and Salford Advertiser*, 16 March 1833. Both cited in the very full and detailed biography of Doherty, R.G. Kirby and A.E. Musson, *The Voice of the People: John Doherty 1798–1854: Trade Unionist, Radical and Factory Reformer*, Manchester 1975, p. 452.

24. *Nottingham Review*, 22 February 1833.

25. *Report of the Great Public Meeting ... 20th May, 1833*, Birmingham, 1833.

26. Kirby and Musson, p. 452.

27. See, for example, *Halifax Guardian*, 8 October 1836.

28. The *Northern Star*, founded by Samuel Neilson in 1792, ran for six years until its suppression in 1798.

29. William Lovett, *Life and Struggles of William Lovett in His Pursuit of Knowledge, Bread and Freedom*, London 1876, p. 127.

30. *Bronterre's National Reformer*, 4 February 1837.

31. Cleave appears in most of the standard histories of Chartism and in accounts of the unstamped press agitation. For a full biography see the entry by I. Prothero and J. Wiener in J.M. Bellamy and J. Saville (eds), *Dictionary of Labour Movement Biography*, vol. IV.

32. Condy speaks for himself in the columns of his newspaper. See also the obituary notices in *Manchester Guardian*, November 1841. There is a collection of cuttings and writings in the Manchester Reference Library; see also J.T. Slugg, *Reminiscences of Manchester Fifty Years Ago*, Manchester 1887.

33. A.J. Plummer, *Bronterre*, London 1971.

34. Kirby and Musson. Among other Irish radical journalists of the early Chartist years, James Whittle, sometimes editor of the *Manchester and Salford Advertiser*, should be mentioned. Although described by Francis Place as 'the physical force delegate from Liverpool' when he represented that town at the first Chartist Convention in 1839, he was in fact on the moderate wing of the movement, and retired from the Convention in March 1839. He reappears in 1841 as a supporter of Lovett's 'new move', a moderate rival to the National Charter Association.

35. R. Challinor and Brian Ripley, *The Miners' Association: A Trade Union in the Age of the Chartists*, London 1968.

36. Royal Commission on the Condition of the Poorer Classes in Ireland, Appendix G, 'The State of the Irish Poor in Great Britain', *Parliamentary Papers*, 1835, vol. xxxiv.

37. *Leeds Mercury* 1829–30, passim (information from John Sanders).

38. For an account of the Glasgow cotton-spinners episode, see Hamish Fraser, 'The Glasgow Cotton Spinners' in J. Butt and J.T. Ward (eds), *Scottish Themes: Essays in Honour of Professor S.G.E. Lythe*. Edinburgh, 1976.

39. Disraeli, the most observant of the novelists who wrote about Chartism, has

one of the factory workers in *Sybil* use the word '(h) immigrants' for the country labourers who were being transferred by some Poor Law authorities into the factory districts – 'they're sold out of slavery, and sent down by Pickford's van into the labour market to bring down our wages' (Book 11, chapter 10, Penguin edn, Harmondsworth 1980, p. 130).

40. Examples of this and other clashes between agricultural workers and seasonally migrant Irish can be found in the replies to the questionnaire sent out by the Constabulary Commissioners in 1836 (HO 73); Georg Weerth spoke of the Irish with their scythes moving in to take the work of the Bradford weavers at harvest time in I. and P. Kuczynski (eds), *A Young Revolutionary in Nineteenth Century England*, Berlin 1971; in 1837 a meeting of unemployed at Leeds complained of the 'swarms of distressed Irish' who took all the haymaking jobs in the district (*Leeds Times*, 8 July 1837). Nevertheless the radicals continually preached a political lesson, like that in an anonymous broadside of 1842:

> The Irish have got no employment at home,
> Then in search of work they are forced to roam;
> 'Tis forty years since they lost their Parliament
> The wealth of their nation abroad is all spent ...

41. *Voice of the West Riding*, 10 August 1833.

42. HO 20/10. Doyle was a Catholic, born in Wexford in 1810.

43. For Ashton, see *Dictionary of Labour Movement Biography*, vol. iii.

44. Arthur Redford, *Labour Migration in England 1800–1850*, 1926; 3rd edn, Manchester 1964, p. 38.

45. *Northern Star*, 30 January 1840.

46. Information from Jonathan Smith of York University.

47. Lovett, p. 95.

48. For this argument, see W. Fagan, *The Life and Times of Daniel O'Connell*, Cork, 1847–48, pp. 244–51.

49. For an account of Feargus O'Connor's early political career in Ireland and in England, see J.A. Epstein, 'Feargus O'Connor and the English Working-Class Radical Movement, 1832–1841; A Study in National Chartist Leadership', Ph.D. thesis, University of Birmingham 1977.

50. Fagan, p. 249.

51. Thomas Ainge Devyr, *The Odd Book of the Nineteenth Century*, New York 1882. Devyr was one of a group of able journalists who worked on the *Northern Liberator*. Born in Donegal of a Methodist mother and a Catholic father, he came to England a strong supporter of O'Connell, but moved into the Chartist Movement and became secretary of the Northern Political Union in 1839. Arrested in November of that year, he jumped bail and went to United States, where he had a long career in radical politics until his death in 1887.

52. HO 20/10.

53. *Bradford Observer*, 25 November 1905: 'Some famous elections at Bradford'.

54. For the Dublin conflict, see Feargus D'Arcy, The Artisans of Dublin and Daniel O'Connell, 1830–47: An Unquiet Liaison', *Irish Historical Studies*, vol. xvii, 1970, pp. 211–43.

55. *Northern Liberator*, 14 April 1838.

56. *The Cotton Spinners' Lament*, Newcastle upon Tyne [1838]. Printed in full in Roy Palmer, *A Ballad History of England*, London 1978, pp. 115–16.

57. *Objects of the Irish Universal Suffrage Association* (1841). Copy in TS 11/601 X/L05744.

58. *Northern Star*, 20 August 1842. See pp. 151–2 for further information on O'Higgins.

59. Letter Brophy to Thomas Cooper, TS 11/600. Brophy was originally a wool-weaver, but worked as journalist and lecturer during the Chartist period. He was one of the '58 others' tried with Feargus O'Connor for conspiracy in 1843. He later became a full-time organizer for the Miners' Association.

60. O'Higgins, 'Ireland and Chartism'.

61. W.H. Dyott, *Reason for Seceding from the Seceders by an ex-Member of the Irish Confederation*, R.I.A. Haliday Tract, vol. 2013, no. 2, 1847. Dyott was a small master-printer in Dublin.

62. *Newcastle Weekly Chronicle*, 29 March 1884. Gammage was born in 1820, and so would have made these discoveries some time in the 1830s.

63. *Newcastle Chronicle*, 19 April 1834, reprinted in Brian Harrison and Patricia Hollis (eds), *Robert Lowery, Radical and Chartist*, London 1979, p. 208.

64. Malcolm Brown, *The Politics of Irish Literature from Thomas Davis to W.B. Yeats*, London 1972, p. 22 and passim for the importance of Emmet in subsequent Irish nationalism.

65. Cited in Treble, n. 93, p. 225.

66. *Northern Star*, 15 January 1845, for one report of a meeting of the Emmet Brigade; David Goodway 'London Chartism', University of London, Ph.D. thesis, 1979, for a fuller account of the London Irish and Chartism.

67. A collection of Thomas Willey's broadsides is in the Madden Ballads Collection, vol. 23 (Cambridge University Library). My thanks to Roy Palmer for this information, and for other references to street literature.

68. W.J. O'Neill Daunt, *Eighty-five Years of Irish History*, London 1886, p. 41.

69. Letter Langridge to Lord Howick, 10 June 1839, HO 40/42 X/J 6904.

70. The lines   Hereditary Bondsmen know ye not
              Who would be free, himself must strike the blow?
represent one of several similarly rhetorical slogans which were common to the Chartist and repeal movements.

71. An incident in the tithe war of the early 1830s in Ireland, when twelve people were killed resisting the militarily enforced collection of tithes. According to O'Connor, he secured a verdict of wilful murder against the authorities concerned in the Coroner's Court, but the bills were ignored at the Assizes. (*National Instructor*, vol. 1, no. 10, 27 July 1850.)

72. *Newcastle Weekly Chronicle*, 27 September 1884.

73. Ibid.

74. Robert Crowe, *Reminiscences of an Octogenarian*, New York [1902], and 'The Reminiscences of a Chartist Tailor', *The Outlook*, 9 August 1902. The editors of the latter journal included a note about the author: 'Mr Crowe's subsequent life, it may be said, has been a carrying on of the work to which he set his hand when he was a boy.... He has been in practically all the labour movements of the past two-thirds of a century.'

75. For George White: Ken Geering, 'George White, a Nineteenth-Century Workers' Leader and the Kirkdale Phenomenon', M.A. thesis, University of Sussex, 1973; for John West: Frederic Boase (ed.), *Modern English Biography*, London 1921, vol. iii. There were many other well-known Irish Chartists, including John Campbell, first secretary of the National Charter Association; George Archdeacon, joint editor of *The English Patriot and Irish Repealer* with James Leach, an Englishman; and John Deegan, card-room hand from Stalybridge, and delegate from there to the first Convention.

76. *Northern Star*, 1 February 1840, named O'Brien, Hoey, Martin, Doyle, White, Deegan, Duffy, O'Connor and 'nine others'. I have not been able to identify the two young Irishmen whom Flora Tristan met among the delegates to the Convention.

77. Earl of Bessborough (ed.), *Lady Charlotte Guest's Journal*, London 1850,

vol. 1, pp. 101–02.

78. Treble, and Norman McCord, *The Anti-Corn Law League*, London 1958; p. 102 and passim.

79. Angus Macintyre, *The Liberator*, London 1983, chapter 8.

80. *The Times*, 6 March 1843.

81. *Northern Star*, 3 February 1844.

82. *The Nation*, 15 August 1847, cited in C. Gavan Duffy, *Four Years of Irish History 1845–9*, London 1883, p. 450.

83. Dyott, p. 87.

84. *United Irishman*, 26 February 1848.

85. *The Gagging Bill* (broadside: n.p., n.d., 1848).

86. 'Parson Lot' [Charles Kingsley], 'Letter to the Chartists, No. 1', *Politics for the People*, 13 May 1848.

87. Thomas Carlyle, *Chartism* (1839) p. 18.

88. In particular, Elizabeth Gaskell, *Mary Barton* and *North and South*; Charles Kingsley, *Alton Locke* and *Yeast*; George Eliot, *Felix Holt, the Radical*. Dickens, who did not write specifically about Chartism, was very much influenced in his presentation of working people by Carlyle, perhaps most evidently in *Hard Times* and *Our Mutual Friend*.

89. Carlyle, p. 4.

90. Sir Charles Gavan Duffy, *Conversations with Carlyle*, London 1896.

91. J. Crabtree, *A Concise History of the Parish and Vicarage of Halifax*, Halifax, 1836, p. 18.

92. HO 20/10, Thomas Cooper, *Life of Himself*, London 1872, and *Northern Star*, passim.

93. Kirby and Musson.

94. Hansard, 12 July 1839, 3rd series, vol. xlix.

95. Burland, MS Annals of Barnsley. In his reply to the letter, Fr Ryan recalled the 'truly Christian piety and devoted attachment and strict attention to the duties of their religion which pervaded my little Flock at Barnsley', and regretted that he 'had neither the power nor the talent to better your political condition'.

5

Seceding from the Seceders: The Decline of the Jacobin Tradition in Ireland, 1790–1850

The period of Irish history that I want to look at here is bounded by the events leading up to the 1798 rising and by the famine. To begin rather dramatically, some of the questions which I am examining may be illustrated by a contrast between the outlooks of two nationalists leaders. In Ireland, as in many other parts of Europe, the outbreak of the French Revolution of 1789 sparked off a radical response. A parade of reformers to the hustings in 1790 included many men who were soon afterwards to become founding members of the Society of United Irishmen, among them James Napper Tandy, described by one observer as 'in all the surliness of republicanism, grinning most ghastly smiles'. The parade also included an anti-slavery banner depicting 'a negro boy, well-dressed and holding high the cap of liberty'.[1] Twelve years later, after the failure of the Irish rising, Tandy, then an exile in France, wrote to one of his family expressing his disapproval of the French suppression of the Toussaint insurrection, saying 'We are all of the same family, black and white, the work of the same creator.'[2]

Half a century later, in the early 1850s, John Mitchel, leader of Young Ireland in 1848, was speaking of Jacobins as 'natural enemies of Law, Property and order'. He suggested that a free Ireland would have slave plantations, and went on later to edit a pro-slavery journal in the United States and to lose two sons fighting for the South in the American Civil War. In his preface to Mitchel's *Jail Journal*, Arthur Griffiths wrote in Mitchel's defence on this question:

> Mitchel has been explained as one who merely hated England, and apologised for as a good man unbalanced by the horrors he witnessed. Even his views on negro slavery have been deprecatingly excused, as if

excuse were needed for an Irish nationalist declining to hold the negro his peer in right.[3]

I am not going to argue for a moment that Mitchel should be taken as the sole voice of Irish nationalist politics in the late 1840s and afterwards. I am not even suggesting that his was by any means a wholly consistent voice – he was certainly not above shouting 'Liberté, fraternité, egalité' when it suited him. Nevertheless, he has often been taken as the true voice of the 'revolutionary separatist' strand of Irish nationalism.

What seems to have happened in these years is first the emergence of the numerically extremely powerful O'Connellite nationalist movement. After the momentous achievements of the campaign for Catholic Emancipation in 1829, the leadership of the movement was largely Catholic middle class and its main achievements were in the field of municipal politics – the removal of the last of the Catholic disabilities as these affected municipal and parliamentary politics and therefore the effective admission of Catholics of the trading and professional classes into the body politic. When, after 1841, it became a movement for the repeal of the union, it was never republican – it did not envisage a break with the British Crown – and it was never revolutionary – O'Connell and his followers deliberately excluded any possibility of the violent overthrow of British rule. Except for a few months in 1848, the nationalist movement of the 1840s deliberately disavowed the experience of 1798 and most of the programme and beliefs of the United Irishmen. This was as much the case with the Young Ireland movement as with the mainstream of the Loyal National Repeal Association of Daniel O'Connell. Although Thomas Davis had begun before his death to plan for a celebration of the life of Wolfe Tone, and had started work on a biography, it was Tone's republicanism rather than his democratic beliefs which inspired this renewed interest.[4] John Mitchel's brief conversion to universal suffrage and the possibility of cooperation with the British Chartists occurred at a moment of crisis and was preceded by a long period of total rejection of any such ideas.

O'Connell's great achievement was to arouse the broadest swathe of opinion that had ever taken part in a nationalist movement. The peasantry, the great majority of the population of Ireland, had been excluded from the parliamentary franchise by the terms of the Catholic Emancipation settlement of 1829 which raised the property qualification for voting from the 40/- freehold to a £10 freehold. Since in Ireland freehold was defined in terms of long leases rather than of fee simple, the pre-1829 franchise had in fact been very broad. Although candidates at that time had to be Protestant, the freeholders, when they broke away from the control of their largely Protestant landlords, could provide a strong indication of Catholic opinion, as the campaign in Clare in 1828–29 amply demonstrated. O'Connell stood for the restoration of at least householder franchise for Ireland, although his commitment to universal male adult suffrage was always in some doubt when it came to Irish as opposed to English political programmes.

In the 1840s the O'Connellite campaign was a cross-class one limited to peaceful mass action. It was not a democratic movement, in that its leadership remained firmly in the hands of O'Connell, his family and his lieutenants. It did not, as did the National Charter Association, have any system for the election of leaders, nor did it include in its programme any political demands other than the repeal of the Act of Union. It was a single-issue campaign, but its organization was bound up with the political career of O'Connell. It can be argued that there were a number of occasions on which the possibilities of pressure for repeal presented by the massive numerical support were sacrificed in the interests of narrower aims. One of these was O'Connell's entry into the Lichfield House compact or Whig alliance with a government totally opposed to repeal, many of whose members were to contribute to the worsening of the effects of the great famine by their dogmatic adherence to free-trade economics. Another was the constant and deliberate refusal to establish joint action with the Chartists. The Lichfield House compact was an attempt to play the game of high politics with associates who respected neither the man nor his programme. The refusal to cooperate with the Chartists – after having been one of the initial signatories of the People's Charter – and the increasing hostility to trade union organization and to factory reform were part of the attempt to put his great influence with the common people of Britain and Ireland at the service of Whig policies.

In a recent study of his famous ancestor, Maurice O'Connell makes the remarkable assertion that Frederick Lucas, the owner and editor of the *Tablet* was 'the only Englishman to support Repeal'.[5] It may have been difficult to find many among the professional politicians who supported it, although there were always a few, but the Chartist movement was committed, under the leadership of O'Connor, to repeal – it was indeed included in the preamble to the 1842 petition:

> That your Petitioners complain of the many grievances borne by the people of Ireland; and contend that they are fully entitled to a repeal of the Legislative Union.[6]

The petition was signed by hundreds of thousands of Englishmen.

O'Connell, more democratic by inclination than many of his associates, was nevertheless always ambivalent about the extent of the franchise reform he envisaged for Ireland. He certainly did not favour sweeping land reform, but rather envisaged a nation which, freed from British rule, would be able to engage in trade and to develop industry and therefore cease to be dependent on England or be a source of cheap labour and cheap food. The O'Connellite programme dominated Irish nationalist politics during the 1830s and 1840s. From the mid 1840s an additional voice was heard associated with the journal *The Nation* and the literary group known as Young Ireland. To begin with they operated within the O'Connellite movement, though many of them were Protestants who remained ambivalent in their attitude to the peasantry. This ambivalence meant that for the most part they rejected democracy more adamantly than did O'Connell. The attempt to find a common platform between the Chartists and the nationalists in the period between 1838 and 1848 foundered more on the Irish rejection of a democratic programme than on the 'racist' or 'imperialist' attitudes of the English, Scottish and Welsh Chartists, or on the personal disagreements between Feargus O'Connor and Daniel O'Connell. These latter were the result rather than the cause of political disagreements.

I want to look briefly here at some of the attempts in the years between Tandy and Mitchel to keep alive the Jacobin tradition that Tandy and his fellow United Irishmen represented; particularly at the attempts of a small group of radicals in the 1840s. It was their failure and the loss of this tradition that stood in the way of effective cooperation between the two movements that threatened the British government in these years.

My own work on Ireland began as, and has to a large extent remained, the view from across the Irish Sea. But it has always surprised me how little awareness most historians of British popular and radical politics have shown of the interaction between mainland British (hereafter British) and Irish politics. Historians of

British 'high politics' have of course been aware of the 'Irish question' as a dangerous stumbling block in the path of unwary politicians, but for most labour historians the Irish question has posed few problems.

To begin with, most twentieth-century labour historians have seen Irish nationalist politics as monolithic as well as unproblematic. The demand for repeal of the union with England and for home rule was so clearly a just one that any genuine radical would support it. If British radicals in the past had failed to form an alliance with Irish nationalists, this was clearly the fault of the British. Either they were racist and uncaring, or they chose leaders who quarrelled with the Irish leaders. Most accounts of Chartism, for example, explain the lack of a joint programme between the repealers in Ireland and the Chartists in the early 1840s by the personal incompatibility of O'Connor and O'Connell, and the basic lack of concern for Ireland felt by the British workmen.[7]

Many of the early historians of nineteenth-century labour movements were concerned to give a solid British respectability to the pioneers. It was this laudable objective which led them to marginalize the women in the early movement, from the unrespectable Owenite women rescued by Barbara Taylor, to the rough and loud-mouthed Chartist viragos. Mark Hovell may be taken to epitomize this attitude. As well as missing out the women altogether, he wrote down the provincial working men and above all the Irish. He contrasts Lovett, 'the sincere, self-sacrificing but somewhat sensitive and resentful London artisan who knew working men and shared their best aspirations', with O'Connor, 'the blustering, egotistical, blarneying, managing but intellectually and morally very unreliable Irishman who probably had never done an honest day's work in his life.'[8]

The anti-Irish bias of so many late nineteenth- and early twentieth-century writers led them to lump together all Irish immigrants, and the sympathy for the victims of imperialist dominion felt by many later writers has led them to lump together all Irish nationalists and to ignore the complexity of nationalist politics. Recent scholarship has been offering correctives to both positions. We know much more about the differences between Irish men and women who came to Britain before the famine and those who came after, for instance, and we may perhaps be rather cautious about the term racism when we note how many of the police who made a point of descending on Irish neighbourhoods to push up their number of arrests in Victorian cities were themselves Irish. Fights there were between Irish and British navvies during the 1840s, but there were many others between Irish and Irish, since the custom of faction-fighting was often imported. By looking more objectively at the differences between Irish people and at the political forms which such differences took, we may be rescuing them from the implicit racism which informs much radical and labour history.

The separation of the history of popular movements and of politics in Britain and Ireland has also resulted in a surprising lack of awareness of the degree to which the history of the two countries is interwoven. The British administration in Ireland learned lessons in crowd control and policing which affected developments in the rest of Britain, while at the level of working-class political action, where so many immigrant Irish were part of the labouring popula-tion, Irish experience was constantly present in conscious and unconscious terms of reference. The whole debate about arming and the possible use of force in the Chartist and immediately pre-Chartist period was carried on while the memory of the 1798 rising was fresh and immediate. Between thirty and a hundred thousand people had been killed and appalling atrocities had been perpetrated within the memory of many of the popular leaders. General Sir Charles Napier, who commanded the army of the North in the early Chartist years, had lived through the rising, as had Daniel O'Con-nell. The terms 'physical force' and 'moral force' in which Chartist tactics were discussed derived from O'Connell's Catholic Eman-cipation campaign, while that campaign had itself derived much of its rhetoric and mass platform tactics from the earlier style of platform agitation of Henry Hunt and the parliamentary refor-mers.[9] The Chartist meeting of 10 April 1848 was intended to be a replay of O'Connell's monster meetings of five years earlier but without the failure of nerve which the Chartists felt had led to the abandonment of the climactic meeting at Clontarf. And, of course, the police 'reforms' of Sir Robert Peel were initiated by a former policer of Ireland.[10]

So I am here looking at some of the interconnections between the two countries, and the effect which these had on British popular politics. Takashi Koseki of Hitotsubashi University is working on a fuller examination of aspects of this question and has published some of his findings in English.[11] I have used some of his findings about the Irish radicals in this essay; I also tried to make more available some of the lesser-known Chartist publications dealing with Ireland in the series of Chartist reprints which I edited in 1987.[12]

The strand of Irish popular politics which I am looking at here is one which seemed to be lost in the period under review. L.M. Cullen has suggested that it resurfaced among the Fenians in a later period, and this may well be so.[13] The phenomenon may be not the death of a Jacobin tradition but rather its suppression or temporary disappearance. Certainly, from the point of view of the possible collaboration between the Irish nationalists and the Chartists, its absence from the politics of Irish nationalism in the O'Connellite period was one of the main inhibitors of that collaboration.

I have used the word 'Jacobin' to describe the set of ideas with which I am concerned. There are problems with this terminology. Historically, the Jacobins have been associated with the Terror, and the word to many has associations only with that period of the French Revolution. In some ways the term 'Painite' is more suitable, especially in the British context. There are problems with the attribution of a set of attitudes to a single writer, however influential, so I have preferred to use the term 'Jacobin', though using it in my own way. I think that the cluster of ideas I am describing are familiar to historians of early nineteenth-century Europe, and of Britain, and that it is not too inaccurate to use the term 'Jacobin' with these provisos.

Briefly, the Jacobin was in his time the ultra-democrat. He was first of all a citizen, who derived his status from his birth into a free society. He related to his fellow-citizens as an equal and as a brother. His watchwords were *liberté, fraternité, egalité*. He was not destined before his birth to a place in any given hierarchy, and as an adult he owed no loyalty to any authority which he had not freely chosen. His obedience to the law was based on his having taken an equal share with his fellows in making it and on all having an equal obligation to obey it. In matters of belief and of private behaviour the Jacobin believed in toleration, limited only by the respect for the same rights in others. His own belief system was likely to be non-authoritarian, possibly agnostic, but he believed that all sectarian religion was anachronistic and likely to give way, as enlightenment spread, to some generalized system of deistic, agnostic or atheistic beliefs. He totally rejected all systems of belief or of government which were based on superstition or terror, whether physical or psychic.

In programmatic terms, Jacobins favoured the minimum of state or government concern with individual behaviour apart from peace-keeping and the protection of property; property included for them property in skills and in labour. Respect for property went with opposition to monopoly and to patronage. Taxation which distributed wealth upward was abhorred, but some degree of distribution downwards towards the sick and otherwise disabled was usually anticipated. Laws were to protect all and to prevent undue influence – the rights of tenants were as important as the rights of landlords, contracts were to be binding on all parties whatever the inequalities of wealth or status between them. Universal suffrage (usually interpreted as universal adult male suffrage) was an essential item in all Jacobin programmes, as was the right of all citizens to hold office. If Rousseau's Geneva, with the equal participation of all citizens in Parliament, was the ideal, most programmes sought for the most participatory and easily influenced form of representative democracy that seemed possible. Education was a central item in the programme, but education that was secular, publicly financed but controlled by the citizens.

Most of the leaders of these movements were men and most of the declarations for universal suffrage meant male suffrage. There were spokesmen and women who articulated a wider system which would include women – Mary Wollstonecraft was in most respects in this tradition – and many, probably the majority, of the radicals of this ilk in the early nineteenth century would have included at least *femmes soles* in the suffrage, although, like the Chartists, they fought shy of making this a priority in their programmes.

Jacobins were almost universally republicans, and many were also nationalists in a Europe in which many small nationalities were oppressed by the great imperial powers. They were opposed to chattel slavery of all kinds, were anti-clerical and anti-aristocratic. They were, as I have said, not opposed to private property as such, only to excessive or monopolistic ownership or control. They expected protection for the property of the poor man as well as the rich, and they mostly assumed the right to control their own work in their home or workshop. Although they may well have respected the market as the place for the display and sale of work, they expected free access to it by buyers and sellers.

Jacobins and Painites were mainly urban, although there was a kind of rural Jacobinism in the mentality of some peasants of the period. Cobbett in many ways articulates several of their characteristic attitudes. Those radicals who went to look for freedom in the

New World often worked out their ideas there in rural surround-ings, as individuals or as members of communities. They were not socialists, although there was in Britain at least some interchange between the Painite and socialist traditions and the concept of 'citizen' is a societal one. Great stress was placed upon the individual and his rights, but these were to be exercised with a sense of social responsibility and fellowship.

But the Jacobins were also potentially revolutionary. The name derives from the French Revolution of 1789, and in fact the pejorative use of it in the nineteenth century is usually illustrated in England or in Ireland by a bloodthirsty character armed to the teeth and sporting a cap of liberty. The philosophy rested on the experience of the American and French revolutions, and on the right of armed revolt against tyranny and oppression, though not on the idea of the expropriation of the expropriators or of the dictatorship of the proletariat.

The Irish rising of 1798 is itself now being rather more variously interpreted than it has been in the past. Tom Dunne, critically reviewing Tim Pat Coogan's *The Hero in Irish History*, complained that:

> He even claims that the chaotic sectarian civil war which was the 1798 'rebellion' was 'the nearest Ireland has ever come to achieving a full unity of its people and a reinstating of its cultural unity'.[14]

These two opposed views show that 1798 can no longer be simply interpreted as the revolt of a united Ireland against foreign oppression. Nevertheless, it was an intensely Jacobin moment at least as far as its leaders went, and it was seen as such by the British authorities. Castleraegh spoke of it as 'A Jacobinical conspiracy with Popish instruments'. How far there was a genuine fusion between a revolutionary Jacobin leadership and the nationalist aspirations of the largely Catholic peasantry will continue to be researched and debated. But the leading figures of the rising who have entered the mythology of Irish nationalist history belong unmistakably to the Jacobin tradition – men like Theobald Wolfe Tone, Lord Edward Fitzgerald, Arthur O'Connor, Thomas Russell, James Napper Tandy, Henry Joy McCracken and Robert Emmet, the outstanding leaders of the United Irishmen.

The programme of the United Irishmen was elaborated during the years immediately following the Revolution in France. They incor-porated the democratic enthusiasm of those years, combined with the revolutionary self-determination which they saw as the legacy of the American Revolution of fifteen years earlier.

All aspirant members of the Society of United Irishmen made this affirmation:

> I, A.B., in the presence of God, do pledge myself to my country that I will use all my abilities and influence in the attainment of an adequate and impartial representation of the Irish nation in Parliament, and as a means of absolute and immediate necessity in the attainment of this chief good of Ireland I will endeavour as much as lies in my ability to forward a brotherhood of affection, an identity of interests, a communion of rights, and a union of power among Irishmen of all religious persuasions without which every reform of Parliament must be partial, not national, inadequate to the wants, delusive to the wishes, and insufficient for the freedom and happiness of the country.[15]

The catechism of the United Irishmen linked the movement to the two great revolutions which had preceded it:

Question	What have you got in your hand?
Answer	A green bough.
Question	Where did it first grow?
Answer	In America.
Question	Where did it bud?
Answer	In France.
Question	Where are you going to plant it?
Answer	In the crown of Great Britain.[16]

By the second half of the 1790s the programme of the Society of United Irishmen included all the points of parliamentary reform which were later to make up the programme of the Chartist movement, with the exception of the secret ballot, that is: (1) universal male adult suffrage; (2) equal electoral districts (500 for Ireland); (3) payment of members; (4) annual parliaments; (5) no property qualifications for membership.

The history of the rising is well-known. The United Irish leaders looked for help to republican France and received it in the form of an attempted invasion, foiled by the 'Protestant wind' at Bantry Bay in 1796, and of a smaller invasion force in 1798. The rising itself involved military engagements on a considerable scale and resulted in something between thirty and a hundred thousand deaths. There were appalling atrocities on both sides, including draconian methods by the British in suppressing and punishing the rising. Hundreds of the leaders at all levels were hanged, transported or driven into involuntary exile. The considered view of the events presented by the British authorities was summed up in the report of the Committee of Secrecy in 1799:

> On consideration of the whole of the evidence, your committee are of opinion that the rebellion originated in a system, framed not with a view of obtaining either Catholic Emancipation, or any reform compatible with the existence of the constitution, but for the purpose of subverting the government, separating Ireland from Great Britain, and forming a democratic republic, founded on the destruction of all church establishment, the abolition of ranks, and the confiscation of property.[17]

In 1803 a further unsuccessful rising was organized by Robert Emmet and Thomas Russell and some of the émigré United Irishmen in France. As the work of Marianne Elliott has shown, this was a more serious conspiracy than has often been allowed.[18] However, it failed and its leaders were publicly executed as traitors.

The events of 1798, then, established a Jacobin, French-associated, democratic revolutionary stance as an essential element in Irish nationalism. Many of those associated with the rising were Presbyterian, non-Anglican Protestants from the north-east, like Henry Joy McCracken and the weaver James Hope; some were ascendancy Protestants who maintained the kind of nationalist stance which may be compared with that of the American colonists; many were Catholics, professional men, small landowners and peasants, particularly in Wexford and the areas around Dublin.

On the night of Emmet's aborted rising the streets of Dublin were being patrolled by volunteers supporting the authority of the British. Among them was a young Catholic barrister, Daniel O'Connell. Many years later he was passing the Grand Hotel in Dublin with a companion and pointed to the building:

> 'I searched every room in that house one July night in 1803.'
> 'What for?'
> 'For Croppies.'[19]

In legend and probably in actuality, most of the croppies were Catholics. The ballad 'The Croppy Boy', written in 1842 and described by Joyce as 'the national anthem of the nationalists', is the story of the entrapment of a Catholic youth by a soldier disguised as a priest.[20] O'Connell's rejection of the rebels had been political not sectarian. The experience of the French Revolution and of 1798 left him with a profound hostility to the use of violence, and he was temperamentally more attached to British constitutionalism than to the more dramatic politics of continental Europe.

144

Most of the leaders of the 1798 rising were killed or executed. A small number of survivors were exiled to France or the United States.[21] Thousands of lesser figures were killed or transported or emigrated to the USA or Britain to avoid arrest. Of those Irish Chartists for whom we have more than minimal biographical information most claimed some connection with 'United men'. It seems to me to be clear that in the pre-famine Irish immigration to Britain there was a considerable political element belonging to this Jacobin tradition. Recent work has shown, and continues to uncover, a strong Irish Jacobin influence among ultra-democrats in the USA.[22]

In Ireland itself, clearly the Jacobins kept their heads down. But in a society in which levels of literacy in English were low, strict censorship does not seem to have been enforced. Accounts of Robert Emmet's life were widely available in Dublin when Thackeray visited the city in 1842, although seemingly absorbed into a general hagiography of national heroes.[23] Thackeray noted that the biography was on sale beside those of St Patrick and Lord Edward Fitzgerald – an interesting combination. The attitude towards Emmet and the other leaders of the by then dominant nationalist discourse, however, was at best guarded.

The O'Connellite movement was undoubtedly the major focus of anti-union and nationalist aims in the 1840s, and was indeed the greatest mass movement in Irish politics of the nineteenth century. Nevertheless, it did not represent the only programme on offer. There were contradictions within the Repeal Association which led to the secession of most of Young Ireland and the foundation of the Confederation. There was also another more radical repeal programme on offer in Ireland, as the lesser-known story of Irish Chartism shows. Among the Irish outside Ireland the alternative Jacobin tradition represented even more of a challenge. Daniel O'Connell himself, possibly the most charismatic popular leader in Europe in the nineteenth century, was in some ways torn between the various varieties of nationalism which were taking off in his lifetime.

Maurice O'Connell makes a distinction between two kinds of nationalism in the Europe of O'Connell's day. On the one hand there was the 'Romantic Nationalism', founded on the philosophy of Rousseau, on the other the ' "cold" rationalism of the enlightenment'. The Young Irelanders he sees as representing the new movement of emotion and sensibility, in which romantic concern for their own national aspirations took precedence over the universalist belief in fundamental human rights, whilst O'Connell embraced an 'old eighteenth century utilitarian nationalism'. He illustrates the difference in attitude by the opposing stance taken on the question of negro slavery in America.[24] As I have already suggested, there were certainly those among the leaders of Young Ireland who were not only not prepared to support the abolitionist movement in the USA, but actively believed in the racial inferiority of the African peoples and in the institution of slavery. The fundamental divide was on a matter of belief, and Maurice O'Connell shows convincingly that Daniel was at the most profound level opposed to the institution of chattel slavery. In this he was following the 'Jacobinical' tradition.

While Daniel O'Connell was trying unsuccessfully to raise the profile of abolitionism within the nationalist movement, it would have been difficult to find a single Chartist who did not strongly oppose chattel slavery, although there were many who regarded the anti-slavery movement as hypocritical. Ernest Jones, who helped found the Union and Emancipation Society in support of the North during the American Civil War, nevertheless characterized the philanthropic millowner as a hypocrite:

> Against the slave trade he had voted,
>   'Rights of Man' resounding still,
> Now basely turning, brazen-throated,
>   Yelled against the ten hours bill.[25]

It was a common argument put forward by the Chartists that wage slavery was different only in degree from chattel slavery and that the high moral tone adopted by abolitionists was often a disguise for the approval of cheap labour, including child labour. In the United States emigrant Chartists in the main supported the anti-slavery movement and many fought on the side of the North in the Civil War, but a few regarded the conflict as irrelevant to the struggle of the labouring people. The most extreme example among the ex-Chartists was John Campbell, who emigrated to the States in 1843. He published a number of books and tracts and took an active part in the labour movement. Among his books was *Negromania: being an examination of the Falsely Assumed Equality of the Various Races of Man*.[26] This work, which made him very unpopular with fellow-radicals, compares the position of the slaves in the South with that of free labourers in the North and in Europe.

It is significant that Campbell was an Irishman, for many of his compatriots took up similar attitudes, comparing the treatment of slaves with that of the labourers in famine-stricken Ireland. Whereas Campbell was almost alone among Chartists in questioning the evils of chattel slavery, there was a strong body of opinion among the Irish nationalists in America and in Ireland, as Maurice O'Connell demonstrates, which either saw anti-slavery as a diversion from the cause of national liberation, or was founded on the firmly anti-Jacobin belief in racial superiority. These attitudes were so powerful and received so much support from the Church hierarchy that Daniel O'Connell was compelled to soft-pedal his own views on the question, in spite of the fact that many thousands of Irishman had joined him in signing an appeal to the Irish in America to support the abolitionist campaign.

The slavery question is only one example of the division within O'Connell's own life and work between his older, rationalist values, which may well be characterized as deriving from the enlightenment by way of Paine and the other deists whose beliefs he had shared in the 1790s, and the nationalism of his repeal movement. This latter was closely tied to the Church and on many issues O'Connell went against his earlier views in order to support it. Slavery was one, non-denominational education was another and provided one of the issues on which he and the Young Irelanders split. In this case it was they who upheld the enlightened rationalist view against the authoritarian educational views of the Catholic Church. But on some of the fundamental political issues which formed the basis of the Chartists' programme neither O'Connell nor Young Ireland was prepared to support a popular democratic programme. The Chartists, British and Irish, believed in manhood suffrage as the basic right of the citizen, in secular education combined with religious toleration, and in secular or associational support for men and women of good will in times of emergency which would be free of the pressures exercised by charitable provision as well as of the social engineering which lay behind the provisions of the 1834 Poor Law Amendment Act. His opposition to a poor law for Ireland which left the administration of relief firmly in the hands of the Catholic Church was one of the issues on which O'Connell differed from most British radicals.

H. Treble, using mainly O'Connellite, Roman Catholic and Anti-Corn Law sources, has convincingly argued that the Irish in Britain held aloof from radical politics, trade unionism and Chartism between the union and the famine.[27] John Belchem and I have argued for a strong element of Irish participation in pre-famine British radical movements.[28] In both cases we have had to rely on material which tends to relate to leaders rather than the crowd. Other writers have used more generally based ideological argument to imply, often reading back from late nineteenth-century developments, that cooperation between British and Irish was impossible because of the innate racism of the British. Without here going into a detailed critique of Treble's arguments, what I am trying to show is a consistent and by no means insignificant element in Irish nationalist politics which could have brought about a degree of cooperation between the two movements in the 1840s which might have made them far more threatening to established authority than either in fact proved. In his comments on Takashi Koseki, L.M. Cullen suggests that the rediscovery of this strand in nationalist thought is important to an understanding of the origins of Fenianism and its successor movements.[29] If this is so, we have to see that just as the O'Connellite repeal movement in England was led from Ireland, so the Jacobin/Chartist element in Irish artisan politics was to some extent kept alive and later fed back into Irish politics from Britain and America. The common people of these nations shared a vocabulary of democratic thought and to some extent a shared experience of republican revolutionary activity dating from the 1790s.

As seen in the previous essay, many of the leaders of British radical movements in the early nineteenth century were Irishmen. The radical platform had included Catholic Emancipation from an early stage and there is evidence of support for O'Connell's campaign of 1829 from many provincial centres as well as from the radical press.[30]

The Reform Act of 1832, in spite of the limited Irish freeholder franchise, nevertheless opened the door for the first time to serious participation by the Irish Catholics in the politics of Westminster. Among those who were returned under O'Connell's leadership was Feargus O'Connor. His proposal for Irish politicians was that they should concentrate only on the question of the repeal of the union and not otherwise recognize the authority of the Westminster Parliament. When the majority of the repealers – who never represented more than 40 of the 104 Irish members – took another tack, following O'Connell into the Lichfield House compact with the Whig government, O'Connor left parliamentary politics in favour of extra-parliamentary activity on an essentially Jacobin programme. The Irish in Parliament after the Reform Bill were indeed faced with a dilemma. Even if the whole number had been won for repeal, which they never were, they could still not expect it to be passed without strong British support. Very few British members supported it – unlike Catholic Emancipation, which had in fact been passed by a house that included no Catholics. The break between O'Connell and O'Connor was on this extremely political issue and not, as it has too often been seen, either a matter of personal incompatibility or simply a matter of O'Connell's hostility to trade unionism. This latter question was only one of many on which O'Connell's increasing association with the Whigs and free traders led him to dissociate himself from the radical and working-class support which he had gained by his campaign for Catholic Emancipation and his spirited and country-wide opposition to the Whig Irish Coercion Act of 1833. O'Connor was unseated in 1835 by an appeal based on the property qualification, but there seems little doubt that he could have got round that – in 1847 when he had far less property he took advantage of one of the commoner legal evasions and took his seat at Westminster. He left parliamentary politics in 1835 to take a leading part in the growing national campaign for universal suffrage which had followed immediately on the Reform Act and was to continue into the Chartist movement of the late 1830s and 1840s, of which he was to be the most important leader.[31]

Daniel O'Connell had emerged during the years of the reform agitation as Ireland's foremost Catholic leader. He gained increasing support from the Church, and was funded by a continuing levy – the O'Connell Tribute – which was collected through the Church. Possibly as the price of this support, he never proposed a complete breach with England, seeing the Crown as the connecting link between Westminster and an Irish Parliament harking back perhaps to the days of Grattan. He was no republican and had been among the Catholic leaders who gave effusive welcome to George IV on his visit to Ireland in 1823, on which occasion the king had presented Lord Fingall, head of the Catholic laity, with the order of St Patrick. Byron, in a savage attack on the episode, asked:

> Will thy yard of blue ribbon, poor Fingall, recall
> The fetters from millions of Catholic limbs?[32]

O'Connell had demonstrated the power of mass non-violent platform agitation in the 1929 campaign and had taken part in the subsequent reform agitation, being seen in Britain as a radical leader of the first order. English reformers included repeal of the union among their demands, as for example in the manifesto of the National Union of the Working Class and Others in 1831. It was called for in the preamble to the second Chartist petition presented to Parliament in 1842, where it was singled out for condemnation by Peel. The hostility which many of the Chartists demonstrated to O'Connell on other issues never extended to the rejection of his demand for repeal.

During the years of the Lichfield House compact or the Whig alliance, O'Connell dropped the repeal campaign. When it became clear that the Whig tenure of office was coming to an end, the Loyal National Repeal Association was founded, but it was not until the Tories, who were returned in the summer of 1841, were firmly in the saddle that it began campaigning in earnest. The massive series of meetings which took place in 1842 and 1843 represented the high point in public activity of the O'Connellite movement. The scale of the movement, which may have involved a higher proportion of the population of the country than that of any other European nationalist movement of the century, was undoubtedly an enormous achievement. It failed completely, however, to move any government or any major figure in the two ruling parties in Britain in the direction of repeal. It did not even appear to add significantly to the difficulties of the British in governing Ireland, since troops were withdrawn from that country to be sent to the disturbed districts of Chartist strength in periods of heightened Chartist activity. Had the Chartist and repeal movements shared a common strategy of resistance to authority, the ruling party, whether Whig or Tory, might well have been forced to make concessions.

The failure to develop a shared strategy has been variously attributed to lack of interest on the part of the Chartists, to the strict adherence by O'Connell to the doctrine of moral force and absolute legality, and to the belated recognition of the value of such a strategy by the leaders of Young Ireland. The fact that for a few months in 1848 something like a rapprochement occurred between the Irish and British movements has usually been attributed to the fact that O'Connell had died in the autumn of 1847. There are, however, important questions of ideology, strategy and politics in the relations between the two movements which have usually been overlooked or over-simplified and which are needed to explain the failure to achieve synthesis or even symmetry.

It is not my purpose here to consider what would have been the outcome of the achievement of all or part of the programme of either movement by the threat of violence or by insurrection. The question is rather why, given the fact that a united or at least a coordinated attack by the Irish in Ireland and in Britain together with the Chartists could have been extremely difficult for the government to handle, and need not have committed either movement to serious compromise, no such combined strategy emerged.

The development of the radical extra-parliamentary movement in Britain was paralleled by a much smaller movement in Ireland, in Dublin in particular. The Dublin artisans seems to have been if anything even better organized on trade questions than those in mainland Britain[33] and it is mainly from among their number that the distinctive radicals emerge who broke with O'Connell on the tactics of repeal politics. Their leader and the most consistent among the Irish Chartists was Patrick O'Higgins.

O'Higgins was a Catholic originally from County Down. He was almost the exact contemporary of Feargus O'Connor, and had a prosperous business in North Anne Street, Dublin, as a merchant dealing in Irish woollen cloth. He had been a strong supporter of O'Connell in both national and Dublin politics, but began to move away from him after 1833. In 1834 Cobbett's visit to Ireland and his tour of the country converted O'Higgins to a Jacobin programme. Cobbett persuaded him that universal suffrage was needed for rural as well as urban workers, and the tour of the countryside completed the conversion. Together with James Whittle, who was later to play a part in the development of the radical press in Britain, O'Higgins started a weekly journal, *The Tribune*, which advocated a programme very much on the lines of the People's Charter. The Lichfield House compact with the Whigs in 1835 was the issue on which the breach with O'Connell was finalized.[34]

In 1837 Feargus O'Connor established the *Northern Star*. It advocated reform on the Jacobin model, opposed the Whig Poor Law Amendment Act of 1834 and strongly supported the arrested leaders of the Glasgow cotton-spinners. In 1838, after an initial hesitation, perhaps partly connected with O'Connell's role in its preparation, the paper came out in full support of the People's Charter, which was to remain on its masthead for the decade of its life as the leading radical journal in Britain. In 1839 a group of Irish radicals formed the Irish Chartist Association, meeting weekly to read the *Star* and the Scottish Chartist journal, the *Scottish Patriot*.

There was clearly considerable interchange between the two countries and the two movements. The influence of O'Connell's successful campaign for emancipation, together with the ensuing national agitation for parliamentary reform, helped to form the tone of the mass platform which campaigned for the extension of reform and reached its high point in Chartism. Cobbett's influence and later that of the Chartists, particularly O'Connor, ensured that an alternative programme existed in Ireland to the movement led by O'Connell.

Attempts by Chartist leaders from England to call large public meetings in Dublin and other Irish centres in the early days of the movement were met with organized resistance from the O'Connellites, but a number of the Dublin and Belfast Chartists joined the movement on the mainland. It must have been a constant temptation to them to leave behind the difficult politics of their own country and to join in the much stronger movement in England or Scotland. Here the influence of O'Connell was far weaker, and many of the Irish immigrants must, like John Doherty, have found no great contradiction in supporting the more radical programme of the Chartists without giving up their older loyalties.

As long as the Whig government was in power O'Connell was obliged to keep the question of repeal in the background. With the Tory victory of 1841, however, he was released from his compact. He was also worried that the leadership of the repeal movement might fall into other hands, particularly that O'Connor might return to Ireland to agitate on the question. The programme of the Irish Chartist Association was taken over in 1841 by the newly formed Irish Universal Suffrage Association, of which Patrick O'Higgins was president.

The IUSA maintained a continuous existence throughout the decade, and left more documentary evidence than its predecessor. As we have seen in the previous essay, its programme consisted of the six points of the Charter and the repeal of the union with Britain – the last, the seventh point, it was insisted,

> though of vital importance to the prosperity of Ireland, can never be achieved until every man of twenty-one years of age and upwards possesses the elective Franchise, nor without the aid and cooperation of the British Chartists, by bringing their moral power to bear upon the FIVE HUNDRED AND FIFTY-THREE British members of Parliament.[35]

Membership of the IUSA included artisans, tradesmen and at least one priest. O'Higgins, in an address to the Roman Catholic Bishops, maintained that the majority of its members were Roman Catholics, and indeed the tactics which O'Connell used to discourage people from joining, which included calling upon the clergy to refuse the sacrament to members and to refuse to baptize their children, could only have been effective against members of the Church. The first secretary, Peter Michael Brophy, went to the mainland of Britain for some time and took a prominent part in the Chartist movement. While there he left the Church and was called an Orangeman by O'Connell for so doing. His successor, W.H. Dyott, a small master-printer, was probably a Protestant. No religious or sectarian discussion was permitted at meetings of the association, and the tone of its publications picked up again the United Irish appeal to all Irishmen to unite to gain their independence. O'Connell accused them of being socialists and infidels as well as Chartists, and perhaps inevitably their replies included the accusation that O'Connell was unscrupulous in the use he made of the Church in collecting his tribute and in attacking those he considered to be his enemies. Although clearly the kind of artisan members of a body such as the IUSA were more likely to be sceptics or dissenters than the population in general, there is no evidence of Protestant sectarianism or of anti-clericalism in any of their publications.

By the time of the establishment of O'Connell's Loyal National Repeal Association, therefore, there already existed an organization aiming at repeal and parliamentary reform. The two organizations were to remain not only apart but opposed to each other until for a brief moment they came together in 1848. This opposition has variously been presented as being based on the personal disagreements between the two leaders, on sectarian differences between the membership of the two bodies, and on the fundamental division between the Chartists, who were prepared to countenance the employment of physical force, and the repealers, who followed O'Connell's view that 'my country's freedom is not worth the spilling of one drop of Irish blood', and whose activity was limited to the use of moral force. The first and third of these factors did have some weight, but the sectarian division, as I have already suggested, has been much over-stated. Catholics almost certainly made up a larger proportion of the membership of the IUSA than they did of the Young Ireland group. On the question of physical versus moral force, it may be noted that the same argument went on within the Chartist movement, and that O'Connell was constantly accused of using massive numbers in a way which in effect threatened the authorities with physical attack. The kind of argument which says 'only my moral force rhetoric is holding back civil war and massive destruction' comes very close to being a threat of force, as was suggested in O'Connell's trial in 1844. The Chartists as well as the repealers had by 1840 made a public disavowal of armed revolt as a deliberate tactic. The Address of the IUSA to the repealers in 1842 urging cooperation in the struggle for repeal asked:

> But *how* repealers is the union to be abrogated? You abjure, like us, physical force. True, you had your Emmet, as we our John Frost: both were pure no doubt, in intention but each – by his want of success – injured the cause he wished to advance.[36]

On the question of relations between Feargus and Dan, it can be shown that mutual hostility developed after the political differences in their programmes rather than being the cause of those differences.

What has been overlooked by most British writers and all but a few Irish labour historians is the political programme of the Chartists and the important ways in which this differed from that of the Loyal National Repeal Association. John Saville, in his book on 1848, does not even mention the Irish Chartists, although their leader was arrested and imprisoned in 1848, but implies throughout that it was lack of concern on the part of the British Chartists that prevented them from leading the Irish in a rising for national liberation. The question of insurrection as a final resort to achieve national independence is of course part of an argument within the Jacobin tradition. The argument was present in Chartism and was to rise again briefly in the repeal movement in 1848. What was never in doubt in the Jacobin tradition was the basic demand for citizenship and the suffrage for all. This had nothing to do with socialism, and again there has been some confusion in the examination of 1848 since many writers have identified the most advanced or 'progressive' thought with those among the Chartists who appeared to be advocating some form of socialism; thus John Saville:

> Feargus O'Connor, who had always remained at a distance from the militants during the summer months [of 1848], now began to state clearly his opposition to the more radical version of the Charter ('I am neither a Socialist nor a Communist. The principle is at variance with the

ruling instinct of man which is selfishness, self-interest, self-reliance and individuality...'.)[37]

Whether there was, in fact, a more radical version of the Charter which was at variance with the Painite or Jacobin reading can be debated. Certainly there were individuals among the Chartists who looked with interest and admiration at the experiments in social administration begun in France, but for most Chartists the great achievement of the February Revolution was the achievement of universal suffrage.

The February Revolution in France undoubtedly affected both the British Chartists and the Irish nationalists. The latter, however, received little encouragement in their attempts to establish relations with the republican government. The Chartists, after sending a deputation to congratulate the French government, found themselves increasingly supporting those radical artisan elements who were soon to be defeated. In June when the street battles occurred, John Mitchel wrote in his journal

> Some people whom the English newspapers call the 'Red Republicans' and Communists attempted another Paris revolution ... but they were swept from the streets with grape and cannister – the only way of dealing with such unhappy creatures.[38]

When he finally settled in the United States, Mitchel soon abandoned his temporary conversion to a limited belief in democracy and became a leading advocate of slavery, and a strong supporter of the South in the Civil War. His passionate belief in Irish nationalism was based not on the universal values espoused by Jacobin ideology but on Irish particularism. There was little in his outlook or philosophy which could have led him to associate with the Chartists in other than an opportunistic way. The same may be said for other leaders of Young Ireland as their later histories show. Thomas Francis Maegher, for example, had announced his conversion to democracy shortly before the abortive attempt at a rising in 1848. He was already by then among the most impassioned of the Young Ireland leaders, and had earned himself the sobriquet of 'Meagher of the Sword' from his rhetorical defence of armed insurrection. He was arrested and sentenced to transportation to Van Dieman's Land. Like Mitchel he managed to escape and make his way to the United States. It was here that Thomas Ainge Devyr, former Chartist and Irish nationalist, who was to spend the rest of his long life engaged in radical politics among the Irish Americans, went in 1854 to hear him lecture. Devyr was amazed to hear his hero talk not about Irish questions but about Australian history, and to deliver an encomium to Queen Victoria, telling his audience of five thousand, many of whom must certainly have expected something rather different, that 'her popularity it is that holds Republican ideas in check'. 'How many good women in England and in Ireland too', demanded Devyr, 'die yearly of famine and the diseases it induces? Is not every brilliant in that woman's hair ... purchased with a human life?'[39]

In so far as Young Ireland can be said to have represented a consistent set of ideas, these were nationalist and particularist rather than democratic or universalist. O'Connell, however, came from a different stable and had certainly embraced broadly democratic principles in his earlier career. By the 1840s, however, he had decided to base his programme on and to seek his support from the Catholic Church, and the attitude of the Church towards separation from Britain was ambivalent. For all its power and influence over the population, the Church in Ireland was an oppressed and victimized organization, albeit far less so by the nineteenth century than it had been earlier. The Church obviously looked to gain freedom from the control of the British establishment, but was hesitant about the degree of separation it wished to see between the two countries. Many in the hierarchy still hoped for the reconversion of Britain and feared that too sharp a rupture could make that less of a possibility. The famous letter of Archbishop McHale in which he upbraided the British for their lack of humanity in helping the victims of the Irish famine ended with a passage blaming this lack of humanity on the teaching of heretical priests and urging the return of Britain to the True Church, when it will

> become once more merry England, and restored to the centre of unity, it will once again respect the splendour of that faith, and the warmth of that charity which was brought to it from Rome.[40]

Freedom of worship was part of a Jacobin programme, but the restoration of the Catholic Church in England was not. O'Connell himself observed the forms of Catholic observance, although one of his more sensitive biographers expressed considerable doubt as to his actual religious conviction.[41] But his great popularity in the country undoubtedly rested at least partly on his strong support for the Church and on his achievement in the campaign for Catholic Emancipation – the only basis on which his affectionate nickname of the 'Liberator' could ever have been given. In pressing for repeal he tried to take with him the greatest possible number of Irish men and women, and his starting point for that support had to be the Church. O'Connell himself was undoubtedly a believer in universal suffrage with the demagogue's faith in his ability to gain massive support. In Ireland, however, he often stopped short at household suffrage, while many of his followers, including most of the prominent members of the Young Ireland group, were even less committed to any extension of political rights. It was against the Young Ireland and later Confederate leadership that the Irish Chartists and many of the Chartists in Britain had their most difficult battles.

In 1842, the year of the foundation of *The Nation*, there was widespread industrial conflict with confrontational activity and rioting in the manufacturing districts of Britain. Among those who faced trial by the end of the year were Feargus O'Connor, Peter Michael Brophy, John Campbell, Christopher Doyle, Bernard McCartney and James Mooney, all Irishmen, all charged with seditious conspiracy. Certainly O'Connor and probably most of the others were members of the IUSA as well as of the National Charter Association. The organization had no bureaucracy, only a small committee elected by ballot of the members. All members were admitted to the councils of the society on payment of an admission fee of two pence and a membership fee of one penny per week. The Loyal National Repeal Association demanded the full payment of its one pound membership subscription before any member could vote, and was organized on a paternalistic model in which the leadership remained firmly in the hands of O'Connell, his lieutenants and his sons. The leakage to the IUSA was firmly plugged by a campaign by the leadership which forbade membership of both, by a series of dissuasive measures, some of them organized through the Church, and by a constant propaganda of hostility in the *Freeman's Journal* and *The Nation*.

On the Chartist side, on the other hand, there were constant attempts in their British journals to enlist support from Ireland and to join forces with the repealers. In provincial centres these efforts were often more successful than in the metropolis where repeal wardens were on the watch for fraternization, although even here there were examples of cooperation which occurred before the officials of the repeal association were aware of them. At least two journals published in Britain by Chartists – the *Poor Man's*

Guardian and Repealer's Friend, edited by Bronterre O'Brien in 1843, and the *English Patriot and Irish Repealer*, edited by George Archdeacon, James Leach and George White in 1848 – were devoted almost entirely to Irish questions. It was no mere personal foible of O'Connor's to insist on the connection between the two movements, but part of a strategy by which the government, whether Whig or Tory, was to be embarrassed and threatened by massive popular support for suffrage extension and repeal.

John Mitchel, Gavan Duffy and the other leading political writers on *The Nation* initially, and vehemently, rejected any suggestion of cooperation with Chartists or democrats at home or abroad. This sentiment may also be found in the writing of most of the Young Irelanders before and after 1848. The brief coming together with the Chartists at the time of Mitchel's arrest in 1848 has to be seen as an exceptional switch of direction taken under the pressure of circumstances, and not as the conversion of Young Ireland to Jacobinism. Their club had been named 'The Eighty-two Club', not 'The Ninety-eight Club', and Mitchel's decision to change the name of his journal to *The United Irishman* came too late to reawaken the internationalism or the democratic programme of the original bearers of that title.

The high tide for O'Connell and for Young Ireland was between 1843 and 1846. Monster meetings involving attendances of up to a million called for repeal, *The Nation* circulated throughout the country, supported by reading rooms and educational/political discussion meetings. The influence of the moral force of mass opinion was implicitly recognized by the British government when O'Connell and a group of his close associates were arrested and tried for conspiracy and misdemeanour in 1843 and 1844. O'Connell was the hero of those years, when more people were involved in the national movement than probably at any other time in Irish history. The Chartists, suspicious of O'Connell and held at arm's length by the leaders of the movement, seem to have suspended independent action in Ireland, although they appeared regularly on platforms in the mainland and O'Higgins wrote on Irish questions in the *Northern Star*. Below the surface, however, there were growing tensions within the repeal movement itself. O'Connell was suspected of organizing his campaigns to embarrass the Tories in the interest of a return of the Whigs. As the realities of the famine began to reveal themselves, O'Connell's open support of the free trade element among Whig politicians put him in bad company, since Peel had adopted a more pragmatic and less ideological attitude to famine relief than was adopted by the Whigs who replaced him in 1846. In July of that year came the open breach between O'Connell and the Young Ireland group, partly on the question of his Whig loyalties and partly on the question of the increasingly violent rhetoric which Young Ireland felt obliged to use. In January 1847 the Young Irelanders seceded from the Loyal National Repeal Association and formed their own organization, the Irish Confederation, to carry out a repeal programme in Ireland and Britain. Confederate clubs brought together many of the artisans who had supported the IUSA and the remains of the O'Connellite repealers, and although the leadership persisted in trying to keep the movements separate, there is plenty of evidence that they came increasingly into cooperation. It should be noted, however, that it was a change on the part of the Young Irelanders that made this possible. Thomas Francis Maegher, who has come down in history as 'Maegher of the Sword', remained, in his own words, 'no democrat' until after the February Revolution in Paris in 1848, when he announced his conversion to democracy.

Takashi Koseki has detailed the relations in Ireland between the Confederates and the Chartists. Mitchel, having taken on board the suggestion that the British government could be severely harassed by a combined rising in Britain and Ireland, announced a temporary conversion to democracy. But it was not until after the February Revolution of 1848 in France that the Confederation leaders began to see the importance for their cause of association with the Chartists. There were other factors. Usually given prominence is the death of Daniel O'Connell in 1847, on his way to Rome. But he had lost influence with the active workers for repeal of the union much earlier. His association with the Whigs and his repudiation of armed action were both seen as inappropriate to the desperate condition of the country. The Young Irelanders moved towards insurrection, but were always haunted by fear of uncontrolled mob action by the Catholic peasantry; meanwhile their creation, the Confederation, moved in Dublin and on the British mainland towards association with the Chartists in England and the Trades' and Citizens' Council in Dublin. The British government, as was its wont when faced with trouble in the sister isle, resorted to a coercion act. The Irish party in the House of Commons offered little resistance, but by 1847 there was again a Chartist member, Feargus O'Connor, who resisted the introduction of coercion, proposed a motion for the repeal of the union and moved for the establishment of a Parliamentary Commission of Inquiry into the effects of the Act of Union of 1800 on the condition of Ireland. It was the actions of O'Connor in the House and the statements on Ireland in the Chartist press that turned Mitchel and his associates reluctantly towards association with the Chartists:

> 'There is one Irishman', Mitchel informed the council of the Confederation in January 1848, 'in the House, indeed, who seems determined to give the Bill [the Irish coercion bill] determined resistance and I honour him for it – I mean the hon. member for Nottingham, Mr Feargus O'Connor.'[42]

By February, as we saw in the previous essay, he was announcing his support for the Chartists.[43]

O'Connor had fought his election in Nottingham with strong emphasis on Ireland and the famine:

> 'I foretold', he said in his speech from the hustings, 'that Lord John Russell would bend to the Irish landlords for political power, rather than grapple with the master evil – the difficulty caused by their dereliction of duty.... Lord John Russell should have made the Irish landlords feed their own poor – should have compelled them, if they are not able to cultivate their estates to give them up to those who were starving for want.[44]

He declaimed a poem satirizing the assumed gratitude of the peasants for famine relief and declared:

> There's the history of Ireland – that it all 'goes in rack-rints and comes back in cold flints', to shoot the producers and kill the poor. And I will ask, from the day that the Saxon first set his polluted foot upon Ireland, what has Ireland cause to be thankful for? Is it nothing that while all other nations are progressing, one nation, most gifted by God, under the guidance of England should be the only nation retrograding?[45]

O'Connor was not changing his tone – it was the Confederates who, far too late in the day, came round to the idea of joint action at the end of 1847 and the beginning of 1848. In Ireland itself the people as a whole never placed their confidence in the Young Irelanders, whose attempts at armed insurrection came to very little. Given the disaster of the famine and the years of starvation and forced emigration which preceded 1848 this is hardly to be wondered at; nevertheless, the question is also one of political leadership. When the Young Ireland group seceded from O'Connell's Association, some of the Irish Chartists looked for a revival of earlier traditions.

W.H. Dyott, the secretary of the IUSA, wrote a pamphlet, *Reasons for Seceding from the Seceders*, exposing the lack of democratic practice among the seceding Confederates. Like many of his fellow-radicals he was later to emigrate to the United States, disillusioned with the failure of the Young Irelanders to direct the misery and discontent of their fellow-countrymen into effective action against their oppressors.

On the British mainland the 'year of revolutions' saw renewed activity among Chartists in some parts of the country, but the high point of revolutionary Jacobinism in the British movement had been several years earlier, in the 1838–39 period. In those years O'Connell was involved in the Lichfield House compact with the Whig government and was only too anxious to distance himself from the Chartists and their programmes. His association with the Whigs in power on the one hand and with the Church in Ireland on the other left no space for the articulation of the belief in democratic political institutions which had clearly formed an important part of his early political creed. Under his leadership and that of *The Nation*, the Irish nationalist movement was never prepared to accept the democratic demands of the European and American radicals. O'Connell's decision to distance himself from the Chartists made possible the wide support for a limited nationalist programme supported by the Church, and thus mobilized sections of the rural peasantry hitherto largely untouched by the demand for repeal. His movement, however, failed completely to achieve its ends. Meanwhile those Irishmen in the 1830s and 1840s who proposed an alternative strategy by combining Irish nationalism with a radical democratic programme were almost all living and working outside Ireland. The potentially powerful combination of British and Irish disaffection was never achieved until after February 1848, when both movements were losing power and the possibility of seriously embarrassing the British government was already past. Foremost among the reasons for this failure to make common cause between the two movements was the suppression or extinction of the Jacobin tradition in Ireland itself.

Notes

1. W. Drennan to Mrs McTier, 1790, Drennan papers 291, cited in R.B. McDowell, *Ireland in the Age of Imperialism and Revolution*, Oxford 1979, p. 348.
2. J.N. Tandy to J. Tandy, 17 June 1802 (ISPO 620/12).

3. Preface to John Mitchel, *Jail Journal* (1854), Gill edn Dublin, n.d., pp. xiii–xiv.

4. Marianne Elliott, *Wolfe Tone, Prophet of Irish Independence*, New Haven and London 1989, p. 413.

5. Maurice O'Connell, *Daniel O'Connell, the Man and His Politics*, Dublin 1990, p. 70.

6. *The National Petition of the Industrious Classes*, Leeds 1842.

7. See, e.g., J.T. Ward, *Chartism*, London 1973, John Saville, *1848, the British State and the Chartist Movement*, Cambridge 1987.

8. Mark Hovell, *The Chartist Movement*, Manchester 1918, p. 67.

9. John Belchem, *Orator Hunt*, Oxford 1985, and see the same author's 'Radicalism as a "platform" Agitation in the Periods 1816–1821 and 1848–1851', unpublished Ph.D. thesis, University of Sussex 1974.

10. For an account of some of the interconnections between policing in the two countries, see Stanley H. Palmer, *Police and Protest in England and Ireland 1780–1850*, Cambridge 1988.

11. Takashi Koseki, 'Chartism and Irish Nationalism 1829–1848: Bronterre O'Brien, the London Irish and Attempts at a Chartist–Irish Alliance', unpublished M. Phil., University of Birmingham 1988, and 'Patrick O'Higgins and Irish Chartism', Working Paper no. 20, Institute of Comparative Economic Studies, Hosei University, Tokyo 1990.

12. Dorothy Thompson (ed.), *Chartism: Working-Class Politics in the Industrial Revolution*. A twenty-two volume facsimile series reproducing contemporary documents of the Chartist movement in Britain, 1838–48, New York and London 1986. Vol. 12, *Chartism in Ireland and Wales*, includes – Patrick O'Higgins, *Chartism and Repeal* (London 1842), Irish Universal Suffrage Association, *Civil and Religious Liberty* (Dublin 1843) and W.H. Dyott, *Reasons for Seceding from the Seceders by an ex-member of the Irish Confederation* (Dublin 1847). Volume 5 in the series, *Small Chartist Periodicals*, includes James Bronterre O'Brien's *Poor Man's Guardian* and *Repealer's Friend* (London 1843).

13. L.M. Cullen, comment on Koseki, 'Patrick O'Higgins and Irish Chartism'.

14. *Irish Literary Supplement*, review by Tom Dunne of Tim Pat Coogan, *The Hero in Irish History*.

15. *Report from the Committee of Secrecy of the House of Commons*, Dublin 1798, pp. 77–8.

16. Cited in Thomas Packenham, *The Year of Liberty*, London 1969, p. 3.

17. *Report from the Committee of Secrecy*, p. 29.

18. Marianne Elliott, *Partners in Revolution*, London 1982.

19. Seán O'Faoláin, *King of the Beggars*, London 1948, p. 121.

20. *The Croppy Boy (a ballad of '98)*, by William McBurney, was written in 1845. Other broadside ballads with this title were on sale in the 1840s.

21. Among those who made new lives in France was Arthur O'Connor, who became a general in the French Army, married a daughter of the philosopher Condorcet and settled to the life of a landed proprietor. He had little sympathy in later life with his Chartist nephew. Among the Americans, Thomas Addis Emmet, brother of Robert, became a successful lawyer and politician.

22. For a valuable account of the activities of some of the United men who remained in England, see Iain McCalman, 'Erin go Bragh: The Irish in British Popular Radicalism, c. 1790–1840', in Oliver MacDonagh and W.F. Mandle (eds), *Irish–Australian Studies*, Canberra 1989, pp. 168–85. For the fate of other United men in France see Elliott, *Partners* and *Tone*. For America, see Richard J. Twomey, 'Jacobins and Jeffersonians: Anglo-American Radical Ideology 1790–1810', in Margaret and James Jacob (eds), *The Origins of Anglo-American Radicalism*, London 1984, pp. 284–300.

23. W.M. Thackeray, *The Irish Sketch Book*, London 1843, chapter 2.

24. O'Connell. See on the same subject, Gilbert Osofsky, 'Abolitionists, Irish Immigrants and the Dilemmas of Romantic Nationalism', *American Historical Review*, vol. 80, no.4, 1975, pp. 895–7; D.C. Riach, 'Daniel O'Connell and American Anti-Slavery', *Irish Historical Studies*, vol. xx, 1976; and Colm Kerrigan 'Irish Temperance and US Anti-Slavery', *History Workshop Journal*, vol. 31, Spring 1991, pp. 105–19.

25. 'The Labourer, a Christmas Carol', *The Labourer*, vol. 1, no. 1, 1847.

26. Philadelphia 1851. For more discussion of the positions on US slavery taken up by some of the Chartist emigrants, see Ray Boston, *British Chartists in America*, Manchester 1971.

27. J.H. Treble, 'O'Connor, O'Connell and the Attitudes of Irish Immigrants towards Chartism in the North of England 1838–48', in J. Butt and I.F. Clarke (eds), *The Victorians and Social Protest: A Symposium*, Newton Abbot 1973, and 'The Attitude of the Roman Catholic Church towards Trade Unionism in the North of England 1833–1842', *Northern History*, vol. V, 1970, pp. 93–113.

28. John Belchem, 'English Working-Class Radicalism and the Irish 1815–1850', in Roger Swift and Sheridan Gilley (eds), *The Irish in the Victorian City*, London 1985, Dorothy Thompson, 'Ireland and the Irish in English Radicalism before 1850', in James Epstein and Dorothy Thompson (eds), *The Chartist Experience: Studies in Working-Class Radicalism and Culture 1830–1860*, London 1982.

29. L.M. Cullen, comment on Koseki, 'Patrick O'Higgins and Irish Chartism'.

30. Belchem, 'English Working-Class Radicalism'.

31. James Epstein, *The Lion of Freedom: Feargus O'Connor and the Chartist Movement, 1832–1842*, London 1982.

32. Byron, *The Irish Avatar*, London 1823.

33. See, for instance, the evidence from Dublin in the Report from the Select Committee on Artizans and Machinery 1824.

34. Koseki, 'Patrick O'Higgins and Irish Chartism'.

35. *Objects of the Irish Universal Suffrage Association*, Dublin 1843.

36. *Civil and Religious Liberty. Address of the Irish Universal Suffrage Association to the Most Rev. and Rt Rev. the Roman Catholic Archbishops and Bishops of Ireland*, Dublin 1843 (reprint 1986, see above n. 12).

37. Saville, p. 69.

38. Mitchel, p. 78. It is interesting to note that one of Mitchel's strongest supporters, the Liverpool Confederate leader Dr Reynolds fled to America in 1848 and served with distinction in the Northern army.

39. Thomas Ainge Devyr, *The Odd Book of the Nineteenth Century*, New York 1882, Pt 2, p. 61.

40. *The Times*, 4 January 1848.

41. O'Faoláin.

42. *Northern Star*, 18 December 1847.

43. The city in Britain in which Irish politics were most closely involved with those of Ireland itself was Liverpool where a higher concentration of Irish lived than in any other British city. As John Belchem has shown in a recent important study, 1848 witnessed some of the same political divisions as existed in Ireland, but with greater space for the confederate viewpoint. ('Liverpool in the Year of Revolution', in John Belchem (ed.), *Popular Politics, Riot and Labour: Essays in Liverpool History 1790–1940*, Liverpool 1992. See also in the same volume Kevin Moore '"This Whig and Tory Ridden Town": Popular Politics in Liverpool in the Chartist Era' for a consideration of Irish influence over a longer period.)

44. *Feargus O'Connor's Speech on the Hustings at Nottingham, 28 July 1847*, Nottingham 1847.

45. Ibid.

6

Queen Victoria, the Monarchy and Gender

During about forty years' work on aspects of nineteenth-century history, the idea of a book on the subject of the queen and her female subjects has often come into my mind – usually with the hope that someone else would write it. Historians of nineteenth-century women have tended to skirt round the fact of a female monarch and the questions of self-definition which this might have raised. In a rather similar way, historians of labour and working-class movements have tended to skirt round the question of republicanism.[1] Why did no significant republican movement emerge in nineteenth-century Britain, in a country with strong anti-legitimist traditions and in which political and social reform were constantly being advocated and to an extent achieved? And why, in a century in which political, professional and business life were being so thoroughly masculinized, was a woman tolerated in the highest public office in the realm for sixty-three years? The two questions were clearly connected, but the answers were not necessarily to be found simply at the level of open political discourse, whether party-political or feminist. Somewhere between 1820 – when Britain seemed to be experiencing something of a republican moment – and 1901, a sea-change occurred. As the Labour theorist Harold Laski wrote in 1931:

> any one who compares the comment of *The Times* upon the death of George IV with the national sympathy in the illness of George V can hardly regard the change in temper as other than a political miracle.[2]

So, when I was asked to write a book on Queen Victoria for a series on nineteenth-century women, I was tempted to take a look, albeit a superficial one, at some of the points during the queen's reign when her gender was important in defining her relationship with her subjects and in establishing the place of the monarchy in the country. I have been mainly concerned with the interaction between the monarchy and popular politics and am well aware that there are very many other and more subtle and complex questions to be raised on this whole question of gender and politics as it related to the throne in the course of the century.

I intend here to concentrate on the period of the queen's accession and to look more briefly at two other key periods in her reign – the decade after her widowhood in 1861, when republicanism again appeared on some political agendas, and the politics and symbolism of the jubilee celebrations of her last two decades.

Victoria's accession to the throne in 1837 marked the beginning of the longest reign in British history. Because it seemed to mark a sharp break with earlier styles of royalty, historians have rather tended to overlook the connections between the young queen and two other princesses, both of whom were dead by the time she came to the throne, but both of whom exercised considerable influence over aspects of the politics of her accession. These were her first cousin, Princess Charlotte, and her aunt, Princess, briefly Queen, Caroline.

George III reigned for almost as long as his granddaughter. As was to happen with her, he saw his sons develop into middle-aged, indeed elderly, men before they stood any chance of inheriting the crown. The Royal Marriage Act of 1772 forbade the marriage of any member of the royal family without the consent of the reigning sovereign, and since George III would only consider royal spouses for his children, most of them embarked on illegal marriages or non-marital partnerships. Although they had by the 1790s produced quite a few children between them, none of these was entitled to succeed. By the mid 1790s, when George III's health had already shown signs of failing, the lack of any legal progeny in the generation below his children began to be seen as a serious problem. His eldest son, George Prince of Wales, was therefore bribed by the payment of his very considerable debts to abandon his Catholic partner, Mrs Fitzherbert, by whom he had a large family, and to enter into holy wedlock with his cousin Princess Caroline of Brunswick. They had a common grandfather in George II, but she had been brought up mainly in Germany and he in Britain. It was an arranged marriage with little evidence of affection on either side, and after the birth of their daughter, Charlotte, in 1796, honour was taken to be satisfied and the royal couple separated, setting up rival establishments and using their daughter as an instrument to gain favour at court, to get money from various sources, and to set up rival political coteries. Twice the prince tried to get the marriage dissolved by instigating 'delicate investigations' into his wife's conduct, but neither attempt succeeded. Both clearly had other sexual liaisons, but those of the prince were the more open and scandalous. As the young Princess Charlotte wrote to her tutor: 'My mother was bad, but she would not have become as bad as she was if my father had not been infinitely worse.'[3]

The young Princess Charlotte does seem to have been extremely popular, however, and when she married Prince Leopold of Saxe-Coburg in 1816 there seemed every possibility of the establishment of a line of succession which could represent a positive and dignified alternative to the increasingly unpopular royal dukes.

The royal dukes (Queen Victoria's 'wicked uncles' as she called them) were a pretty dreadful lot. After George himself came William, Duke of Clarence (later to reign as William IV). Like his brother he had a long-standing relationship with a well-known actress, Mrs Jordan, and they had produced nine children. Next came the Duke of Kent, also by now in a long-term, though in his case childless, relationship with Mme de St Laurent. He was a professional soldier, like his brothers constantly in debt, and renowned for the fanatical and cruel punishments he inflicted on the men serving under him. His conduct in fact provoked mutinies among the officers and men serving under him and he was removed from his command. Next to him came Ernest Augustus, Duke of Cumberland. He too was known as a fanatical disciplinarian. He was also a high Tory and an ultra-Protestant who was to speak against Catholic Emancipation in the House of Lords and later to become involved in a scandal when it emerged that he had accepted the position of high master in the Orange Order. He was in addition implicated in a number of other scandals including the murder or suicide of his personal valet under very strange circumstances. Whatever the truth of these various stories, and some were certainly invented, they were part of the image he presented to the public. After him came the Dukes of Sussex and of Cambridge. Had George had no heir, the brothers would have ruled in this order on his death, since none had a legitimate heir at the time of Princess Charlotte's marriage.

The princess soon became pregnant, but died in childbirth after a long and probably mishandled labour had resulted in a still-born son.

The death of the princess produced a huge wave of national mourning. Some of the first examples of commemorative cottage china are mourning images and vessels produced at the time of her death. George Eliot records the story of a French musician of her acquaintance who first came to England at this time and was unable to get employment because he was wearing a bright green coat and everyone else was in mourning colours. Shelley seized the occasion to compare the death of the princess with the death of English liberty epitomized by the savage sentences carried out on the leaders of the Pentridge rising,[4] and Byron, republican though he was, wrote that 'those who weep not for kings shall weep for thee' and later the famous lines

> Of sackcloth was thy wedding garment made;
> Thy bridal fruit was ashes; in the dust
> The fair-haired daughter of the Isles is laid
> The love of millions. . . .[5]

In mourning for the princess people were clearly touched by the tragedy of early death and death in childbirth, but there was a lot more in the reaction, and it helps to explain the remarkable movement which swept the country two years later in support of her mother, Princess Caroline.

Before this was to occur, however, came the undignified rush by the royal dukes to fill the vacancy left by the death of Charlotte and her son. Their non-royal partners were cast aside and suitable brides taken aboard. Clarence left Mrs Jordan and the nine young Fitzclarences to marry a German princess. The Duke of Kent abandoned Mme de St Laurent and took as his wife the sister of Princess Charlotte's husband, a youngish widow with a son and a daughter by her first marriage. Ernest Augustus was in fact already married, although his marriage was so far childless. It was generally expected that the Duke of Clarence would produce an heir – he already had produced one large family and had a daughter by his new wife. He produced another in 1819, an annus mirabilis for young royals, and three young cousins followed. The Duke of Cambridge produced a son, George, in March – optimistically christened with the Hanoverian royal name. In May came Victoria and three days later a son was born to the Duke and Duchess of Cumberland, also christened George. There were thus five children, of whom Victoria was third in line. The Clarences were to produce still-born twins later, but neither of their two surviving little girls lived much beyond infancy. At the time of the accession of George IV in 1820, however, it still seemed likely that, although he himself was childless and would remain so, his successor, the Duke of Clarence, would provide a legitimate heir to follow him. Victoria, whose father had fallen a victim to the best medical practice of the time and had died eight months after her birth, was not by any means the most likely candidate for the position of heir to the throne.

George IV's accession to the throne in 1820 provoked the widespread national movement of support for his wife known as the 'Queen Caroline agitation'. The movement has puzzled historians. It was among the most widespread popular movements of the century, taking the form of passionate support for one or other of the participants in a squalid domestic row between characters who were without either integrity or charisma.[6] The explosion of feeling and action occurred in 1820, when at last the death of George III brought his son, who had been acting as Regent on and off for a good many years, to the throne as George IV. He was determined that his wife should not share the throne with him, and a series of financial and social arrangements was entered into between them by which she was to be persuaded to remain on the European continent and not return to Britain, although she was to be acknowledged as queen. The single item on which the agreements broke down was the king's absolute refusal, from which he refused to be budged, to allow the queen's name to be included among those for whom prayers were asked in the Anglican liturgy. On this apparently minor point all the negotiations broke down, the queen announced her intention to return to Britain from her voluntary exile overseas, and the government started proceedings in the House of Lords to strip her of her titles and allow George his divorce. The story has been told in a number of places and its significance discussed. It affected the life of Victoria, although she was barely a year old at the time, forming an essential part of the background to her accession and a key to some of the attitudes and expectations which were developing towards the Crown among the British people.

Anticipation of the return to Britain of the queen produced demonstrations of loyalty towards her throughout the kingdom. Among the effusions was an ode of welcome written by a nineteen-year-old Cambridge undergraduate, Thomas Babington Macaulay. The first and last stanzas give the flavour of the whole campaign.

Let mirth in every visage shine,
And glow in every soul.
Bring forth, bring forth the oldest wine,
And crown the largest bowl.
Bear to her home, while banners fly
From each resounding steeple,
And rockets sparkle in the sky,
The Daughter of the People.
E'en here for one triumphant day, .
Let want and woe be dumb,
And bonfires blaze and schoolboys play,
Thank Heaven! our Queen is come!

Though tyrant hatred still denies
Each right that fits thy station,
To thee a people's love supplies
A nobler coronation:
A coronation all unknown
To Europe's royal vermin:
For England's heart will be thy throne,
And purity thine ermine;
Thy proclamation our applause,
Applause denied to some;
Thy crown our love; thy shield our laws,
Thank Heaven, our Queen is come.[7]

Macaulay and his father were ardent supporters of the queen, and neither of them was a political innocent. When the news arrived in Cambridge that the king's attempt to have his wife stripped of her titles through a bill of pains and penalties had failed because of insufficient support in Parliament, and that the bill had been withdrawn, Macaulay wrote to his father:

All here is ecstasy. 'Thank God, the country is saved' were my first words when I caught a glimpse of the papers on Friday night. 'Thank God the country is saved' is written on every face and echoed by every voice.[8]

This sense that a victory had been gained over a morally corrupt king by the nation's insistence that he honour the customs of the country and the sacrament of marriage seems to have been an important part of the enthusiasm with which the queen's 'victory' was greeted. There was rejoicing throughout the country. Reluctant conservative clergy in remote villages were forced to allow church bells to ring out. In London and the manufacturing districts windows which were not lit up in celebration were stoned. In Miss

Mitford's Berkshire hamlet, a retired publican – 'a substantial person with a comely wife' –

> introduced into our peaceful vicinage the rebellious innovation of an illumination on the Queen's acquittal. Remonstrance and persuasion were in vain; he talked of liberty and broken windows – so we lighted up. Oh how he shone that night with candles and laurel and white bows and gold paper, and a transparency (originally designed for a pocket handkerchief) with a flaming portrait of Her Majesty, hatted and feathered in red ochre.[9]

Politically, the Queen Caroline episode is hard to decode. There is no doubt that some of the more radical elements piled in to gain access to the streets after the set-back to popular agitation which had been given by the Peterloo massacre barely a year earlier. On that occasion a large but peaceful demonstration for parliamentary reform had been attacked and cut down by the yeomanry cavalry, twelve people had been killed and many more injured. The yeomanry had been congratulated by ministers of the government and the organizers of the demonstration had been arrested and imprisoned. The reformers withdrew and for a time abjured large public demonstrations. A 'loyal' demonstration in support of the legitimate queen of their country may well have seemed a safer way to attack authority, and one which the military could have found some difficulty in suppressing. Richard Carlile, for example, a leader of the campaign against press censorship, was serving a prison sentence for blasphemous libel during part of the Caroline agitation and was editing his journal *The Republican* from jail. He was, he said, 'as careless about the whole system of monarchy as it was possible for a man to be'. Nevertheless, he was an ardent supporter of the queen in his journal, describing her as 'a virtuous and true heroine'.[10] William Benbow, another outspoken republican, published a broadside calling attention to the moral and courageous actions of women in past history which ended 'And a QUEEN will now bring down the corrupt conspirators against the Peace, Honour and Life of the Innocent'.[11] In the area of high politics, it was the radicals who took the queen's side. An anonymous pamphleteer addressing the Earl of Harewood in Yorkshire in 1820 complained that the peers, by throwing out the bill of pains and penalties, had succumbed to the clamour of the London crowd and to the activities of revolutionary demagogues who could, he maintained, 'procure addresses by cartloads'. 'A democratic peer', he continued, 'is the most crazy of all political maniacs' – the duty of a peer being to stand by his king.[12] The interesting aspect about it is that among the population as a whole the division did appear to be along class lines. Macaulay may have seen rejoicing on every face in Cambridge, but when the towns-people organized a demonstration to celebrate, it was attacked by a mob of eight hundred undergraduates chanting 'King, king, king!'[13]

Why did the queen elicit all this popular support? Some of it may have been instrumental, but the gifts and addresses which flowed in from such urban groups as the Kidderminster carpet-weavers, the Coventry watchmakers and many others indicate a widespread concern beyond that of the active politicians. Perhaps the most novel aspect of the campaign, however, and one which provides some sort of key to part of it, was its specifically female dimension. Clearly the queen was seen not only, in Macaulay's phrase, as the victim of 'tyrant hatred' but also as the victim of male tyranny and sexual double standards. At least seventeen female petitions were sent, including one from 17,652 'married ladies of the metropolis'. The sympathy expressed in most of these petitions was for 'a woman wronged'.

The British Crown and the British national image has always had strong associations with female figures. In folk and popular mythology England did better under queens, from Boadicea through Good Queen Bess to Queen Anne. Perhaps the support for Caroline was also from a population which wanted a figurehead on the throne rather than an active politician, a figurehead, moreover, who could command respect and who could embody to some extent the accepted virtues of marriage, fidelity and parenthood – virtues proper to a benevolent and disinterested head of state. Caroline undoubtedly profited from the popularity of her daughter as well as from the unpopularity of her husband and his brothers. After the near hysteria of the celebration of her acquittal, however, she sank again into the background and the pathetic farce of the coronation in which the doors of the cathedral were barred against her seems to have roused little public protest. Her death soon after the coronation saved George IV from further embarrassment, although the re-routing of her funeral cortège through the city on its way to the coast did again briefly provide the opportunity for the organiza-tions of the London artisans to defy the military and assert some control of the streets.[14]

It may well be that a very strong element in the whole Caroline affair was the assertion by the crowd, including the women, of the belief that the British monarch, unlike 'Europe's royal vermin', was not above the law and customs of the country. George, and in a different way his successor William IV, openly flouted the marriage laws, and even more so the customary expectations of the partnership, particularly those of the women.

At the time of the Caroline agitation, the Princess Victoria was only one of the possible successors to the throne. She was brought up by her widowed mother in a very female environment, her greatest friend and companion being her half-sister Feodora. Although not deliberately cut off from her royal uncles, she was spared in her early years the manipulation to which the Princess Charlotte had been subject.

By the time of the accession of William IV, in 1830 however, all his children had died and twelve-year-old Victoria was clearly his heir. Next in line was the least popular and most sinister of her uncles, Ernest Augustus, Duke of Cumberland. It is not the purpose of this essay, or of my work, to examine the question of how much of a 'Hanoverian conspiracy' there was against the princess. At least one commentator has pooh-poohed the idea completely, and Victoria herself in her old age vehemently denied the existence of any such plot. By then, however, she had become extremely defensive about her family, even its least savoury members. Anyone who has read at all extensively in the contemporary press and literature must be aware that it was widely believed that a Hanoverian conspiracy existed. Prince Albert believed that the attempts on Victoria's life which took place in the 1840s were inspired by supporters of Ernest Augustus, and at the time of her accession and coronation the papers are full of hints and rumours.[15] Until Victoria's accession the Hanoverian monarchs had ruled over Hanover and Britain. Hanover, however, was governed by the Salic law under which females were not recognized as rulers in their own right. Victoria therefore could not become Queen of Hanover. The royal title would in any case go to Ernest Augustus, and there is no doubt that many high Tories would have preferred the British Crown to go to him as well. There had, in their earlier years, been some attempts to pair his son George with Victoria and thus to assure the joint succession. George – who went blind in his early teens – did succeed to the throne of Hanover, from which he was later removed in the process of Prussian aggrandizement, but attempts to promote marriages between Victoria and either of her two Hanoverian cousins did not succeed. Those who wished for a male Hanoverian succession, therefore, rested their hopes upon the person of Ernest Augustus.

As Walter Bagehot pointed out in his book on the constitution, legitimacy was not, at this time, a strong element in the history of the British throne.[16] The three most recent dynasties had all been invited to the throne in spite of the existence of candidates with a more directly legitimist claim. The great principle which had governed their selection had been their embracing of Protestantism, a principle which was a key element in Cumberland's political philosophy. He had opposed the granting of Catholic Emancipation in 1829, which he and his supporters saw as the betrayal of the coronation oath, and Victoria's unsuitability as a woman was reinforced by her known liberalism on this and other political questions which she was held to have imbibed from her uncle Leopold, the chief male influence in her life. In a famous letter written by him shortly before the death of William IV, Leopold urged her to rely on the liberal ministers:

> For them, as well as for the Liberals at large, you are the *only* Sovereign that offers them *des chances d'existence et de durée*. With the exception of the Duke of Sussex, there is *no one* in the family that offers them anything like what they can reasonably hope from you, and your immediate successor with the mustaches is enough to frighten them into the most violent attachment for you.[17]

For the Whigs and liberals inside the political system and certainly for the radicals whose number was rapidly increasing outside, the young queen was much to be preferred to her immediate successor with the mustaches. This was certainly not the case among many Tories, however, as Major General Sir Charles Napier, commander of the Northern Division of the army, was to note when he described in a letter to his brother a dinner he attended soon after her coronation:

> Our dinner was a *black* affair. I would not have gone if I had not first ascertained ... that Lord Scarborough, the Whig Lord Lieutenant of the county, was to go, and so concluded that it could not be a party dinner: yet it was so. The first toast *Church and State*, made it clear we were a Tory party, for the acclamations were immense.
>
> The next toast was *The Queen*. Glasses were filled, but not a sound of applause followed. Her Majesty's health was drunk in significant silence. 'No man cried God bless her' except myself. Then came *The*

Queen Dowager and the rest of the royal family: instantly the room shook with shouts of applause.[18]

Napier, although liberal, indeed radical, in his politics, was not a republican. For many republicans, however, the danger of a Hanoverian reaction seemed very real, and support for a young, female monarch of reputedly liberal views must have appeared very much the lesser evil. This view was articulated flippantly by *Cleave's London Satirist and Gazette of Variety* at the time of the coronation, when its reports might have been considered to have departed from their 'comparatively stern and republican nature'. The editorial justified their welcome of 'a young, lovely, accomplished and generous-hearted girl to the British throne' on the grounds of chivalry and the 'queenophobia' to be found elsewhere. *Cleave's* was soon publishing critical cartoons and squibs about Victoria and her husband and family, but at the moment of her accession this criticism was held off.

A detailed study of the folk presentation of the queen would be interesting. Ballads at the time of her accession, coronation and marriage attributed attitudes to her which would have astounded her. She was held to be sternly opposed to the 1834 Poor Law, to support political reform, and in 1840 to have intervened personally to secure the commutation of the death sentences on the Welsh Chartist leaders. Clearly her age and her gender led to expectations of attitudes very different from those of her predecessors – described by a contemporary as 'an idiot, a voluptuary and a buffoon'. Lady Wharncliffe, meeting the young Victoria, had expressed herself 'delighted with our little future Queen.... I look to her to save us from Democracy, for it is impossible that she should not be popular when she is older and more seen.'[19] The assurance of popularity certainly gained strength from the memory of Princess Charlotte, as the Duke of Buckingham and Chandos noted at the time of Victoria's accession: 'The bitter disappointment caused by the untimely fate of the last female heiress presumptive gave deeper feelings to the interest with which she was regarded.'[20]

A queen, especially a young one – and Victoria at the time of her uncle's death was only just old enough to rule without a regent – was clearly a less threatening figure to English radicals or to the disaffected Irish than a Hanoverian Protestant duke would have been. She was able to pick up some of the support which had existed for Charlotte and Caroline. But there was no feminist press at the time and it is very difficult to see how far her victory was seen by other women as in any sense a gender victory. A small ray of light on this matter comes from the autobiography of H.G. Wells. His mother was, he records, so great an admirer of Queen Victoria, even copying her style of dress, that she helped to make her son a republican. But in describing his mother's education at a small private school in the 1830s he made this comment:

An interesting thing about this school of Miss Riley's, which was in so many respects a very antiquated eighteenth-century school, was the strong flavour of early feminism it left in her mind. I do not think it is on record anywhere, but it is plain to me from what I have heard my mother say that among schoolmistresses and such like women there was a stir of emancipation associated with the claim, ultimately successful, of the Princess Victoria ... to succeed King William IV. There was a movement against that young lady based on her sex, and this had provoked in reaction a wave of feminine partisanship throughout the country. It picked up reinforcement from an earlier trouble between George IV and Queen Caroline.[21]

With her marriage two years after her accession, Victoria became the first British monarch, perhaps the first public figure of any kind, to combine both the public and private roles – roles whose separation was to become part of the ideology of the age over which she presided. Although she produced nine children during her marriage, she never renounced her primacy as occupant of the throne. If her pregnancies prevented her from honouring public engagements and Albert stood in for her, it was always as her deputy. He held no official title, apart from an honorary 'Royal Highness' until 1856, when he became officially the prince consort. Unlike her married women subjects, Victoria was not subject to the law of *coverture*: she did not take her husband's name, put any of her property under his control or lose her right to make contracts or engage in any transactions in her own right. Indeed, it was she who proposed marriage to Albert, a fact on which cartoonists and street balladists did not hesitate to comment:

Since the Queen did herself for a husband propose,
  The ladies will all do the same I suppose;
Their days of subserviency now will be past
  For all will 'speak first' as they always did last!
Since the Queen has no equal, 'obey' none she need,
  So of course at the altar from such vow she's freed:

> And the women will all follow suit, so they say –
> 'Love, honour' they'll promise, but never 'obey'.[22]

Clearly the extent to which the queen actually fulfilled the role of mother as well as that of head of state may have been pretty notional. Nevertheless, throughout the years of their marriage, she and Albert were constantly pictured, in an age of rapidly expanding cheap visual material, in a family situation, surrounded by their children. On semi-state occasions such as the opening of the Great Exhibition in 1851, the queen appeared surrounded by the little royals all got up in highland dress.

It is not easy to gather how far this combination of roles in the head of state affected the aspirations of her female subjects. There was plenty of knock-about comedy about the royal fecundity and the secondary role of the prince. A music-hall song of 1842 reminded the royal couple of the teachings of Malthus and reported an imaginary conversation in which 'V unto A so boldly did say' –

> The state is bewildering about little children,
> And we are increasing, you know we have four,
> We kindly do treat 'em
> and seldom do beat 'em
> So Albert, dear Albert, we'll do it no more
>   Do it no more
>   Do it no more,
> No Albert, dear Albert, we'll do it no more.[23]

The circumstances of Victoria's accession, combined perhaps with the image of a young mother, to some extent disarmed radical republicanism in the turbulent early decades of her reign. The Chartist agitation, although it had strong elements of republicanism in it, never put the issue at the top of the agenda in the way in which most radical movements in Europe did at the time. The parallel Irish agitation for repeal of the union with Britain actually adopted the Crown as part of its campaign, something which seems in many ways paradoxical.

Although most Chartists would have declared themselves to be republicans, they did not identify the throne as the seat of reaction or even as a serious threat to reform. Perhaps Ernest Jones's utopian poem, 'The New World or the Revolt of Hindostan', written in 1849 whilst he was in prison for sedition, sums up the Chartist attitude. Describing the overthrow of the British government by the forces of democratic revolution, he pictured the results:

> While prostrate Mercy raised her drooping head
> Thus came the people, thus the gold-kings fled;
> None fought for them, none spoke, they slunk away
> Like guilty shadows at appearing day;
> They were not persecuted but forgot:
> Their place was vacant and men missed them not.
> And Royalty, that dull and outworn tool!
> Bedizened doll upon a gilded stool –
> The seal that Party used to stamp an Act
> Vanished in form as it had long in fact.[24]

In 1848, when crowns were tumbling all over Europe, the revitalized Chartist movement produced the slogan 'France has the Republic, England shall have the Charter'. George Eliot wrote to John Sibree in that year: 'Our little humbug of a queen is more endurable than the rest of her race because she calls forth a chivalrous feeling and there is nothing in our constitution to obstruct the slow progress of *political* reform.'[25] Gender, it would seem was important but perhaps not decisive.

In the parallel O'Connellite Irish repeal movement the effect of the monarch's gender is more obvious. O'Connell was not a republican, indeed he had served as a volunteer against the rising of the republican United Irishmen in 1798. Nevertheless, in calling for the repeal of the union he was going against the policies of all but a small group of mainly Irish members in the House of Commons, and was challenging the power of the British government to rule Ireland. But he called his movement the Loyal National Repeal Association, began its membership requirements with an oath of loyalty to the queen, and issued campaign buttons which showed the Irish harp surmounted by a crown and bearing the twin slogans GOD SAVE THE QUEEN and REPEAL OF THE UNION.[26] He was never stinting of his admiration for the 'darlin' little queen' and saw her as a 'golden bridge' that was to unite the two countries once Ireland achieved its separate parliament.

In a famous essay published in 1867, Walter Bagehot described the monarchy as a tamed and domesticated institution:

A *family* on the throne is an interesting idea also. It brings down the pride of sovereignty to the level of petty life. No feeling could seem more childish than the enthusiasm of the English at the marriage of the Prince of Wales. They treated as a great political event, what, looked at as a matter of pure business, was very small indeed. But no feeling could be more like common human nature as it is, and as it is likely to be. The women – one half of the human race at least – care fifty times more for a marriage than a ministry.[27]

Such observations he felt explained the interest shown by the general public in the doings of 'a retired widow and an unemployed youth', that is, Victoria and her eldest son Albert Edward. However, almost before his book hit the shops, issues arose which led to a revival of republicanism. These issues, too, were closely associated with questions of gender.

Prince Albert had died in 1861. His sudden death at the early age of forty-two left his wife distraught and grief-stricken. She retired to her Scottish estate in Balmoral, and for a time refused to undertake any public duties. This was the expected reaction of a woman of her time, and her mourning, though by modern standards extravagant and bizarre – the prince's room was left as it had been at the time of his death; shaving water was regularly brought to it and his clothes laid out for the rest of the queen's life; busts, memorials and icons of all kinds were distributed to the palace staff; and an enormous mausoleum was prepared in the grounds of Windsor Castle to receive a life-sized marble statue – was nevertheless only marginally more extravagant than that practised by many of her subjects in similar circumstances. Nevertheless, the queen was different. She refused to fulfil her public duties – for example, she only opened Parliament six times during the remaining forty years of her reign, and withdrew into absolute retirement – even to the extent of taking part in the magnificent marriage of her eldest son in 1863 from a screened room away from any contact with the ceremony or her guests.

Such retirement on the part of a widow was quite in keeping with the sensibility of the time. It was, indeed, defended on many sides. But the correct behaviour would also have been for her to retire from office, making way for her son, already of age and of the appropriate sex for a monarch. And the problem here was Bertie, her heir. Victoria was convinced that he was quite unfit to rule and that he would bring disrepute, even ruin, to the Crown. She refused, therefore, to abdicate in his favour. Her daughter Princess Louise later remarked that 'Had it not been for Bertie's unsuitability, charity and the family would have been enough for her.'

The 1860s then saw in some ways a replay of the situation at Victoria's accession. Again arguments were raised against a female monarch; again a suitable male candidate was at hand. As the decade progressed and the queen remained invisible, republican arguments began to emerge. The country was doing perfectly well without a monarch, why spend all the money on an unnecessary institution? The prince was not popular with liberals – Kipling was later to describe him as 'a corpulent voluptuary of no importance' – whilst the middle years of the decade began to be filled with rumours about the queen's relations with her former servant John Brown.

The John Brown episode illustrates better than almost anything else in her reign the double standards of morality that were applied to men and women.[28] There seems no reasonable doubt from the evidence at the time, and even more from items which have come to light since, that a few years after her husband's death the queen began a relationship with Brown that lasted until his death in 1884. That the relationship was a sexual one, certainly in its early years, also seems clear enough. It was a relationship of mutual love and respect, was entered into some years after her husband's death, involved no betrayal of other relationships, although it was clearly distressing to her children, and had no effect on the politics of the country. Nevertheless, its nature has always been strenuously denied in official circles, royal historians have fallen over backwards to ridicule the idea that it was more than an ordinary mistress–servant relationship, and even radical historians have presented it as a severe moral lapse. Compared with the treatment of the sexual behaviour not only of her predecessors but also of her successor, the contrast is clear – Edward is referred to as 'the merry monarch' and streets in London are named after his mistresses; indeed Alexandra Road, named after his wife, has recently been renamed Langtree Terrace, perhaps to match the nearby pub which has been changed from 'The Princess of Wales' to the 'Lily Langtree'.

The refusal of the queen to abdicate, her retirement from public duties and rumours of her association with Brown undoubtedly fuelled a revival of republicanism. Gladstone, who has been credited at this time with saving the monarchy, noted in a memorandum to his foreign secretary at the end of the decade that the fund of goodwill towards the queen and her son was diminishing 'and I do not see from whence it is to be replenished. To speak in rude and general terms, the Queen is invisible and the Prince is not respected.'[29]

These years saw a small flood of republican pamphlets and journals. The two best-known pamphlets are probably *What Does*

She Do With It? by Solomon Temple, builder (who may or may not have been George Otto Trevelyan), and Charles Bradlaugh's *Impeachment of the House of Brunswick*, ostensibly written to show up the villanies of past Hanoverians, particularly George IV when Prince of Wales, but clearly aimed at the present bearer of the title. Like much – indeed most – British republican writing then and later, these stressed the expense of monarchy and attacked the extravagancies and failings of actual figures, rather than arguing the case for a republic as a more rational and democratic form of government. Republican clubs developed and later writers recalled the atmosphere as one of increasing rejection of royalty. James Ramsay Macdonald looked back at the turn of the century to the 1860s when

> The throne seemed to be tottering ... the Queen and the Prince of Wales had no hold on the popular mind; there was a spirit of democratic independence abroad: the common man believed in the common man.[30]

Within the Liberal Party, too, republican voices were heard. 'The Republic must come', Joseph Chamberlain wrote to his friend Sir Charles Dilke in 1871, 'and at the rate at which we are moving, it will come in our generation.'[31] In the same year, *Fraser's Magazine* reported that in London

> Men – decent steady artisans ... speaking amid applauding circles of shopmates wished that the whole tribe of royalty were under the sod; while women, mothers themselves, prayed that its women might be made unfruitful, so that the race of royal paupers might not be increased.[32]

The fall of the French Second Empire in 1870 further fuelled the republican campaign. Addressing a meeting in his home town of Birmingham at the time Chamberlain said amid cheers that he felt no great horror at the idea of the possible establishment of a republic in Britain. Dilke went further in a famous speech in Newcastle in which he declared:

> If you can show me a fair chance that a republic here will be free from the political corruption that hangs about the monarchy, I say, for my part – and I believe the middle classes in general will say – let it come.[33]

The case being made increasingly against the monarchy was its cost and its lack of function. The true extent of the queen's actual involvement with politics only came to be realized after her death when her letters and other documents began to be published. Dilke, who suffered in his own career through royal displeasure, complained in 1879 that 'the Queen *does* interfere, constantly',[34] but the strong monarchism of all her ministers, including Gladstone, who once declared that 'the Queen alone is enough to kill any man', allowed her actual influence to be concealed behind a bland public image. It seems probable that the increasing polarization of male and female roles may have helped to reinforce the non-political image of the queen, since mid Victorian men found it difficult to associate political action with a female.

Although many, particularly among conservative politicians, would have preferred a male monarch, objections to the queen seemed rarely to have been made on grounds of gender, at least in public. Lord Howden wrote privately to Lord Clarendon that it would have been well for the queen

> for her own interest, happiness and *reputation*, to have abdicated on the day her son came of age. She would *then* have left a great name and a great regret.[35]

Among republicans the gender issue was also handled with some care. John Bright, the Quaker Liberal politician who was at one time seen by the republicans as a possible first president of the British republic, earned the Queen's gratitude by his defence of her retirement:

> A woman – be she the Queen of a great realm, or be she the wife of one of your labouring men – who can keep alive in her heart a great sorrow for the lost object of her life and affection is not at all likely to be wanting in a great and generous sympathy for you.[36]

His response to the suggestion that he should be president was cautious in the extreme:

> As to the *opinions* on the question of Monarchy or Republicanism, I hope and believe it will be a long time before we are asked to give our opinion; our ancestors decided the matter a long time since, and I would suggest that you and I should leave any further decision to our posterity.[37]

The specific event which is usually held to have defused the growing republican feelings was the serious illness of the Prince of Wales in the winter of 1871. In that year he was brought down with an attack of typhoid fever – the illness which was thought, though probably mistakenly, to have killed his father ten years earlier. The queen kept watch by his bedside and the whole nation held its breath until the crisis was past and the heir to the throne was on the road to recovery. A signal of the nation's change of heart may be seen in the fact that a motion critical of royal expenditure introduced into the House of Commons shortly before the prince's illness gained 53 votes, whereas for a similar one soon after his recovery Dilke was unable to find a seconder.

This is not an essay on British republicanism, except as it was affected by the presence of a female monarch. There are some general points to be made, however. As Bright's response indicated, there was, even among radical and labour politicians, a residual constitutional rhetoric which saw the Crown as an essentially British institution which had on occasion – mostly in the distant past in which myth and history fuse – been the defender and preserver of British liberties. The Chartist factory reformer Samuel Kydd, for example, took the pseudonym 'Alfred' for his lengthy defence of the factory children, and, as we have seen, Boadicea and Good Queen Bess were figures invoked in defence of liberty by ultra-radicals. There was a strong folk belief in the virtue of female monarchs –

> When Britain really ruled the waves –
> (In good Queen Bess's time)

– and the longer Victoria remained on the throne, the more she became associated with Britain's undoubted commercial and imperial expansion, the more she fitted into these folk myths. Memories of the English Republic were not, for the Irish or for the common people of England, memories of liberty; even the radicals who revered the Commonwealthsmen rarely referred back to the Protector. After the low period of the 1860s, more skilful political handling emphasized the strong points in the country's monarchism, and the queen went on to achieve an astonishing amount of popularity.

By the early 1870s Chamberlain found his own support dropping away, and settled for the compromise which was offered in various forms by a wide range of politicians. 'There is really', he maintained, 'not any great practical difference between a free constitutional monarchy such as ours and a free republic.'[38] The feeling demonstrated during the prince's illness seemed to have made it clear that republicanism was not a vote-winner.

Victoria's gender certainly facilitated her transformation in the last two decades of her reign into the figure of the mother of Empire. Although the presence of a woman in the highest office of state was on numerous occasions used by reformers and feminists as an argument in favour of women's rights to a greater part in the public life of the nation, the queen herself gave no support to such arguments. Apart from her support of the work of Florence Nightingale and the reform of the nursing profession, she was increasingly associated with conservative views both in party and gender politics. It was as a mother figure that she was presented as head of the Empire and Empress of India. This image helped to legitimate the mother image which has come down as part of the legacy of her reign – the stern guardian of family morals, the watchful parent and grandparent who controls the behaviour of children and grandchildren of both sexes. In those years she lent strength to those, women as well as men, who supported the status quo and women looking for greater freedom and all those working for greater democracy in politics and liberalization in morals found a great deal of what they had to contest embodied in the attitudes associated with her name.

If Victoria's presence on the throne affected the social and political position of her female subjects, it would seem to have been, apart from a brief period at the time of her accession, in the realm of family politics rather than in that of legal and political status. If, at the end of her reign, women had greater rights to their own property when married and received greater lip-service, at least, as moral leaders within the home, these achievements have to be seen against the background of the greater exploitation of women in the labour market and the reduction of their authority in most aspects of public life below that of the throne. By the end of her life, Victoria's image was firmly placed as that of the materfamilias, an image which to some extent actually masked her own close concern with affairs of state. The words of the 'Jubilee Hymn' composed by the Bishop of Wakefield in 1897 illustrate this:

> O Royal Heart, with wide embrace
> For all her children yearning!
> O happy realm, such mother-grace
> With loyal love returning!
> Where England's flag flies wide unfurled,
> All tyrant wrongs repelling;
> God Make the world a better place
> For Man's brief earthly dwelling.[39]

Over the sixty-three years of her reign, Victoria moved from presenting a strong challenge to conservatism – indeed to reaction and to male political dominion – towards the presentation of a purely moral and familial role for women. In her persona of a purely private figure she in fact deceived, as the son of her private secretary pointed out, 'the general public, including radicals and even republicans for a time' as to the extent of her power and influence.[40] Her reign and her public face did, however, contribute to the limitation of the power of the monarchy as well as to the disarming of British republicanism by identifying the monarchy with private and familial rather than with public and political responses. It was, after all, not for political ambition or the attempt to re-establish the powers enjoyed by earlier monarchs that her great-grandson was forced to abdicate, but for a rejection of standards of marital and familial behaviour demanded by the Church and by respectable opinion.

Notes

1. There is no one book on British republicanism. An overview is given in John Cannon, 'The Survival of the British Monarchy' *Transactions of the Royal Historical Society*, 5th series, no. 36, 1986, pp. 143–64. For the early period, see John Belchem, 'Republicanism, Popular Constitutionalism and the Radical Platform in Early Nineteenth-Century England', *Social History* vol. 6, no. 1, January 1981, pp. 1–32. For the later period see Royden Harrison, 'The Republicans: A Study of the Proletarian Left 1869–73', in his *Before the Socialists*, London 1965, pp. 210–50, and Edward Royle, *Radicals, Secularists and Republicans 1866–1915*, London 1980, pp. 198–206. Kingsley Martin, *The Crown and the Establishment*, London 1962, is a lively account of some of the issues involved. All biographies of Chamberlain and Dilke have some account of their involvement, and see Feargus D'Arcy, 'Charles Bradlaugh and the English Republican Movement, 1868–73', *Historical Journal*, vol. xxv, 1982, pp. 367–83. Apart from the press and the biographies of some of the people involved, these have been my main sources for my account of republicanism.

2. Harold Laski, *The Labour Party and the Constitution*, London 1931, p. 24.

3. F. Max Muller, (ed.), *Memoirs of Baron Stockmar by his Son*, tr. from the German, (1873), vol. 1, p. 2.

4. Percy Bysshe Shelley, *Address to the People on the Death of Princess Charlotte* (1817), first surviving edn London 1840.

5. Byron lines are from *Childe Harold's Pilgrimage*, Canto 4, cclxic and clxx.

6. The fullest and most recent account of the Queen Caroline affair is in Iain McCalman, *Radical Underworld: Prophets Revolutionaries and Pornographers in London, 1795–1840*, Cambridge 1988. A good short account which includes material from outside London is Thomas Laqueur, 'The Queen Caroline Affair: Politics as Art in the Reign of George IV', *Journal of Modern History*, vol. 54, 1984, pp. 417–66. See also Craig Calhoun, *The Question of Class Struggle: Social Foundations of Popular Radicalism during the Industrial Revolution*, Chicago 1982.

7. G.O. Trevelyan (ed.) *Life and Letters of Lord Macaulay*, 2 vols, Oxford 1961, vol. 1, p. 92.

8. Ibid., vol. 1, p. 93.

9. Mary Russell Mitford, *Our Village: Sketches of Rural Character and Scenery*, (1812–32), London 1867, 2 vols, vol. 1, p. 3.

10. McCalman, and for a brief mention, Joel M. Wiener, *Radicalism and Freethought in Nineteenth Century Britain: The Life of Richard Carlile*, Westport, Conn., 1983, pp. 57–8.

11. William Benbow leaflet *Glorious Deeds of Women* (PRO HO 40ff., 195).

12. Broadside, *To The Right Honorable the Earl of Harewood*, 20 November 1820.

13. Laqueur, p. 444.

14. Prothero, *Artisans and Politics in Early Nineteenth Century London*, Folkstone 1979, pp. 147–55.

15. Robert Rhodes James, *Albert Prince Consort*, London 1983, p. 136.

16. Walter Bagehot, *The English Constitution* (1867), London 1963, pp. 88–9.

17. Viscount Esher and A.C. Benson (eds), *The Letters of Queen Victoria: A Selection of Her Majesty's Correspondence between the Years 1837–1861*, 1907, vol. 1, p. 72.

18. Sir William Napier (ed.), *The Life and Opinions of General Sir Charles James Napier*, London 1857, vol. 2, p. 84.

19. Caroline Grosvenor and Lord Stuart of Wortley (eds), *The First Lady Wharncliffe and Her Family 1799–1856*, London 1927, 2 vols, vol. 2, p. 791.

20. Richard Grenville, Second Duke of Buckingham and Chandos, *Memoirs of the Court and Cabinets of William IV and Victoria*, London 1861, p. 122.

21. H.G. Wells, *Experiment in Autobiography*, London 1934, vol. 1, pp. 45–6.

22. Ballad reprinted in Charles Hindley, *Curiosities of Street Literature*, London 1871; reprinted with introduction by Leslie Shepherd, London 1966.

23. Cited in Peter Leslie, *A Hard Act to Follow*, London 1978 pp. 47–8.

24. Ernest Charles Jones, 'The New World', *Notes to the People*, vol. 1. no. 1, 1851.

25. George Eliot to John Sibree, – March 1848, in Gordon S. Haight (ed.), *Letters of George Eliot*, Oxford 1954, 2 vols, vol. 1, p. 254.

26. The O'Connell campaign button is reproduced in John Ashton, *Gossip in the First Decade of Victoria's Reign*, London 1903, p. 133.

27. Bagehot, p. 85.

28. For a more, detailed examination of the evidence and an account of the Queen's relationship with John Brown, see my *Queen Victoria, Gender and Power*, London 1990, chapter 4.

29. Gladstone to Granville, 3 December 1870, in Agatha Ramm (ed.), *The Political Correspondence of Mr Gladstone and Lord Granville*, London 1952. Mary Ponsonby, wife of the queen's private secretary, wrote to her husband in September 1871: 'If they don't take care, Gladstone will show his teeth about Royalty altogether and I wouldn't answer for it lasting long after that' (*Mary Ponsonby: A Memoir, Some Letters and a Journal* London 1927, p. 68).

30. *Democracy*, 23 February 1901.

31. S. Gwynn and M.G. Tuckwell, *The Life of the Rt Hon. Sir Charles W. Dilke*, London 1917, 2 vols, vol. 1, p. 140.

32. [A Working Man], 'English Republicanism', *Fraser's Magazine*, n.s., vol. 3, January–June 1871, pp. 755–6.

33. Gwynn and Tuckwell, p. 139.

34. Cited in Frank Hardie, *The Political Influence of Queen Victoria*, Oxford 1935, p. 243.

35. Lord Howden to the Earl of Clarendon, 4 June 1964, cited in Sir Herbert Eustace Maxwell, *Life of Clarendon*, London 1913, 2 vols, vol. 2, p. 292.

36. Cited in Elizabeth Longford, *Victoria RI*, London 1966, pp. 469–70.

37. John Bright to a gentleman inquiring whether he would accept the post of first President of the English Republic if it were to be offered to him. Rochdale, 7 April 1872, in H.J. Leech (ed.), *The Public Letters of the Rt Hon. John Bright MP*, London 1885, p. 153.

38. J.L. Garvin, *Life of Joseph Chamberlain*, London 1932, 2 vols, vol.1, p. 152.

39. 'Jubilee Hymn', words by Bishop How, music by Sir Arthur Sullivan.

40. Arthur Ponsonby, *Henry Ponsonby, Queen Victoria's Private Secretary*, London 1942, p. 124.